MW01026225

The Princess of Wales with her six-month-old son Prince William

American Ancestors and Cousins of

The Princess of Wales

The New England, Mid-Atlantic, and Virginia Forebears,
Near Relatives, and Notable Distant Kinsmen,
Through Her American Great-Grandmother,
of Lady Diana Frances Spencer, Now Her Royal Highness
The Princess of Wales

Gary Boyd Roberts &
William Addams Reitwiesner

GENEALOGICAL PUBLISHING CO., INC.
Baltimore, 1984

1001 N. Calvert Street
Baltimore, Maryland 21202

Library of Congress Catalogue Card Number 84-81095
International Standard Book Number 0-8063-1085-5
Made in the United States of America

Photographic Credits

Frontispiece: *Courtesy of British Information Services*
4th Baron Fermoy: *Courtesy of Norfolk Fire Service, King's Lynn, England*
Mrs. Shand-Kydd: *Courtesy of The Press Association, Ltd.*

Contents

Chapter Five

The American Relatives of H.R.H. The Princess of Wales, *by William Addams Reitwiesner*

Preface

In 1981 the courtship, engagement, and marriage of the Prince of Wales and Lady Diana Frances Spencer captured the world's romantic imagination. Popular interest in the Princess of Wales has remained almost constant since, and was much increased with the birth in June 1982 of a son and probable future sovereign, Prince William Arthur Philip Louis. (As this volume goes to press, moreover, the Prince and Princess of Wales are expecting a second child, due in the autumn of 1984.) Almost immediately after the royal courtship was seriously reported, the authors of this book, having noticed that one great-grandmother of Lady Diana was a New Yorker, began to trace this latter's American ancestry and near relatives, and to gather data on more distant kinships to notable figures in American history. Some of our discoveries were reported shortly after the engagement was announced—in the *New York Times* and the *Washington Post*, in *Time* and *Newsweek*, and through the Reuters and UPI news agencies. English coverage was provided by David Williamson in articles in the *Genealogists' Magazine* and the *Sunday Times Magazine*. John Chancellor used much of our material during NBC's coverage of the royal wedding, Abby Van Pelt provided an entrée to the American near relatives, the English Speaking Union sponsored an Ohio lecture tour in the fall of 1981, and in 1982 the authors produced early versions of two of the chapters included in this volume. These were Gary Boyd Roberts' article on "The New England Ancestry of H.R.H. The Princess of Wales," published in the April and October 1982 issues of *The New England Historical and Genealogical Register*, and William Addams Reitwiesner's privately distributed "The American Ancestors and Relatives of Her Royal Highness The Princess of Wales." Mr. Roberts' article was one of the most favorably received in the *Register*'s history, and in the summer of 1983 popular interest in the Princess's American ancestors was rekindled by wide reporting of a distant kinship between the Princess and 10th cousin Nancy Reagan.

Almost since first hearing of Lady Diana Spencer, then, many Americans have been aware that the Princess of Wales has genealogical links to this country. Not only, however, is the Princess one-eighth (or more properly, three-sixteenths) American, the granddaughter of a Harvard graduate and U.S Army captain during World War I, great-granddaughter of a member of Mrs. Astor's "400," great-great-granddaughter of a Wall Street millionaire, great-great-great-granddaughter of Ohio pioneers, great-great-great-great-granddaughter of a graduate of Yale, and great-great-great-great-great-granddaughter of a builder of Independence Hall, a revolutionary soldier, and a privateer; she also has ancestors who lived in six of the thirteen original colonies (Massachusetts, Connecticut, New Jersey, Pennsylvania, Maryland, and Virginia), near relatives in Newport, New York City, Philadelphia, Washington, D.C., Ohio, and throughout the country, several hundred distant kinsmen well known in U.S. history (beginning with the revolutionary martyr Nathan Hale, a 1st cousin six times removed), and probably between twenty and thirty million living distant American cousins. Given the keen interest in both the Princess and these connections, the authors have much expanded their early work and in this volume consolidate for the first time all of their findings to date.

American Ancestors and Cousins of The Princess of Wales is designed to answer three questions:

1) Who are the Princess's American ancestors and am I (any reader) among her twenty–thirty million distant kinsmen in this country? You are among the latter if you descend from *any* of the former, and all of the Princess's known American ancestors are covered herein.

2) Which notable historical figures are among the Princess's and my (if you share any common ancestors) distant kinsmen? and

3) Who are the Princess's nearest 500 American relatives (second, third, fourth or fifth cousins)?

The authors think many readers will indeed find themselves distantly related to the Princess of Wales and Prince William. They also believe that many readers will know of other notable kinsmen and other facts regarding persons treated in this work. All such additions or corrections are welcome.

Gary Boyd Roberts
William Addams Reitwiesner

American Ancestors and Cousins of

The Princess of Wales

Chapter One

THE NEW ENGLAND ANCESTRY OF H.R.H. THE PRINCESS OF WALES

I

The marriage of the Prince of Wales and Lady Diana Frances Spencer has introduced a large slice of Americana into the genealogy of the British royal family. Their children, including a probable future sovereign, will be ancestrally one-sixteenth American. For the Princess's maternal grandfather, the 4th Baron Fermoy, was not only a graduate of St. Paul's School and Harvard who lived in the United States until his father's death in 1920 and served during World War I as an American Army captain in France; he was also by a few minutes the eldest male offspring of an Irish lord's second son and the daughter of an American millionaire. This daughter, the Princess's American great-grandmother, twice divorced, known generally as Mrs. Frances Burke Roche, died at age eighty-nine in New York City in 1947. She and her sister, Mrs. Peter Cooper Hewitt, were in the 1890s two of Mrs. Astor's "400" and remained prominent in New York and Newport society thereafter. Their millionaire father, who loathed his daughter's "foreign" marriage, was Frank Work, half Scottish, raised in Chillicothe, Ohio, Wall Street speculator, horseowner, and protege of Commodore Vanderbilt. Worth $15,000,000 at his death in 1911, Work may well qualify as a tycoon and "robber baron." His mother, born near Baltimore, was largely of Philadelphia, Maryland, and New Jersey ancestry, but one of her almost certain great-great-grandfathers, Joseph Boude, was an innkeeper and distiller in seventeenth-century Marblehead, Massachusetts. Frank Work's wife, Ellen Wood, the Princess's American great-great-grandmother, was the daughter of a prosperous porkpacker and early settler of Chillicothe, born in what is now West Virginia, the ancestry of whose parents has not yet been determined. Ellen's mother was the daughter of Dr. Joseph Strong, 1770–1812, a Philadelphia surgeon born in Connecticut who graduated from Yale in 1788 and whose own wife was the daughter of a privateer, also of Philadelphia, born probably in Scotland.

Dr. Joseph Strong, the Princess's "gateway ancestor" to New England, was the son of a revolutionary soldier and patriot, a first cousin of the martyr spy Nathan Hale, a second cousin once removed of both Vermont hero Ethan Allen and the second wife of William Floyd, signer of the Declaration of Independence from New York, and a fourth cousin once removed of both Joseph Warren of Bunker Hill and William Williams, signer of the Declaration of Independence from Connecticut. Dr. Strong's father, grandfather, and great-grandfather were Coventry selectmen who represented their town in the Connecticut General Assembly. His ancestry, consisting totally of New Englanders and their Great Migration and English forebears, is fully known for five generations, and of the thirty-two possible sixth-generation ancestors, first names or more are known for twenty-eight. Geographically diffuse, this ancestry is nonetheless concentrated, before any move to Coventry or nearby Windham, in five areas—Northampton, Massachusetts; Hartford, Windsor, and Farmington, Connecticut; Boston, Dorchester, Roxbury, Charlestown, Lynn, Salem, Beverly, Wenham, and Ipswich, Massachusetts; Duxbury and Bridgewater, Massachusetts; and Norwich, New London, Preston, and Stonington, Connecticut. The migration pattern was generally from Massachusetts to Connecticut, or from Hartford or Windsor to Northampton. Dr. Strong's immigrant male ancestors (sons who came with their fathers are excluded) number nineteen—John Strong, Thomas Ford, William Holton, Samuel Allen, Thomas Woodford, Robert Blott, Henry Woodward, John Lee, Stephen Hart, Thomas Bishop, John Cogswell, Adam Hawkes, John Fobes, William Gager, Robert Hibbard, John Luff, Edward Walden, James Morgan, and Robert Parke. Most were farmers, but William Gager was a surgeon, Robert Hibbard a bricklayer, and John Luff a weaver. Two ancestresses, Elizabeth (Charde) Cooke and Alice (Freeman) Thompson, wives of Thomas Ford and Robert Parke respectively, were widows who brought children by their first husbands to New England; and two more, Elizabeth (Gore) Gager, daughter-in-law of William Gager, and Constant Mitchell, wife of John Fobes, seem to have had New England siblings. Dr. Strong had no *Mayflower* descent, but Constant Mitchell was probably a daughter of Thomas Mitchell and Margaret Williams of the Leyden company. The English place origins or parents of thirteen of the twenty-three immigrant forebears who left American progeny or kinsmen are known or have been suggested, and Dr. Strong's matrilineal immigrant ancestress, the above-named Alice (Freeman) (Thompson) Parke, was of gentry origin and noble and royal descent.

The twenty-three just-listed immigrant forebears of Dr. Joseph Strong, and their American descendants and kinsmen are numerically almost comparable (note, however, the absorption of Woodford's progeny into Blott's, of Lee's into Hart's, and of Hibbard's into Luff's) to the twenty-three *Mayflower* families now being covered, through the early eighteenth century, in *Mayflower Families Through Five Generations*. Assuming an average birth year of 1610 for Dr. Strong's twenty-three immigrant sires, assuming thirty years per generation and thirteen generations of descendants, the last three of which are living, assuming three children per family in each generation (a fair average, I think, when both village and urban, pre- and post-industrial revolution families are considered), deducting almost 50 percent for overlap and intermarriage, and perhaps adding the likely progeny of the Marblehead Boudes as well, the living descendants of the Princess of Wales's New England ancestors now number probably between twenty and thirty million Americans. Among these are 250—and no doubt many more—of the several thousand most notable individuals in American history, a fair sample of the Yankee, and especially Connecticut and Connecticut Valley Yankee, contribution, over 350 years, to the nation at large.

The purpose of this chapter is to detail and document the above summary. Additionally I wish to suggest that partial American ancestry for a Princess of Wales should not surprise us; nor should fully known ancestry well covered in printed works for a pioneer migrant from this region, millions of distant American relatives for any of his descendants, or kinships thereby to a large number of major historical figures. Considering these points one at a time we may first note that the number of marriages between American women, often heiresses, and Britishers—titled, noble, gentle, intellectually distinguished, or just rich—between roughly the Civil War and World War I, was probably over one thousand. Two hundred or more can be listed by simply examining *Burke's Peerage* in some detail. Some intermarriage, moreover, has continued. Not only were the stepmother of Neville Chamberlain and the mothers of Sir Winston Churchill and Harold Macmillan American (for Jennie Jerome's ancestry, and Churchill's kinships to Franklin D. Roosevelt, Douglas MacArthur, and Henry Wallace, see *The New York Genealogical and Biographical Record*, 73 [1942]:159-172, 219-221); so too were the mother of Erskine Hamilton Childers, President of the Republic of Ireland, 1973–1974, the wife of Rudyard Kipling, the first wife of Sir Thomas Beecham, 2nd Baronet, and the first and fourth wives of Bertrand (3rd Earl) Russell. Some of the transatlantic marriages of the last century, of course, were childless, but grandchildren, great-grandchildren, and great-great-grandchildren of others are now spread throughout much of the British upper classes, peerage families especially. And these marriages are in addition to various colonial unions which, although considerably fewer and involving much less American ancestry, have produced many British descendants. Robert Porteus, Jr. (ca. 1705–1754) of Virginia, a graduate of Peterhouse, Cambridge in 1730, and later rector of Cockayne Hatley, Bedfordshire, England, for whom see chapter four of this work, was a second cousin of George Washington, a second cousin once removed of Meriwether Lewis, and a third cousin of Thomas Nelson, signer of the Declaration of Independence. Porteus's British descendants include H.M. Queen Elizabeth The Queen Mother and the 6th Baron Carrington, recent foreign secretary. John Singleton Copley, the American painter, and Susanna Farnum Clarke, his wife, the latter a descendant of New England Appletons, Winslows, Hutchinsons (including the noted Mrs. Anne [Marbury] Hutchinson), and John Chilton of the *Mayflower*, left a large British progeny through their son, the 1st Baron Lyndhurst. Included are the Honorable Lavinia Mary Strutt, wife of the late 16th Duke of Norfolk, and the Honorable Pamela Beryl Digby, wife successively of Randolph Churchill (Sir Winston's son, by whom she was the mother of the current Winston Churchill, M.P.), theatrical producer Leland Hayward, and Averill Harriman. The descendants, firstly on Antigua, then in the British peerage, baronetage, and gentry, of Samuel Winthrop, a son of Governor John Winthrop of Massachusetts Bay, are outlined by Ellery Kirke Taylor in *The Lion and the Hare* (Ann Arbor, 1939), charts Q-T. And New England migration to Canada has produced transatlantic kinships as well. Not only were Sir Charles Tupper, 1st Baronet, and Sir Robert Laird Borden, the only Canadian prime ministers from Nova Scotia, of New England ancestry; so also was Gladys Henderson Drury, a descendant of Governor Thomas Dudley of Massachusetts Bay and Reverend John Rogers, 6th president of Harvard College, and wife of William Maxwell Aitken, 1st Baron Beaverbrook, the financier, newspaper owner, and member of Churchill's war cabinet (see *Burke's Genealogical and Heraldic History of the Landed Gentry*, 18th ed. [London, 1969], 2:165, and Tracy Elliot Hazen, *The Hazen Family in America* [Thomaston, Conn., 1947], 93, 94, 185, 186). Beaverbrook's daughter married firstly Ian Douglas Campbell, later 11th Duke of Argyll, great-nephew of a son-in-law of Queen Victoria, and left a daughter who was the third wife of novelist Norman Mailer. Such examples are not endless, but the cumulative result is an Anglo-American kinship much reinforced since our seventeenth-century migration. As genealogies are compiled on the progeny of later, especially nineteenth-century British immigrants to the United States also, this reinforcement seems even stronger.

No more surprising than American ancestry for many members of the British upper class—into which the royal family is likely to marry—is almost completely traceable ancestry for a New England pioneer migrant. In "New Sources for Seventeenth-Century New England and the Pioneer Population of 1750 to 1850: A Review Essay," *The New England Historical and Genealogical Register* (henceforth the *Register*), 135 (1981): 57-68, I discussed the ease with which the best pre-1960 sources for seventeenth-century New Englanders can be gleaned from Clarence Almon Torrey's *New England Marriages Prior to 1700*. Footnote 2, page 58, moreover, mentioned the multi-ancestor genealogies by M. W. Ferris, Ernest Flagg, M. L. Holman, D. L. Jacobus and E. F. Waterman, E. B. Sumner, L. A. W. Underhill, and F. C. Warner. Of the thirteen major sources for the ancestry of Dr. Joseph Strong listed below, eight are multi-ancestor works by one of these authors. The remaining five are traditional agnate descendant single family genealogies, of which the 1871 Strong volume, a major source for many Connecticut

Valley families (see *The Connecticut Nutmegger*, 12 [1979]: 375), and the 1980 Adam Hawkes volume are outstanding. A few errors or omissions in the 1901 Hibbard genealogy and *The Parke Scrapbooks* were corrected by use of Windham, Connecticut, deeds and probate district records, all Northampton marriage records were confirmed by examining the copy by Walter E. Corbin at the New England Historic Genealogical Society (henceforth NEHGS), and Coventry, Norwich, Windham and other Connecticut vital records were found (especially the birth and death dates for Caleb Bishop) or confirmed by using the microfilm copy, also at NEHGS, of the Barbour Collection (see the *Register*, 134 [1980]: 8, 9). A few other sources are noted in the ancestor table below, and Dr. Joseph Strong was admittedly a college graduate and member of one of his town's leading families. Nonetheless, being able to trace the bulk of his New England ancestry and finding definitive accounts of almost all his immigrant ancestors in major multi-ancestor genealogies of the last few generations is not unusual. Not only does Torrey's work identify almost all pre-1960 material on probably 99 percent of seventeenth-century New Englanders; the multi-ancestor works listed and indexed by immigrant in Donald Lines Jacobus's "My Own Index" section of *Index to Genealogical Periodicals*, vol. 3, 1947–1952 (New Haven, 1953), and (listed only) the *Register*, 135 (1981): 196-198, cover probably over 2,500 Great Migration immigrants. These works, 130 in all, range from good to excellent. Additionally, the considerable number of high quality New England single-family genealogies, the various town histories with nearly definitive genealogical sections (for a short list see the *Register*, 135 [1981]: 58, footnote 3, 60), the large New England periodical literature, and various compilations of primary sources, especially the above cited Barbour Collection for Connecticut and the printed vital records volumes for Massachusetts towns (an exhaustive list, prepared by Edward W. Hanson and Homer Vincent Rutherford, appears in the *Register*, 135 [1981]: 183-194) all contribute to an unparalleled regional excellence in printed genealogical sources. Once the origin of a migrant New Englander is found, sometimes admittedly a formidable task, much of his known ancestry is likely to be well covered in print. And since New England primary sources, on which printed ones are based, are superb until the mid-eighteenth century, if the migrant leaves New England before 1800, as did Dr. Joseph Strong, and his parents and grandparents are known through a good printed genealogy, vital or Bible record, wills, deeds or other sources, probably most of his remaining New England forebears are readily traceable also.

Almost all descendants of pioneers from New England who moved north, west, or south in the century between 1750 and 1850 will have at least twenty known Pilgrim or Great Migration ancestors. Some will have fifty or more, and many contemporary New Englanders of largely Yankee ancestry will have well over two hundred. Many immigrants of the decades between 1620 and 1650 now doubtless have over a million living descendants—again assuming thirteen generations, three now living, three children and thirty years per generation, and considerable cousin intermarriage. Thus the number of distant American kinsmen of anyone with sizable New England ancestry is enormous. Probably never, however, has it equalled more than half of the national population—because of extensive intermarriage and overlapping, which grow exponentially as the progenies of more immigrants are considered; because New Englanders by no means migrated everywhere; and because many Americans are totally of mid-Atlantic, southern, or nineteenth- or twentieth-century immigrant ancestry. Good statistical studies in genealogy are rare. As social historians explore these issues more exactly, many figures may change. However, as regards the probability of ancestry in common with the Princess of Wales for anyone with a considerable number of New England forebears, since the Princess has probably between twenty and thirty million New England-derived distant American relatives, as noted above, I should now estimate it as high as 20 or 25 percent.

However we attempt to calculate the likely *total* number of the Princess's New England-derived relatives, specific distant kinships to at least 250 of the several thousand most notable individuals in American history are clear. These 250, listed below with outlines of their descents from ancestors of Dr. Joseph Strong, include ten presidents or their wives (the two Adamses, Fillmore, Hayes, Cleveland, T. Roosevelt, Wilson, Coolidge, F. D. Roosevelt, and Truman); various "tycoon" families (Armours, Colts, Marshall Fields, Firestones, Fords, H. L. Hunts, McCormicks, J. P. Morgans, Potter Palmers, Pillsburys, C. W. Posts, Rockefellers, Scribners, Strauses, Tiffanys, Vanderbilts, and Whitneys); a sizable number of literary figures or their spouses, especially those leaders associated with Harvard, the mid-nineteenth-century "flowering of New England," abolition or reform (later Adamses, Alcotts, Beechers, Holmeses, Emerson, Longfellow, E. E. Hale, Bancroft, Prescott, Motley, T. D. Weld, Susan B. Anthony, and Elizabeth Cady Stanton); and numerous twentieth-century entertainment, media, or sports figures or their spouses (C. D. Gibson, Caruso, Valentino, Lillian and Dorothy Gish, John and Ethel Barrymore, Orson Welles, Humphrey Bogart, Spencer Tracy, Shirley Temple, Anthony Perkins, Julie Harris, Lee Remick, Dina Merrill, Sidney Lumet, Eddie Duchin, Henry Luce, Lowell Thomas, Edward R. Murrow, Ben Bradlee, George Gallup, the Alsops, Walter C. Camp, and "Gene" Tunney). Also included are five U.S. vice-presidents (Colfax, Morton, Sherman, Dawes, and Rockefeller), eight secretaries of state (Washburne, Root, Lansing, Stimson, Acheson, Dulles, Herter, and Vance), two presidents of Harvard (Kirkland and Lowell), seven presidents of Yale (Elisha Williams, the two Timothy Dwights, Woolsey, Hadley, Seymour, and Brewster), and a wide variety of twentieth-century literary figures (among others Frank Norris, L. F. Baum, Clarence Day, Hart Crane, F. Scott Fitzgerald, J. P.

Marquand, Robert Penn Warren, Archibald MacLeish, Barrett Wendell, Van Wyck Brooks, Samuel Eliot Morison, Arthur Schlesinger, Jr., and Erle Stanley Gardner, or their wives). So inclusive, these 250 seem a fair sample of the Yankee, and especially Connecticut and Connecticut Valley Yankee, contribution to American history. Involved in both the Revolution and the formation of the Federalist mercantile elite of Salem and Boston, whose second generation was in large part responsible for "the flowering of New England," Unitarianism, abolitionism, and early feminism, these notable kinsmen of Dr. Joseph Strong and their immediate forebears also moved, as did he and his children and grandchildren, to New York City and/or the Midwest. There they helped to found both the industrial oligarchy of the immediate post-Civil War decades, and its own second generation offspring, inter-city turn-of-the-century "society," headed by the 400 in New York. A few less wealthy but locally notable kinsmen produced political leaders, especially in upstate New York and Ohio. In this century "society" settled into an "eastern establishment" much represented by these 250 (note the just-listed secretaries of state); literature and the arts and sciences have continued to expand and flower, both within and outside New England and its colleges; and much business opportunity has moved to the South or the West (note the California-based entertainment and media figures above). Unfortunately, space considerations preclude documenting each generation in the descents of these 250 notable figures from various ancestors of Dr. Joseph Strong. One major source has been my own research, including various pamphlets and "The Mowbray Connection" (23 volumes, manuscript collection at NEHGS and elsewhere, for some discussion of which see *The Connecticut Nutmegger*, 10 [1977]: 3-12, and *The Detroit Society for Genealogical Research Magazine*, 41 [1978]: 141; 42 [1979]: 191), collected and compiled since 1966. All descents outlined below have been rechecked, however, and much additional research undertaken as well.

The remainder of this chapter consists of (1) a detailed genealogical summary of the seven generations between Dr. Joseph Strong and the Princess of Wales; (2) an ancestor table of Dr. Strong, again covering seven generations; and (3) the list of 250 notable figures who share part of his New England ancestry, together with an outline of the generations between each of the 250 and every nearest common forebear. Before proceeding to this specific data and documentation, however, I wish to acknowledge several colleagues, partial sponsors, and individuals or media who have encouraged this research into the American and New England ancestry of the Princess of Wales. First among my colleagues, who exhausted sources at the Library of Congress and the National Archives, and undertook research with me in Chillicothe, is William Addams Reitwiesner of Silver Spring, Maryland, whose monograph, "The American Ancestors and Relatives of Lady Diana Frances Spencer," was sent to various scholars and libraries in the spring of 1981 and is incorporated, with revisions and deletions, as chapter five of this work. Mr. Reitwiesner and I are also major contributors to the American section of a forthcoming book on the Princess's entire known ancestry for twelve or more generations, to be edited by David G. Williamson and published by Charles Skilton, Ltd. This last project I discussed in *The Genealogist* (New York), 2 (1981): 244-256; the work will be essentially a companion to Gerald Paget's *The Lineage and Ancestry of H.R.H. Prince Charles, Prince of Wales,* 2 vols. (London and Baltimore, 1977).

Secondly, I wish to acknowledge Neil D. Thompson, who undertook much research in New York City vital records and wills; Timothy Field Beard and Gunther Pohl, for additional work in New York; John R. Grabb, Mrs. Marie Taylor Clark, and Mrs. Carol Willsey Bell, for extensive Ohio research; Francis James Dallett and Roger D. Joslyn for research, now published, on the Boude family of Boston, Marblehead, Philadelphia, and Baltimore; Benjamin H. Gaylord and Wayne C. Hart, for partial underwriting of research into notable Holton and Hart descendants respectively; and the English Speaking Union, for sponsoring an Ohio lecture tour on the American ancestry of the Prince and Princess of Wales, a trip that allowed me to undertake research in Chillicothe and Columbus. Among media outlets whose articles or broadcasts generated much reader response and new information, I wish to acknowledge *Time* magazine, the *Washington Post,* NBC, Reuters and UPI news agencies, and in London the *Sunday Times Magazine*. A seven-generation ancestor table of the Princess appeared in David G. Williamson's "The Ancestry of Lady Diana Spencer," *Genealogists' Magazine*, 20 (1981): 192-197, 281, 282. And among persons who encouraged this research I wish to acknowledge Lady Fermoy, the Princess's grandmother, who wrote to Mr. Reitwiesner; Abby Van Pelt of Philadelphia, the Princess's second cousin, with whom Mr. Reitwiesner and I have formed an ongoing friendship; and my colleagues at NEHGS in Boston.

II

The Descent from Dr. Joseph Strong to H.R.H. The Princess of Wales

1. Dr. Joseph Strong, b. South Coventry, Conn., 10 Mar. 1770, d. Philadelphia, Penn., 24 Apr. 1812, a graduate of Yale College in 1788 who studied medicine under Dr. Lemuel Hopkins of Hartford, 1788-1790, and Dr. Benjamin Rush at the School of Medicine, University of Pennsylvania, 1791-1792. Strong first practiced at Middletown, Conn., was a surgeon's mate in the legion of General Anthony Wayne in the Ohio campaign against the Indians (appointed 4 May 1792, resigned 1 May 1796) and lived thereafter in Philadelphia. A leading local physician, he was also a major promoter of the Philadelphia Society for the Encouragement of Domestic Manufactures, invented the axle tourniquet for the control of bleeding during surgical operations (patent dated 29 Jan. 1801), and died intestate, aged 42 years, 1 month, and 14 days, of yellow fever. See "Biography of Dr. Joseph Strong, 1770–1812, Philadelphia Physician," by Lockwood Anderson Barr (a great-great-grandson) (typescript, NEHGS [Pelham Manor, N.Y., 1940]; published, somewhat condensed, in *Yale Journal of Biology and Medicine*, 13 [1941]: 429-450); Franklin Bowditch Dexter, *Biographical Sketches of the Graduates of Yale College*, vol. 4, 1778-1792 (New York, 1907), 620, 621; and pp. 414-416 of the Strong genealogy listed below. Dr. Strong m. in Philadelphia (at the First Baptist Church, according to *Pennsylvania Archives*, 2nd ser., vol. 8 [Harrisburg, 1880; reprinted as *Record of Pennsylvania Marriages Prior to 1810*, vol. 1, Baltimore, 1968], 771, where he is mistakenly called Dr. "John" Strong) 8 Sept. 1796 Rebecca Young, b. Philadelphia 5 May 1779, who m. (2) Peter Gardiner (by whom she had a son, Richard J. Gardiner, b. Philadelphia 15 Feb. 1818) and moved to Chillicothe, Ohio, between 1818 and 1823. Mrs. Gardiner d. Piqua, Ohio (to which her son, William Young Strong, had moved from Chillicothe) 8 June 1862, and is undoubtedly the "Mrs. Gardner" buried, without a stone, in the lot of her son-in-law, John Wood, in Grandview Cemetery, Chillicothe (Marie Taylor Clark, *Tombstone Inscriptions of Grandview Cemetery, Chillicothe, Ohio, Ross County* [Chillicothe, 1972], 2). Mrs. Rebecca Young Strong Gardiner was the daughter of Capt. Peter Young of Philadelphia, revolutionary privateer, of unknown origin, b. perhaps in Scotland ca. 1739 (described as aged 42 on 11 Dec. 1781), whose will was dated 13 Oct. 1776 and proved 12 Nov. 1784, and Eleanor ———, his wife, whose origin is also unknown but who died after 21 Oct. 1796. See L. A. Barr, "Captain Peter Young (1738-1784), Mariner of Philadelphia," (typescript, the Library of Congress and elsewhere [Pelham Manor, N.Y., 1945]).

2. Eleanor Strong, b. Philadelphia ca. 1802-3, d. New York City 9 July 1863, aged 60 (death records, Borough of Manhattan, City of New York, in custody of Municipal Archives, 31 Chambers Street, New York, N.Y., 10007, but said to be aged 61 at death in the obituary notice of Thursday, 9 July 1863 in the *New York Evening Post*—see Gertrude A. Barber, "Deaths Taken From the *New*

York Evening Post [from July 1, 1863 to August 6, 1864]," vol. 40, 1941, p. 3, typescript), m. St. Paul's Episcopal Church, Chillicothe 13 Mar. 1823 (see vol. 1 of its parish register, now in the custody of Rev. William V. Brook, Jr., rector of said church, 33 E. Main Street, Chillicothe, 45601, and on microfilm at the Ross County Historical Society, Chillicothe, and several typescript copies of Ross County marriages) John Wood, b. Va., probably in or near Shepherdstown, Berkeley County (now Jefferson County, W. Va.) 29 July 1785, d. Chillicothe 29 Jan. 1848 (M.T. Clark, *op. cit.*). John Wood's tombstone mistakenly gives 1847 as his year of death, but his will (see Ross County will book E and F, 76) was dated 21 Jan. 1848 and proved 3 Feb. 1848, and an executor's notice, dated 9 Feb. 1848, appeared in the *Scioto Gazette*, a Chillicothe newspaper, on Wednesday, 23 Feb. 1848, p. 3, col. 4. No baptism for Eleanor, usually called Ellen, is listed in the records of Old Christ Church, Philadelphia, where siblings were baptised 3 Nov. 1797 (Lucy), 6 Nov. 1801 (Joseph Jr. and Peter Young Strong), and 11 Mar. 1812 (William Young Strong, Rebecca Strong, and Lavinia Strong, this last undoubtedly the "child of Joseph Strong" buried the next day), and no orphan's court record in Philadelphia or other documentary source can be found that lists all children of Joseph Strong and Rebecca Young. There is, however, no doubt of Eleanor's parentage. She was very likely named for her maternal grandmother and aunt (an Eleanor Young b. 13 Nov. 1767), and two of her sons were named William Bond Wood (after William Key Bond, 1792-1864, noted judge and congressman, who married Lucy Strong, Eleanor's oldest sister) and Joseph Strong Wood (after his maternal grandfather). Two of Eleanor's children, Thomas James Wood and Ellen Wood (see below), were baptized at St. Paul's, Chillicothe, on the same day (22 July 1832) as Josephine Bond, their first cousin. The New York death record of Ellen Wood states that she was born in Pennsylvania, and that of her daughter Ellen Work, gives "mother's birth place" as Philadelphia. The Strong genealogy listed below, a printed work of very high quality in which I can find only one mistake regarding this family (there is no evidence that Dr. Joseph Strong ever lived in Chillicothe), lists (p. 415) Ellen as Joseph and Rebecca's fourth child, between Peter Young Strong and William Young Strong, whose births are given in the records of Old Christ Church, alongside their baptisms, as 28 Apr. 1801 and 26 June 1806 respectively (another brother, William Strong, b. 12 Dec. 1804, d. 8 Sept. 1805). L.A. Barr misread the burial date of the "child of Joseph Strong" and thought that Lavinia (b. 19 Aug. 1810) survived and was identical with Ellen, an obviously wrong inference. Lastly among evidence for Eleanor's parentage is the already mentioned burial of a "Mrs. Gardner," undoubtedly her mother, in the Grandview Cemetery lot of John Wood. Before Mrs. Gardiner died in 1862 she had probably expressed a wish to be buried in Chillicothe. All of her children except R.J. Gardiner had moved away, but Ellen Wood, then of New York City, doubtless saw to her mother's burial alongside the latter's son-in-law and at least one grandson.

John Wood and his bachelor brother George Wood (1792-1861, for whom see the obituary in the *Scioto Gazette*, Tuesday, 29 Jan. 1861, p. 3, col. 2) were early Chillicothe merchants who made a sizable fortune as porkpackers. According to a Bible record partly confirmed by the research of Capt. Gerard Hadden Wood, a great-grandson of John and Ellen, the parents of the brothers, and of their sister, Susannah James Wood, 1798–1872, who as Susan J. Wood m. in Ross County 11 Mar. 1819 Thomas Hoffman, and had two children, were another George Wood, who died in Kentucky 23 Aug. 1802, and Elizabeth Conner (1766–13 Oct. 1818).

These last were married "about 1784" probably in Berkelely Co., Va., although no such marriage is listed in Guy L. Keesecker, *Marriage Records of Berkeley County, Virginia, for the Period of 1781-1854* (Martinsburg, W. Va., 1969), and after her husband's death Elizabeth Wood moved to Franklin County, Ohio, "six miles from Columbus." Siblings of the three Chillicothe pioneers were Thomas Wood (1788-1834, who married Elizabeth Ramsay and left five children), Charles Conner Wood (1790-1838), William Wood (b. 1796), and Anna Maria Wood (b. 1800). John Wood was in Chillicothe by 13 Nov. 1809, when an advertisement appeared in the *Scioto Gazette* for a new store owned by Wood and Thomas James. For further details of John Wood's career in Chillicothe, and of Frank Work's as well, see the *Ross County Historical Society Newsletter*, July, 1981, 1-4, 12. The Chillicothe home of John Wood still stands, at 95 West Fourth Street, as does the rather elegant house of his widow, at 85 South Paint Street. Eleanor Strong Wood built this last shortly after her husband's death, and sold it 2 June 1856, after which she and her daughter Ellen moved to New York City, where one of her sons was probably working for Frank Work. For further information on the Wood and Hoffman families see *History of Franklin and Pickaway Counties, Ohio, with Illustrations and Biographical Sketches of Some of the Prominent Men and Pioneers* (Cleveland, 1880), 293; *Portrait and Biographical Record of Fayette, Pickaway, and Madison Counties, Ohio, Containing Biographical Sketches of Prominent and Representative Citizens* (Chicago, 1892), 237, 238, 830, 831; and Aaron R. Van Cleaf, *History of Pickaway County, Ohio, and Representative Citizens* (Chicago, 1906), 875.

3. ELLEN WOOD, b. Chillicothe 18 July 1831 (calculated from her age at death), baptized at St. Paul's 22 July 1832, d. New York City 22 Feb. 1877 (death certificate 258528, Ellen Work, Health Dept., Borough of Manhattan, City of New York), m. New York City 19 Feb. 1857 (marriage records, Borough of Manhattan, City of New York, also in custody of the Municipal Archives) Frank Work, millionaire speculator, broker, banker, horseowner, and protege of Commodore Vanderbilt, b. Chillicothe 10 Feb. 1819, d. New York City 16 Mar. 1911 (death certificate 8825, Frank Work, Health Dept., Borough of Manhattan, City of New York), son of John Work or Wark (almost certainly 28 Oct. 1781–16 Apr. 1823), an immigrant of Scottish parentage born in Plymouth, England, and Sarah Duncan Boude (15 Dec. 1790–17 Dec. 1860) of Elkridge Landing, Maryland, for whom see the next chapter and Francis James Dallett, "The Inter-Colonial Grimstone Boude and His Family" in *The Genealogist* (New York), 2 (1981): 74-114, 257. John Work and his wife were in Ohio probably before 1815. He died in Chillicothe; she, much later, in Columbus. Sarah Duncan Boude was a daughter of Joseph Boude (1740-post 1793/4) of Philadelphia and Baltimore, stated by a grandson to have been a revolutionary soldier, and Barbara Black; granddaughter of Thomas Boude (ca. 1700-1781) of Philadelphia, and Sarah Newbold (1700-1780); great-granddaughter of Grimstone Boude of Boston, Perth Amboy, and Philadelphia (d. 1716) and his second wife Mary ——— (d. post 1731, m. 2nd George Campion); and great-great-granddaughter almost certainly of Joseph Boude of Boston and Marblehead, Mass. (d. ante 1683) and Elizabeth ——— (d. 1670). So Frank Work too has some New England ancestry. His name was given as Frank "H" Work on his daughter's marriage record (see citation below) and he was called "Franklin" when his brother, John Clinton Work, was made his guardian 23 Apr. 1833 (Franklin Co. probate record 0895, now missing but abstracted in *The Ohio Genealogical Quarterly*, 5 [1941]: 447—"John Work

chosen as guardian of Franklin, aged 14 yrs. and Elizabeth, aged 15 yrs., minor heirs of ——— Work." This entry was found by Mrs. Carol Willsey Bell. Elizabeth Work, who died childless in 1847, m. James Kooken, Jr., 1809-1872, of Columbus and New York City, for whom see the above cited 1880 *History of Franklin and Pickaway Counties, Ohio*, between 592 and 593). For Frank Work's rather colorful career as a speculator and horseowner see his obituary in the *New York Times*, 17 Mar. 1911, p. 9, col. 5, and Henry Hall, ed., *America's Successful Men of Affairs, An Encyclopedia of Contemporaneous Biography*, vol. 1 [New York, 1895], 743. His equally colorful will, with 15 codicils, was dated 5 Jan. 1901, proved 29 Apr. 1911, is recorded in Liber 909 of New York County Wills, pp. 295-308, and is several times treated in the *New York Times* during the first half of 1911 (most notably on 29 Apr., p. 1, col. 3). Mrs. Burke Roche, below, was left no definite legacy, only an allowance as trustees saw fit and only so long as she remained separated from Aurel Batonyi; the Burke Roche grandsons to receive their share had to become American citizens, keep permanent legal U.S. residence, and take the surname Work; and his granddaughter, then Mrs. Cynthia Burke Roche Burden, to receive her share must not marry a foreigner or visit Great Britain during the lifetime of her father. Most of these stipulations were ignored, and Work's daughters and grandchildren divided the estate equitably among themselves and the other heirs.

4. FRANCES ELEANOR (usually called FRANCES ELLEN) WORK, b. New York City 27 Oct. 1857, d. there 26 Jan. 1947 (death certificate 2372, Mrs. Frances Burke Roche, Health Dept., Borough of Manhattan, City of New York), known generally as Mrs. Burke Roche, socialite, one of Mrs. Astor's "400" (Cleveland Amory, *Who Killed Society?* [New York, 1960], 525) m. 1) Christ Church, New York City 22 Sept. 1880 (Christ Church marriage records, now in the custody of Father Joseph Zorawick, Rector of Christ and St. Stephen's Church, 120 W. 69th St., New York, NY 10023. No civil record can be found.) Hon. James Boothby Burke Roche, b. Twyford Abbey, Middlesex, England 28 July 1851, B.A. Trinity College, Cambridge, 1877 (see J. A. Venn, comp., *Alumni Cantabrigienses, Part II [from 1752 to 1900]*, vol. 5 [Cambridge, 1953], 338), Member of Parliament for East Kerry 1896-1900, 3rd Baron Fermoy from 1 Sept. 1920 until his death two months later, at Artillery Mansions, Westminster, 30 Oct. 1920. Mrs. Burke Roche was granted an American divorce at Wilmington, Delaware 3 Mar. 1891 and m. 2) in New York City 4 Aug. 1905, as his second wife, Aurel Batonyi, a Hungarian-born groom and horse trainer from whom she was also divorced, on 5 Nov. 1909. For Mrs. Burke Roche's matrimonial career and fuller details on her sons, granddaughter, and great-granddaughter below, see part one of the fifth chapter of this work, plus various entries in the *Times* (London) and the *New York Times*, both indexed, recent editions of *Burke's Genealogical and Heraldic History of the Peerage, Baronetage, and Knightage* and *Debrett's Peerage, Baronetage, Knightage and Companionage* (the articles Fermoy and Spencer in both) and of the British *Who's Who* and *Who Was Who*, and the *Genealogists' Magazine*, 20 (1981): 192-197, 281.

5. EDMUND MAURICE BURKE ROCHE, 4th Baron Fermoy, b. Chelsea, England 15 May 1885, d. King's Lynn 8 July 1955, British M.P. for King's Lynn 1924-35 and 1943-5, m. St. Devenick's, Bieldside, Aberdeenshire, Scotland 17 Sept. 1931 Ruth Sylvia Gill, b. Dalhebity, Bieldside, Aberdeenshire 2 Oct. 1908, still living,

Woman of the Bedchamber to Queen Mother Elizabeth since 1960. Lord Fermoy and his twin bachelor brother, the Hon. Francis George Burke Roche (d. Newport, R.I. 30 Oct. 1958), both lived after their parents' divorce with their mother in the U.S., prepared at St. Paul's School, Concord, N.H., 1899-1905, and graduated from Harvard College in 1909. Lord Fermoy worked in various departments of the Delaware, Lackawanna and Western Railroad from the fall of 1909 until World War I, in which he served in France as a U.S. Army captain. After his father's death in 1920 he returned to England. For further details see Arthur Stanwood Pier, *St. Paul's School, 1855-1934* (New York, 1934), 325, 327, 331, 332, and 342, the several twentieth-century alumni directories of St. Paul's, and the decennial (1919), 25th (1934), 30th (1939), 40th (1949), 45th (1954), and 50th (1959) anniversary reports of the 1909 class of Harvard College. The last two Harvard class reports mention Lord Fermoy's friendship with the royal family at Sandringham.

6. The Honorable FRANCES RUTH BURKE ROCHE, b. Park House, Sandringham, 20 Jan. 1936, m. 1) at Westminster Abbey 1 June 1954 Edward John Spencer, Viscount Althorp, 8th Earl Spencer since 9 June 1975, b. Sussex Square, London 24 Jan. 1924, Royal Equerry 1950-4. Viscount Althorp and his wife obtained a divorce in 1969 and she m. 2) 2 May 1969, as his second wife, Peter Shand Kydd.

7. Lady DIANA FRANCES SPENCER, now H.R.H. The Princess of Wales, b. Park House, Sandringham 1 July 1961, m. at St. Paul's Cathedral 29 July 1981, H.R.H. Prince Charles Philip Arthur George, Prince of Wales, b. at Buckingham Palace 14 Nov. 1948.

8. H.R.H. PRINCE WILLIAM ARTHUR PHILIP LOUIS of Wales, b. St. Mary's Hospital, Paddington, London 21 June 1982.

III

An Ancestor Table of Dr. Joseph Strong, Preceded by the Major Printed Sources Used in its Compilation

Anderson, Ruby Parke. *The Parke Scrapbook*. 3 vols. Baltimore, 1965, 1966, n.d. 1:1, 2; 2:24-26, 30, 51; 3:14, 15, 46 (Parke, Morgan, Hibbard, Bishop, Strong).

Dwight, Benjamin Woodbridge. *The History of the Descendants of Elder John Strong of Northampton, Mass*. 2 vols. Albany, N.Y., 1871. Reprint. Baltimore, 1975. Pp. 14-19, 228-230, 308-310, 330, 331, 414-416, 769, 770, 986, 987.

Ferris, Mary Walton. *Dawes-Gates Ancestral Lines*. 2 vols. Milwaukee, 1931-1943. 1:293-302 (Ford); 187-189 (Cogswell); 2:840-849 (Woodward).

Flagg, Ernest. *Genealogical Notes on the Founding of New England: My Ancestors' Part in that Undertaking*. Hartford, 1926. Reprint. Baltimore, 1973. Pp. 210 (Woodward); 258, 259 (Hart).

Hibbard, Augustine George. *Genealogy of the Hibbard Family*. Hartford, 1901. Pp. 8-16, 19-21, 26, 27.

Holman, Mary Lovering. *Ancestry of Col. John Harrington Stevens and His Wife Frances Helen Miller*. 2 vols. Concord, N.H., 1948-1952. 1:348-353 (Strong); 354-356 (Ford); 390, 391 (Holton); 400-402 (Woodward); 407-410 (Woodford); 411-413 (Blott).

Jacobus, Donald Lines and Edgar Francis Waterman. *The Granberry Family and Allied Families*. Hartford, 1945. Pp. 169-172 (Bishop); 199, 200 (Cogswell); 249, 250 (Hawkes); 216-218 (Fobes); 223-225 (Gager) (the entire American ancestry of Caleb Bishop); 282, 283 (Morgan); 285-288 (Parke); 333 (Thompson).

———. *Hale, House, and Related Families*. Hartford, 1952. Reprint. Baltimore, 1978. Pp. 447-452 (Allen); 808, 809 (Woodford); 480-482 (Blott).

Lee, Leonard and Sarah Fiske Lee. *John Lee of Farmington, Hartford Co., Conn., and His Descendants*. 2d ed. Meriden, Conn., 1897. Pp. 44-48, 53-58, 467-470 (Hart, Lee, Strong).

Smith, Ethel Farrington. *Adam Hawkes of Saugus, Mass., 1605-1672: The First Six Generations in America*. Baltimore, 1980. Pp. 1-31.

Sumner, Edith Bartlett. *Descendants of Thomas Farr of Harpswell, Maine, and 90 Allied Families*. Los Angeles, 1959. Pp. 32, 33 (Blott); 68-71 (Cogswell); 165-167 (Hebard or Hibbard); 192, 193 (Luff); 303 (Walden).

Underhill, Lora Altine Woodbury. *Descendants of Edward Small of New England and the Allied Families with Tracings of English Ancestry*. Rev. ed. Boston, 1934. Pp. 509-511 (Mitchell).

Warner, Frederick Chester. "The Ancestry of Samuel, Freda and John Warner." 5 vols. Boston, 1949. Typescript, NEHGS and elsewhere. Pp. 646-649 (Strong); 214, 215 (Ford); 309, 310 (Holton); 796, 797 (Woodford); 72 (Blott); 804, 805 (Woodward); 487, 488 (Parke); 666, 667 (Thompson).

Some use was also made of Orrin Peer Allen, *The Allen Memorial, Second Series: Descendants of Samuel Allen of Windsor, Conn., 1640-1907* (Palmer, Mass., 1907); Alfred Andrews, *Genealogical History of Deacon Stephen Hart and His Descendants, 1632-1875* (Hartford, 1875); Rev. Edward Payson Holton and Harriet Scofield, "A Genealogy of the Descendants in America of William Holton (1610-1691) of Hartford, Conn. and Northampton, Mass.," 2nd ed., 1965 (typescript, NEHGS); E. O. Jameson, *The Cogswells in America* (Boston, 1884); Nathaniel H. Morgan, *Morgan Genealogy: A History of James Morgan of New London, Conn. and His Descendants from 1607 to 1869* (Hartford, 1869). An older multi-ancestor work, Frank Farnsworth Starr, *Various Ancestral Lines of James Goodwin and Lucy (Morgan) Goodwin of Hartford, Connecticut*, 2 vols. (Hartford, 1915), covers the Woodfords (2:183-191) and Blotts (2:193-201) in considerable detail. A second such work, not quite as good as those already listed, Louis Effingham DeForest, *Our Colonial and Continental Ancestors: The Ancestry of Mr. and Mrs. Louis William Dommerich* (New York, 1930), covers the Ford (99-101), Allen (40, 41), Woodford (217, 218), Blott (51), Hibbard (107-110), and Luff (129, 130) families. For Parkes see also Selim Walker McArthur, *McArthur-Barnes Ancestral Lines* (Portland, Me., 1964), 97-101.

In the following table Dr. Strong is given the number 1, his parents 2-3, grandparents 4-7, great-grandparents 8-15, great-great-grandparents 16-31, great-great-great-grandparents 32-63, and great-great-great-great-grandparents 64-127. For the parents of any given ancestor (say 10), refer to the individuals with double that number (the father) and double that number plus one (the mother) (i.e., 20 and 21); for the child of an ancestor, refer to the individual with half that number (5). If this last is female, her number will be odd, and to find her child divide by two and discard the remaining 1/2 (thus the child of 5 is 2).

1. Dr. Joseph Strong, 1770-1812.

2. Benajah Strong, b. Coventry, Conn. 13 Oct. 1740, d. there 25 Nov. 1809, selectman of Coventry and member of the Connecticut General Assembly in 1781 who responded to the Lexington Alarm under Capt. Elias Buell of Coventry and served as private and corporal. He thus qualifies as a revolutionary soldier and patriot and is listed in the *DAR Patriot Index* (Washington, 1967), 657. Four descendants, three through Dr. Joseph Strong, are treated in the *Daughters of the American Revolution Lineage Books*, 81 (1925): 202 (Mrs. Elisa Anderson Hewett, #80532), 109 (1929): 146 (Mrs. Fannie States Babcock Leonard, #108485), and 150 (1936): 285, 286 (Mrs. Mary Anderson Barr and her daughter, Mrs. Corinne Barr Uhler, #s 149910 and 149913). Benajah m. 1) at Coventry 9 Mar. 1769

3. Lucy Bishop, b. Norwich, Conn. 21 Dec. 1747, d. Coventry 27 Nov. 1783.

4. Joseph Strong, Jr., b. Northampton, Mass. 25 July 1701, d. Coventry 9 Apr. 1773, also a Coventry selectman and member of the Connecticut General Assembly, m. at Coventry 12 May 1724, a second cousin

5. Elizabeth Strong, b. Northampton 27 Sept. 1704, d. Coventry 1 May 1792.

6. Caleb Bishop, b. Norwich 16 Mar. 1715/6, d. Guilford, Conn. 16 Feb. 1785, m. Norwich 19 Apr. 1739

7. Keziah Hibbard, b. Windham, Conn. 19 May 1722, death date unknown. For documentary proof of Keziah's parentage (for the Hibbard genealogy and *Parke Scrapbooks* both contain errors) see Windham, Conn. land records (on microfilm at the Connecticut State Library in Hartford), H, 198-200, in which

deed of 21 June 1743 Caleb Bishop and wife Kezia sell to her brother Nathan Hebard the one-ninth part of a parcel of land left them by "our honored father Ebenezer Hebard."

8. JOSEPH STRONG, b. Northampton 2 Dec. 1672, d. Coventry 23 Dec. 1763, town treasurer and selectman of Coventry, first representative from Coventry in the Connecticut General Assembly, m. 1) at Northampton in 1694

9. SARAH ALLEN, b. Northampton 22 Aug. 1672, d. before 15 Sept. 1724.

10. PRESERVED STRONG, b. Northampton 29 Mar. 1680, d. Coventry 26 Sept. 1765, m. at Northampton 23 Oct. 1701 his step-sister

11. TABITHA LEE, b. Farmington, Conn. ca. 1677/8, d. Coventry 23 June 1750.

12. SAMUEL BISHOP, Jr., b. Ipswich, Mass. Feb. 1678/9, d. Norwich 18 Nov. 1760, m. at Norwich 2 Jan. 1705/6

13. SARAH FOBES, b. Norwich 24 June 1684, d. there 11 Mar. 1759.

14. EBENEZER HIBBARD, b. Wenham, Mass. May 1682, d. Windham Oct. 1732, not 1752, as given in all published accounts. The probate file on Ebenezer Hebard (#1843, Windham Probate District, also at the Connecticut State Library) includes documents of Jan. 1732/3, Mar. 1734, and Feb. 1736/7. See also the *Register*, 51 (1897): 316-321 for the Hibbards. Ebenezer m. at Windham 10 Mar. 1709

15. MARGARET MORGAN, b. Preston, Conn. 28 July 1686, death date unknown.

16. THOMAS STRONG, b. Hingham, Mass. ca. 1637, d. Northampton 3 Oct. 1689, m. 2) at Northampton 10 Oct. 1671, as her first husband

17. RACHEL HOLTON, b. Hartford, Conn. ca. 1650, death date unknown. She m. 2) at Northampton 16 May 1698 Nathan Bradley.

18. NEHEMIAH ALLEN, b. ca. 1634, d. Northampton 27 June 1684, m. at Northampton 21 Sept. 1664, as her first husband

19. SARAH WOODFORD, bapt. Hartford 2 Sept. 1649, d. Northampton 31 Mar. 1712/3. She m. 2) at Northampton 1 Sept. 1687 Richard Burke and 3) at Northampton 11 July 1706 Judah Wright.

20. JEDEDIAH STRONG, bapt. Taunton, Mass. 14 Apr. 1639, d. Coventry 22 May 1733, m. 1) at Northampton 18 Nov. 1662

21. FREEDOM WOODWARD, bapt. Dorchester July 1642, d. Northampton 17 May 1681.

22. JOHN LEE, b. England (perhaps near Colchester, Essex) ca. 1620, d. Farmington 8 Aug. 1690, immigrant on the *Francis* in 1634, in Hartford 1635, in Farmington 1641, m. at Farmington 1658, as her first husband

23. MARY HART, b. England ca. 1630/1, d. as the result of a fall from a horse, South Hadley, Mass. 10 Oct. 1710. She m. 2) at Northampton 5 Jan. 1691/2, as his second wife, Jedediah Strong, #20 above.

24. SAMUEL BISHOP, b. Ipswich ca. 1645, d. there shortly before 2 Mar. 1687, graduate of Harvard College in 1665 (see John Langdon Sibley, *Biographical Sketches of Graduates of Harvard University*, 2, 1659-1677 [Cambridge, 1881], 189), m. at Ipswich 10 Aug. 1675, as her first husband

25. HESTER COGSWELL, b. Ipswich ca. 1656, d. after 17 Jan. 1703/4. She m. 2) at Ipswich 16 Dec. 1689 Thomas Burnham.

26. CALEB FOBES, b. probably at Duxbury, Mass., d. Preston 25 Aug. 1710, m. 1) at Norwich 30 June 1681

27. SARAH GAGER, b. New London, Conn. Feb. 1651, death date unknown.

28. ROBERT HIBBARD, Jr., bapt. Salem, Mass. 7 May 1648, d. Windham 29 Apr. 1710, m. Wenham 1673
29. MARY WALDEN, b. Wenham ca. 1655, d. Windham 7 Mar. 1736.
30. JOSEPH MORGAN, b. Roxbury, Mass. 29 Oct. 1646, d. Preston 5 Apr. 1704, m. at New London 26 Apr. 1670
31. DOROTHY PARKE, b. New London 6 Mar. 1652, d. at Preston date unknown.
32. JOHN STRONG, b. Chard, Somerset, England ca. 1610, d. Northampton 14 Apr. 1699, immigrant probably in 1635 (when he was in Hingham, Mass.), in Taunton, Mass. in 1638, in Windsor, Conn. in 1645, and in Northampton in 1660. He was the son of John Strong (ca. 1585-ante 26 Nov. 1627) of Chard and grandson of George Strong of Chard, whose will, dated 26 Nov. 1627 and proved 16 Feb. 1636 mentions "my grandchild John Strong." He m. 2) ca. 1636
33. ABIGAIL FORD, bapt. Bridport, Dorset, England 8 Oct. 1619, d. Northampton 6 July 1688.
34. WILLIAM HOLTON, perhaps the William bapt. Holton St. Mary's, Suffolk, England 20 Oct. 1610, son of Edward Holton, d. Northampton 12 Aug. 1691, immigrant probably on the *Francis* in 1634, an early settler of Hartford, to Northampton about 1655. His wife (m. ca. 1632) was perhaps
35. MARY ———, d. Northampton 16 Nov. 1691.
36. SAMUEL ALLEN, b. (perhaps near Chelmsford, Essex) England ca. 1608, bur. Windsor 28 Apr. 1648, immigrant probably of the 1630s, in Windsor 1640/1, almost certainly a brother of Thomas Allen of Middletown, Conn. He m., as her first husband
37. ANN ———, d. Northampton 13 Nov. 1687, who m. 2) William Hulbert.
38. THOMAS WOODFORD, b. England, d. Northampton 6 Mar. 1666/7, immigrant on the *William and Francis*, in Roxbury 1632/3, in Hartford 1639/40, in Northampton 1655/6, m. Roxbury before 1639
39. MARY BLOTT, b. England before 1615, d. probably at Hartford or Northampton before 27 May 1662.
40. Same as 32 above.
41. Same as 33 above.
42. HENRY WOODWARD, perhaps the Henry bapt. Childwell, Lancashire, England 22 Mar. 1607, son of Thomas Woodward and Elizabeth Tynen of Much Woolton, Lancashire (who were married 23 May 1592), killed by lightning at Northampton 7 Apr. 1683, immigrant in the *James* to Boston in 1635, in Dorchester 1639, in Northampton 1659, m. probably in Dorchester ca. 1640
43. ELIZABETH ———, d. Northampton 13 Aug. 1690.
46. STEPHEN HART, perhaps the Stephen bapt. Ipswich, Suffolk, England 25 Jan. 1602/3, son of Stephen Hart, d. Farmington between 16 and 31 Mar. 1682/3, immigrant probably in 1630/1, in Cambridge 1632, in Hartford 1636, in Farmington 1645. He is called "my cousin" in the will of Judith Morris, widow, of Dedham, Essex, England, dated 25 Jan. 1645 (see the *Register*, 48 [1894]: 118, 119). His first wife, #47, the mother of his children, is unknown.
48. THOMAS BISHOP, b. England ca. 1618, d. Ipswich 7 Feb. 1670/1, immigrant, in Ipswich by 1636, m.
49. MARGARET ———, d. Ipswich shortly before 29 Mar. 1681.
50. WILLIAM COGSWELL, bapt. Westbury Leigh, Wiltshire, England Mar. 1618/9, d. Ipswich 15 Dec. 1700, m. probably at Lynn, Mass. ca. 1649
51. SUSANNA HAWKES, twin, b. Charlestown, Mass. 13 Aug. 1633, d. Ipswich before 5 Aug. 1696.

52. JOHN FOBES, d. Bridgewater, Mass. 1660, immigrant, in Plymouth, Mass., 1636, later in Duxbury, in Bridgewater, 1656, m. as her first husband

53. CONSTANT MITCHELL, birth and death dates unknown, who m. 2) 1662 John Briggs of Portsmouth, R.I. Nahum Mitchell, in his *History of the Early Settlers of Bridgewater, in Plymouth County, Massachusetts, including an Extensive Family Register* (Boston, 1840, reprint Baltimore, 1970), 162, called Constant a sister of Experience Mitchell of Duxbury, an identification D. L. Jacobus was inclined to accept. If so, her parents were almost certainly Thomas Mitchell of Leyden, Holland (aged 56 on 15 Aug. 1622, from Cambridge, England) and Margaret Williams, his second wife, widow of Christopher Stocking, who were married in Amsterdam 9 May 1606. See *The American Genealogist*, 56 (1980): 97, 98.

54. JOHN GAGER, b. England by 1625, d. Norwich 10 Dec. 1703, m. probably at Norwich

55. ELIZABETH GORE, b. England ca. 1627, d. after 10 Jan. 1703/4, apparently an immigrant, sister of Hannah Gore, first wife of Stephen Gifford of Norwich, and of Mary Gore, this last a daughter of Samuel Gore, "citizen and grocer of London, deceased [on 19 May 1643]."

56. ROBERT HIBBARD, perhaps the Robert bapt. St. Edmunds, Wiltshire, England 13 Mar. 1613, son of John Hibbard, d. Beverly, Mass. 7 May 1684, immigrant, in Salem 1638, in Beverly 1670/1, m. Salem, ca. 1640

57. JOAN LUFF, d. Beverly, Mass. shortly before 6 Apr. 1696.

58. EDWARD WALDEN, d. Wenham June 1679, immigrant, in Ipswich 1648, early settler of Wenham. His wife, #59, not named in his will, is unknown.

60. JAMES MORGAN, b. England ca. 1607, d. New London 1685, immigrant to Boston, in Roxbury 1640, New London 1651, m. at Roxbury 6 Aug. 1640

61. MARGERY HILL, whose origin and birth and death dates are unknown.

62. THOMAS PARKE, b. 13 ——— 1616 Hitcham, Suffolk, England, d. Preston 30 July 1709, m. Roxbury, Mass. before 28 Oct. 1644

63. DOROTHY THOMPSON, bapt. Preston Capes, Northamptonshire, England 5 July 1624, d. after 5 Sept. 1707.

66. THOMAS FORD, b. England ca. 1590, d. Northampton 28 Nov. 1676, immigrant in the *Mary and John* to Nantasket 1630, in Dorchester shortly thereafter, in Windsor 1636, in Hartford 1644, in Northampton 1672, m. (perhaps his second wife) Bridport, Dorset 19 June 1616, as her second husband

67. ELIZABETH CHARDE, b. England, bur. Windsor 18 Apr. 1643. She had m. 1) at Thorncombe, Dorset 2 Sept. 1610 Aaron Cooke, bur. Bridport 29 Dec. 1615. See *The American Genealogist*, 11 (1934-1935): 179, 180; 16 (1939-1940): 41-43; 56 (1980): 233.

78. ROBERT BLOTT, b. England, d. Boston, Mass. between 27 Mar. and 22 Aug. 1665, immigrant, in Charlestown 1634, later perhaps in Concord, in Boston 1648. His first wife, #79, the mother of his children, is unknown.

82. Same as 66 above.

83. Same as 67 above.

100. JOHN COGSWELL, b. Westbury Leigh, Wiltshire, England ca. 1592, d. Ipswich 29 Nov. 1669, immigrant on the *Angel Gabriel* to Pemaquid, Maine in 1635, in Ipswich later that year. He was a son of Edward Cogswell of Westbury Leigh (will dated 23 June 1615, proved 12 Jan. 1615/6) and Alice ——— (will dated 25 June 1615, proved 11 May 1616), and grandson of Robert Cogswell,

bur. Westbury Leigh 7 June 1581, whose widow, Alice Cogswell, was buried Dilton, Wiltshire 1 Aug. 1603. John m. at Westbury Leigh 10 Sept. 1615

101. Elizabeth Thompson, b. England, d. Ipswich 2 June 1676, daughter of Rev. William Thompson, vicar of Westbury from 1603 until his death in 1623, and his first wife, Phillis ———, who was buried there 19 July 1608.

102. Adam Hawkes, bapt. Hingham, Norfolk, England 26 Jan. 1605, as Adam, son of John Hawke, d. Lynn, Mass. 13 Mar. 1671/2, immigrant in the Winthrop Fleet, soon thereafter in Charlestown, in Lynn 1638, m. 1) Charlestown ca. 1631, as her second husband

103. Mrs. Ann Hutchinson, b. England ca. 1595, d. Lynn 4 Dec. 1669. She was perhaps Ann Brown, sister of Nicholas Brown of Reading and daughter of Edward Brown and Jane Lide (daughter of Thomas Lide) of Inkbarrow, Worcestershire (see the *Register*, 103 [1949]: 182). Her first husband was perhaps Thomas Hutchinson of Charlestown.

108. William Gager, b. Suffolk, England, d. Charlestown 20 Sept. 1630, immigrant in the Winthrop Fleet. His wife, #109, is unknown.

110. Samuel Gore of London, England, probably the Samuel Goare who married Elizabeth Hill of Rotherhithe, a district of London, 18 Jan. 1625/6, as found in Boyd's Marriage Index at the Society of Genealogists in London. A grocer, Gore was probably also the "Samuel Goore" who "became free of the Grocer's Co. London 16 May 1622. Late apprentice to Henry Dodd." See the *Register*, 115 (1961): 252, 253, 256.

114. John Luff, d. Salem ca. 1667/8, immigrant on the *Mary and John* to Boston, 1633, in Salem 1636, m.

115. Bridget ——— living 1671, aged 84.

124. Robert Parke, bapt. Postingford, Suffolk, England 3 June 1580, d. Mystic (Stonington) Conn. 14 Mar. 1664/5, immigrant in the Winthrop Fleet, soon thereafter in Roxbury, in Wethersfield, Conn. 1639, in New London 1649, in Stonington 1658. He was a son of Robert Parke of Gestingthorpe (will dated 12 Feb. 1592/3, proved 3 Apr. 1593) and Alice Chaplin (married Sudbury, Suffolk 1579), grandson of William Parke of Gestingthorpe (will dated 25 Mar. 1551, proved 13 May 1551), and great-grandson of another William Parke of Gestingthorpe, d. 1531. This last was likely a son of a third William Parke of Gestingthorpe, living 1484, probable son of John Parke of that place, heir of his father in 1455, son of another John Parke of Gestingthorpe, heir of his father in 1414, son of Robert Parke of Gestingthorpe, d. 1400, and Margaret ———, d. 22 Aug. 1408. The immigrant m. 1) Semer, Suffolk 9 Feb. 1601/2

125. Martha Chaplin, bapt. Semer, Suffolk, England 4 Feb. 1583/4, d. probably by 1643 (whether she came to New England is unknown), her husband's first cousin and a daughter of William Chaplin of Semer, Suffolk, who was buried there 15 Oct. 1629, and Agnes ———, his first wife, buried at Semer 26 Sept. 1602. William Chaplin and his sister Alice Chaplin, wife of Robert Parke of Gestingthorpe, above, were children of another William Chaplin, of Tarnes Farm, Long Melford, whose will was dated 15 Nov. 1575 and proved 25 Jan. 1577/8, and an unknown first wife. Robert Chaplin (1602-1643/4) of Bury St. Edmunds, Suffolk, a brother of Mrs. Martha Chaplin Parke, was the father of a lord mayor of London, the grandfather of a baronet, and an ancestor of all viscounts Chaplin and Canterbury, all barons Manners, and various other British peers. See *The American Genealogist*, 33 (1957): 11-13, and sources cited therein;

Joseph James Muskett, *Suffolk Manorial Families* (Exeter, 1910) 3:102-120; and recent editions of *Burke's Peerage, Baronetage and Knightage* (the Chaplin article especially).

126. JOHN THOMPSON, gent., of Little Preston, Northamptonshire, England, d. London 6 Nov. 1626 m. 2) before 1 May 1616, as her first husband

127. ALICE FREEMAN, birth and death dates unknown, immigrant, m. 2) shortly after 30 May 1644 Robert Parke, #124 above. Alice was a daughter of Henry Freeman of Cranford, Northamptonshire, b. 1560, and Margaret Edwards (m. by 25 Dec. 1591), granddaughter of Thomas Freeman of Irchester, Northamptonshire (will dated 24 Mar. 1585, proved 11 May 1586) and of Edward Edwards of Alwalton, Huntingtonshire (will dated 25 Dec. 1591, proved 16 Sept. 1592) and Ursula Coles (bur. Alwalton 2 Feb. 1606), and great-granddaughter of Henry Freeman of Irchester (will dated 6 Aug. 1580, proved 29 Apr. 1585) and Joan Rudd, of Peter Edwards of Peterborough, Northamptonshire, and Alwalton (b. ca. 1490, d. ca. 1552) and his second wife, Susanna Samwell (m. ca. 1535), and of Richard Coles of Preston Capes (d. 11 Sept. 1575) and Jane Bond (m. 1527, living 1576). An ancestor table of Alice Freeman for 32 generations is outlined in Henry James Young, *The Blackmans of Knight's Creek: Ancestors and Descendants of George and Maria (Smith) Blackman*, rev. ed., (Carlisle, Pa., 1980), 55-134. Through Susanna Samwell, Alice Freeman and Dr. Joseph Strong have two royal descents, both outlined in an appendix at the end of this work. The first, carefully developed by Clarence Almon Torrey and George Andrews Moriarty, Jr., is from Ethelred II, King of England, d. 1016, and Malcolm II, King of Scots, d. 1034, via earls of Northumberland and Dunbar and the Merlay, Gobion, Morteyn, and Giffard families. See *The American Genealogist*, 13 (1936-1937): 1-8; 14 (1937-1938): 145, 146; and 29 (1953): 215-218, and the *Register*, 75 (1921): 131-136 and 79 (1925): 358-378, and the 19-volume manuscript collection of G.A. Moriarty at NEHGS. The second royal descent, compiled by H. J. Young from F. N. MacNamara, *Memorials of the Danvers Family (of Dauntsey & Culworth)* (London, 1895), William F. Carter, *The Quatremains of Oxfordshire* (Oxford, 1936), volume 8 of the Moriarty manuscript collection, and a few other sources, is from Hugh Capet, King of France, d. 996, through counts of Hainault, Roucy, Montdidier, and Clermont, and the Clare, Wake, Duston, Grey of Rotherfield, Breton, Quatremain, Bruley, Danvers, Langston, and Giffard families. The former of these royal descents is outlined in F. L. Weis and W.L. Sheppard, Jr., *Ancestral Roots of 60 Colonists Who Came to New England Between 1623 and 1650*, 5th ed. (Baltimore, 1976), lines 34, 41-43, and 29A. The additional royal descent outlined in 29A, however, through the Corbet, Harley, and Besford families, has been disproved; see *The Genealogist* (New York), 1 (1980): 27-39. The second, Capetian royal descent of Alice Freeman is charted in Henry James Young, *The Carolingian Ancestry of Edmond Hawes, Alice Freeman, and Thomas James* (Carlisle, Pa., 1983), 7-8. Sir John Throckmorton (d. 1445) of Coughton, Warwickshire, and John Danvers (d. ca. 1448) of Colthorp, Oxfordshire, great-great-great and great-great-grandfathers respectively of Susanna Samwell, were each ancestors of several dozen immigrants to the American colonies. These kinships are explored in "The Mowbray Connection," 7: 162-166, 174, 175. Among other New England colonists Alice Freeman's nearest kinsman was Rev. William Sargent (1602-1682) of Malden, Mass.; see Weis and Sheppard, *Ancestral Roots*, line 43.

IV

Two Hundred Fifty Notable Distant Kinsmen of Dr. Joseph Strong & H.R.H. The Princess of Wales

The following alphabetically listed 250 distant kinsmen of Dr. Joseph Strong and the Princess of Wales all receive, or undoubtedly will receive, considerable coverage in the *Dictionary of American Biography, Notable American Women,* or *Webster's Biographical Dictionary.* Immediately after each name are the notable kinsman's birth and death years and a word or phrase that denotes his or her area of achievement. If the figure himself, not a spouse, shares ancestry with Dr. Strong an outline then follows, generation by generation, beginning with the figure's parents, then grandparents, then great-grandparents, etc. (names only, as space considerations preclude dates or places), and using semicolons to separate generations, of the descent from the ancestor or ancestors shared with Dr. Strong (a pair unless the kinship is of the half blood). These last are identified by their numbers in the preceding ancestor table (see pages 27-32), and no mention is made of earlier or later marriages of any listed ancestors of the 250. Whenever a figure has two or more distant kinships to Dr. Strong, as is frequently the case, all lines are followed in every generation, with commas separating individual couples therein and the couples themselves listed in standard genealogical order, parents of husbands preceding those of wives. Whenever cousins marry, I state in parentheses or brackets following the names of parents, which child of that surname was theirs in the earlier listed (but chronologically next) generation. In the case of marriage between cousins of different generations, the common ancestors are generally mentioned only once, followed by all children in that figure's ancestry. See, for example, number 95. This format is much like that used in the *Daughters of the American Revolution Lineage Books.* Whenever a figure's spouse is the kinsman of Dr. Strong, the name of the husband or wife immediately follows, in parentheses, the designation of the figure's occupation or achievement. The spouse's ancestry is then treated exactly as a kinsman's, and following the final indication of shared ancestry with Dr. Strong the parentheses are closed. If both a notable figure and his or her spouse were distant kinsmen of Dr. Strong, only the former's kinship is treated. Charted pamphlets outlining these and some other kinships between the Princess of Wales and notable Americans have been deposited in the library of NEHGS.

1. LYMAN ABBOTT, 1835–1922, Congregational clergyman & reformer; Jacob Abbott III & Harriet Vaughan; Jacob Abbott, Jr. & Betsey Abbott; Jacob Abbott & Lydia Stevens (parents of Jacob, Jr.), Joshua Abbott & Elizabeth Chandler (parents of Betsey); Joseph Abbott & Deborah Blanchard (parents of Jacob), Nathaniel Abbott, Jr. & Penelope Ballard (parents of Joshua); Nathaniel Abbott & Dorcas Hibbard (parents of Joseph & Nathaniel, Jr.); Joseph Hibbard & Elizabeth Graves; 56-7.

2. DEAN GOODERHAM ACHESON, 1893–1971, U.S. Secretary of State under Truman (wife, Alice Stanley; Louis Crandall Stanley & Jane Cornelia Mahon; John Mix Stanley & Alice English; Seth Stanley, Jr. & Huldah Catlin; Seth Stanley & Ruth Clark; Noah Stanley & Ruth Norton, John Clark & Elizabeth Newell; Thomas Stanley, Jr. & Esther Cowles, John Newell & Elizabeth Hawley; Samuel Cowles, Jr. & Rachel Porter, Samuel Newell & Mary Hart; Thomas Porter & Sarah Hart, Thomas Hart & Ruth Hawkins; 46-7 [parents of Sarah & Thomas]).

3. JOHN ADAMS (JR.), 1735–1826, 2nd U.S. President; John Adams & Susanna Boylston; Peter Boylston & Anne White; Benjamin White & Susanna Cogswell; 50-1.

4. JOHN QUINCY ADAMS, 1767–1848, 6th U.S. President, son of 3 above & Abigail Smith.

5. CHARLES FRANCIS ADAMS, 1807–1886, diplomat, son of 4 above & Louisa Catherine Johnson.

6-7. BROOKS ADAMS, 1848–1927, historian, & HENRY (BROOKS) ADAMS, 1838–1918, novelist & historian, sons of 5 above & Abigail Brown Brooks.

8. AMOS BRONSON ALCOTT, 1799–1888, educator and transcendentalist (wife, Abigail May; Joseph May & Dorothy Sewall; Samuel May & Abigail Williams; Joseph Williams, Jr. & Martha Howell; Joseph Williams & Abigail Davis; Stephen Williams & Sarah Wise; Joseph Wise & Mary Thompson; 126-7).

9. LOUISA MAY ALCOTT, 1832–1888, novelist, daughter of 8 above.

10. NELSON WILMARTH ALDRICH, 1841–1915, U.S. Senator & Republican leader, financier, & art collector (wife, Abby Pearce Truman Chapman; Francis Morgan Chapman & Lucy Anne Truman; Amos Chapman & Amy Morgan, Jonathan Truman & Mary Willett; Israel Morgan & Elizabeth Brewster, John Willett & Elizabeth Leffingwell; William Morgan, Jr. & Temperance Avery, Elijah Brewster & Elizabeth Fitch, Samuel Leffingwell & Hannah Gifford; William Morgan & Mary Avery, Joseph Brewster & Dorothy Witter, Pelatiah Fitch & Elizabeth Choate, Samuel Gifford & Mary Calkins; John Morgan & Elizabeth Jones, Ebenezer Witter & Dorothy Morgan, Samuel Choate & Mary Williams, Stephen Gifford & Hannah Gore; 60-1 [parents of John], 30-1 [parents of Dorothy], Stephen Williams & Sarah Wise, 110-1; Joseph Wise & Mary Thompson; 126-7).

11. HORATIO ALGER (JR.), 1834–1899, novelist, writer of boys' stories; Horatio Alger & Olive Augusta Fenno; James Alger, Jr. & Hannah Bassett; James Alger

& Martha Kingman; Jonathan Kingman & Mary Keith; Joseph Keith & Elizabeth Fobes; Edward Fobes & Elizabeth Howard; 52-3.

12. ETHAN ALLEN, 1738–1789, commander of the "Green Mountain Boys," revolutionary soldier & Vermont patriot; Joseph Allen & Mary Baker; Samuel Allen & Mercy Wright; 18-9.

13-14. JOSEPH (WRIGHT) ALSOP (V), b. 1910, & STEWART (JOHONNOT OLIVER) ALSOP, 1914–1974, newspaper columnists & political analysts; Joseph Wright Alsop IV & Corinne Douglas Robinson; Joseph Wright Alsop III & Elizabeth Winthrop Beach; Joseph Wright Alsop, Jr. & Mary Alsop Oliver; Joseph Wright Alsop & Lucy Whittlesey, Francis Johonnot Oliver & Mary Caroline Alsop; Chauncey Whittlesey, Jr. & Lucy Wetmore, Richard Alsop, Jr. & Mary Wyllys Pomeroy (parents of Mary Caroline); Chauncey Whittlesey & Elizabeth Whiting, Eleazer Pomeroy and Mary Wyllys; Samuel Whittlesey & Sarah Chauncey, Benjamin Pomeroy & Abigail Wheelock; Nathaniel Chauncey & Abigail Strong, Joseph Pomeroy & Hannah Seymour; 32-3, Medad Pomeroy & Experience Woodward; 42-3.

15. SUSAN BROWNELL ANTHONY, 1820–1906, reformer & suffragette; Daniel Anthony & Lucy Read; Humphrey Anthony & Hannah Lapham; Joshua Lapham & Hannah Sherman; John Lapham, Jr. & Mary Russell; Joseph Russell & Elizabeth Fobes; 52-3.

16. PHILIP DANFORTH ARMOUR, 1832–1901, founder of Armour & Co., Chicago meat packers (wife, Malvina Belle Ogden; Jonathan Ogden & Mary Elizabeth Gorham; Timothy Gorham & Martha Smith Merrill; Miles Gorham & Abigail Morris; John Gorham & Lydia Dorman; Benjamin Dorman & Sarah Tuttle; Samuel Tuttle & Sarah Hart; Stephen Hart, Jr. & Anne Fitch; 46-7).

17. LOUIS STANTON AUCHINCLOSS, b. 1917, novelist; Joseph Howland Auchincloss & Priscilla Dixon Stanton; John Winthrop Auchincloss & Joanna Hone Russell; Charles Handy Russell & Caroline Howland; Samuel Shaw Howland & Joanna Hone; Joseph Howland & Lydia Bill; Ephraim Bill & Lydia Huntington; Joshua Huntington & Hannah Perkins; Simon Huntington III & Lydia Gager; 54-5.

18. RAY STANNARD BAKER, 1870–1946, author, editor, diplomat; Joseph Stannard Baker & Alice Potter; Luther Alexander Baker & Mercy Stannard, James Addison Potter & Mary Miller Denio; Joseph Stannard & Phebe Denison, John Denio & Harriet Amelia Stiles; Christopher Denison & Elizabeth Kelsey, Ezra Stiles, Jr. & Sybil Avery; Samuel Denison & Mary Lay, Samuel Avery & Sybil Noyes; Robert Lay, Jr. & Mary Stanton, Humphrey Avery & Jerusha Morgan, William Noyes & Sybil Whiting; Thomas Stanton, Jr. & Sarah Denison, William Morgan & Margaret Avery, John Noyes & Mary Gallup; George Denison & Bridget Thompson, James Morgan, Jr. & Mary Vine, William Gallup & Sarah Chesebrough; 126-7, 60-1, Nathaniel Chesebrough & Hannah Denison; George Denison & Bridget Thompson, above.

19. ABRAHAM BALDWIN, 1754–1807, Georgia congressman, U.S. Senator, founder & first president of Franklin College, later the University of Georgia; Michael Baldwin & Lucy Dudley; William Dudley & Ruth Strong; 16-7.

20. GEORGE BANCROFT, 1800–1891, historian, diplomat, Secretary of the Navy (1st wife, Sarah Hopkins Dwight; Jonathan Dwight, Jr., & Sarah Shepard; Levi Shepard & Mary Pomeroy; Seth Pomeroy & Mary Hunt; Ebenezer Pomeroy & Sarah King, Jonathan Hunt, Jr. & Martha Williams; Medad Pomeroy & Experience Woodward, John King & Sarah Holton, Samuel Williams & Theoda Parke; 42-3, 34-5, William Parke & Martha Holgrave; 124-5).

21. Joel Barlow, 1754–1812, poet & diplomat (wife, Ruth Baldwin, sister of Abraham Baldwin, 19 above).

22. Frederick Augustus Porter Barnard, 1809–1889, president of Columbia University, 1864–1889, a founder of Barnard College; Robert Foster Barnard & Augusta Porter; Sylvester Barnard & Sarah Grosse; Abner Barnard & Rachel Catlin; Ebenezer Barnard & Elizabeth Foster; Joseph Barnard & Sarah Strong; 32-3.

23. (Mrs.) Ethel Barrymore (Colt), 1879–1959, actress (husband, Russell Griswold Colt; Samuel Pomeroy Colt & Elizabeth Mitchelson Bullock; Christopher Colt, Jr. & Theodora Goujaud DeWolf; Christopher Colt & Sarah Caldwell; John Caldwell & Margaret Collyer; Hezekiah Collyer, Jr. & Jennett Evans; Hezekiah Collyer & Hepzibah Wadsworth; Jonathan Wadsworth & Hepzibah Marsh; John Marsh, Jr. & Sarah Lyman; Richard Lyman, Jr. & Hepzibah Ford; 66-7).

24. John Barrymore, 1882–1942 (2nd wife, Blanche Marie Louise Oelrichs, the actress Michael Strange; Charles May Oelrichs & Blanche DeLoosey; Henry Ferdinand Oelrichs & Julia Matilda May; Frederick May & Julia Matilda Slocum; John May & Abigail May; Samuel May & Abigail Williams [parents of Abigail], grandparents of Mrs. Amos Bronson Alcott, see 8 above).

25. L(yman) Frank Baum, 1856–1919, author of *The Wonderful Wizard of Oz;* Benjamin Ward Baum & Cynthia Ann Stanton; Oliver Stanton & Rhoda Underwood; Robert Stanton & Elizabeth Palmer; Joshua Stanton & Hannah Randall; William Stanton & Anna Stanton; Thomas Stanton, Jr. & Sarah Denison (parents of William); George Denison & Bridget Thompson; 126-7.

26. Moses Yale Beach, 1800–1868, inventor, co-founder of the *New York Sun* (wife, Nancy Day; Henry Day & Mary Ely; William Ely & Drusilla Brewster; William Brewster & Damaris Gates; Benjamin Brewster & Elizabeth Witter; Ebenezer Witter & Dorothy Morgan; 30-1).

27. Sir Thomas Beecham, 2nd Bt., 1879–1961, composer & conductor (1st wife, Utica Welles; Charles Stuart Welles & Ella Celeste Miles; Henry Spalding Welles & Amelia Beardsley; Henry Welles & Sarah Spalding; John Spalding & Wealthy Anne Gore; Obadiah Gore, Jr. & Anna Avery; Obadiah Gore & Hannah Parke, Richardson Avery & Sarah Plumb; Thomas Parke III & Hannah Witter, William Avery & Anna Richardson; Thomas Parke, Jr. & Mary Allyn, Samuel Richardson & Anna Chesebrough; 62-3, Nathaniel Chesebrough & Hannah Denison; George Denison & Bridget Thompson; 126-7).

28. Lyman Beecher, 1775–1863, Presbyterian clergyman; David Beecher and Esther Lyman; John Lyman & Hope Hawley; Ebenezer Lyman & Experience Pomeroy; Thomas Lyman & Ruth Holton, John Pomeroy & Mindwell Sheldon; Richard Lyman, Jr. & Hepzibah Ford, 34-5, Medad Pomeroy & Experience Woodward, Isaac Sheldon & Mary Woodford; 66-7, 42-3, 38-9.

29. Henry Ward Beecher, 1813–1887, Presbyterian & Congregational clergyman, publicist & abolitionist, son of 28 above & Roxana Foote.

30. Edward Bellamy, 1850–1898, utopian socialist, author of *Looking Backward;* Rufus King Bellamy & Maria Louisa Putnam; Jonathan Bellamy & Phebe Stiles; Samuel Bellamy & Anna Steele; Daniel Steele & Anna Guernsey; John Steele & Mary Newell; Samuel Newell & Mary Hart; Thomas Hart & Ruth Hawkins; 46-7.

31. (Mrs.) Ruth (Fulton) Benedict, 1887–1948, anthropologist (husband, Stanley Rossiter Benedict; Wayland Richardson Benedict & Anne Elizabeth Kendrick; Asahel Clark Kendrick & Anne Elizabeth Hopkins; Sewall Hopkins &

Prudence Hart; Mark Hopkins & Electa Sargeant, Thomas Hart, Jr. & Mary Hungerford; Timothy Hopkins & Mary Judd, Thomas Hart & Hannah Coe; John Hopkins & Hannah Strong, Hawkins Hart & Sarah Royce; John Strong, Jr. & Mary Clark, Thomas Hart & Ruth Hawkins; 32 & Marjorie Dean, 46-7).

32. COUNT FOLKE BERNADOTTE, 1895–1948, diplomat, United Nations mediator in Palestine in 1948 & grandson of Oscar II, King of Sweden (wife, Estelle Romaine Manville; Hiram Edward Manville & Henrietta Estelle Romaine; Charles Brayton Manville & Jennie A. Long; Addison Manville & Salome Calkins; Seth Calkins & Nancy Holmes; Samuel Calkins III & Anna Dean; Samuel Calkins, Jr. & Damaris Strong; Samuel Calkins & Hannah Gifford, Josiah Strong & Joanna Gillette; Stephen Gifford & Hannah Gore, John Strong, Jr. & Elizabeth Warriner; 110-1, 32 & Marjorie Dean).

33-34. HUMPHREY (DEFOREST) BOGART, 1899–1957, actor, whose 4th wife was LAUREN BACALL, originally Betty Joan Perske, b. 1924, actress; Belmont De Forest Bogart & Maud Humphrey; John Perkins Humphrey & Frances Churchill; Harvey Humphrey & Elizabeth Rogers Perkins; Jonathan Humphrey & Rachel Dowd, Dyer Perkins & Charlotte Sophia Woodbridge; Isaac Humphrey & Esther North, John Perkins, Jr. & Bethia Baker, Samuel Woodbridge & Elizabeth Rogers; John North & Esther Stanley, John Perkins & Elizabeth Bushnell, Dudley Woodbridge & Sarah Sheldon; Nathaniel Stanley & Sarah Smith, Joseph Perkins & Martha Morgan, Ephraim Woodbridge & Hannah Morgan, Isaac Sheldon III & Elizabeth Pratt; Samuel Smith & Ruth Porter, 30-1 (parents of Martha), John Morgan & Rachel Deming (parents of Hannah), Isaac Sheldon, Jr. & Sarah Warner; Thomas Porter & Sarah Hart, 60-1, Isaac Sheldon & Mary Woodford; 46-7, 38-9.

35. CHARLES JOSEPH BONAPARTE, 1851–1921, U.S. Attorney-General & Secretary of the Navy, civil service reformer; Jerome Napoleon Bonaparte, nephew of Napoleon I, & Susan May Williams; Benjamin Williams & Sarah Copeland Morton; Joseph Williams III & Susanna May; Joseph Williams, Jr. & Martha Howell, Benjamin May & Mary Williams; Joseph Williams & Abigail Davis (parents of Joseph, Jr.), Stephen Williams, Jr. & Mary Capen (parents of Mary); Stephen Williams & Sarah Wise (parents of Joseph & Stephen, Jr.); Joseph Wise & Mary Thompson; 126-7.

36. BENJAMIN CROWNINSHIELD BRADLEE, b. 1921, executive editor of *The Washington Post* since 1968; Frederick Josiah Bradlee, Jr. & Josephine de Gersdorff; Carl August de Gersdorff & Helen Suzette Crowninshield; Ernst Bruno de Gersdorff & Caroline Choate; George Choate, Jr. & Margaret Manning Hodges; George Choate & Susanna Choate; Stephen Choate & Mary Low (parents of Susanna); David Low, Jr. & Susanna Low; David Low & Mary Lamb (parents of David, Jr.); Caleb Lamb & Mary Wise; Joseph Wise & Mary Thompson; 126-7.

37. KINGMAN BREWSTER (JR.), b. 1919, president of Yale University, 1963–1977, diplomat; Kingman Brewster & Florence Foster Besse; Charles Kingman Brewster & Celina Sophia Baldwin; Elisha Huntington Brewster & Sophronia M. Kingman; Elisha Brewster & Sarah Huntington; Jonathan Brewster, Jr. & Zipporah Smith, Jonathan Huntington & Sarah Huntington; Jonathan Brewster & Mary Parish, Ephraim Smith & Hannah Witter, Simon Huntington & Sarah Huntington (parents of Sarah); Daniel Brewster & Hannah Gager, Ebenezer Witter & Dorothy Morgan, Ebenezer Huntington & Sarah Leffingwell (parents of Sarah); 54-5, 30-1, Simon Huntington III & Lydia Gager; 54-5.

38. LOUIS BROMFIELD, 1896–1956, novelist & playwright (wife, Mary Appleton Wood; Chalmers Wood & Ellen Appleton Smith; John Cotton Smith & Harriette Appleton; Thomas Mather Smith & Mary Greenleaf Woods; Daniel Smith & Mary Smith; Cotton Mather Smith & Temperance Worthington [parents of Mary]; William Worthington & Temperance Gallup; William Gallup & Sarah Chesebrough; Nathaniel Chesebrough & Hannah Denison; George Denison & Bridget Thompson; 126-7).

39. VAN WYCK BROOKS, 1886–1963, man of letters (2nd wife, Gladys Durant Rice; Charles Clarence Rice & Jeannie Terry Durant; Edward Payson Durant & Jeannie Terry; George Washington Durant & Mary Lucinda Harrington; Allen Durant & Parthenia Holdridge; Edward Durant, Jr. & Mary Allen; Edward Durant & Judith Waldo; Cornelius Waldo, Jr. & Faith Peck; Cornelius Waldo & Hannah Cogswell; 100-1).

40. MCGEORGE BUNDY, b. 1919, foreign affairs adviser to J. F. Kennedy, president of the Ford Foundation (wife, Mary Buckminster Lothrop; Francis Bacon Lothrop & Eleanor Abbott; William Sturgis Hooper Lothrop & Alice Putnam Bacon, Gordon Abbott & Katherine McLane Tiffany; Thornton Kirkland Lothrop & Anne Maria Hooper, Jeremiah Abbott & Ellen Maria Bangs; Samuel Kirkland Lothrop & Mary Lyman Buckminster, Thomas S. Abbott & Betsey Lovejoy; John Hosmer Lothrop & Jerusha Kirkland, Joseph Buckminster, Jr. & Mary Lyman, Jeremiah Abbott & Elizabeth Stickney; Samuel Kirkland & Jerusha Bingham, Joseph Buckminster & Lucy Williams, Nathaniel Abbott, Jr. & Penelope Ballard; Daniel Kirkland & Mary Perkins, William Williams, Jr. & Hannah Stoddard, Nathaniel Abbott & Dorcas Hibbard; Joseph Perkins & Martha Morgan, William Williams & Elizabeth Cotton, Joseph Hibbard & Elizabeth Graves; 30-1, Isaac Williams & Martha Parke, 56-7; William Parke & Martha Holgrâve; 124-5).

41. RICHARD EVELYN BYRD (JR.), 1888–1957, naval officer and explorer, discoverer of the South Pole (wife, Marie Donaldson Ames; Joseph Blanchard Ames & Helen Andrews; Elisha Ford Ames & Orilla B. Parke; Elijah Ames & Abigail Ford; Job Ames & Mary Dyke; Daniel Ames & Hannah Keith; Timothy Keith & Hannah Fobes; Edward Fobes & Elizabeth Howard; 52-3).

42. ALEXANDER CALDER, 1898–1976, sculptor (wife, Louisa James; Edward Holton James & Mary Louisa Cushing; Robertson James & Mary Lucinda Holton, Robert Maynard Cushing & Olivia Donaldson Dulany; Edward Dwight Holton & Lucinda Millard, John Perkins Cushing & Mary Louisa Gardner; Jesse Millard & Lucinda Loomis, Robert Cushing & Anne Maynard Perkins; Abiathar Millard & Tabitha Hopkins, John Cushing IV & Deborah Barker; Ebenezer Hopkins & Susanna Messenger, John Cushing III & Elizabeth Holmes; Daniel Messenger & Lydia Royce, Nathaniel Holmes & Sarah Thaxter; Nehemiah Royce & Hannah Morgan, Joseph Holmes & Elizabeth Clapp; 60-1, Roger Clapp & Joanna Ford; 66-7).

43. WALTER CHAUNCEY CAMP, 1859–1925, Yale football coach, promoter of American football; Leverett Lee Camp & Ellen Sophia Cornwell; Elah Camp & Orib Lee, Chauncey Cornwell & Mary Goodrich Cosslett; Nathan Ozias Camp & Phebe Spencer, Eber Lee & Huldah Bishop, Robert Cornwell & Sarah Hart; Elah Camp & Phebe Baldwin, David Bishop & Andrea Fowler, Elijah Hart, Jr. & Sarah Gilbert; Ezra Baldwin & Ruth Curtis, Benjamin Fowler & Andrea Morgan, Elijah Hart & Abigail Goodrich, Ebenezer Gilbert & Mercy Cowles; Jonathan Baldwin & Thankful Strong, John Morgan & Elizabeth Jones, Thomas Hart, Jr. & Mary Thompson, Samuel Cowles III & Sarah Wadsworth; 32-3, 60-1, Thomas

Hart & Ruth Hawkins, Samuel Cowles, Jr. & Rachel Porter; 46-7, Thomas Porter & Sarah Hart; 46-7.

44. ENRICO CARUSO, 1873–1921, opera singer (wife, Dorothy Benjamin; Park Benjamin III & Ida Crane; Park Benjamin, Jr. & Mary Brower Western; Park Benjamin & Mary Judith Gall; David Benjamin & Lucy Parke; John Benjamin, Jr. & Margaret Jameson, Zebulon Parke & Anna Killam; John Benjamin & Phebe Larabee, Ezekiel Parke & Mercy Safford; Greenfield Larabee, Jr. & Alice Parke, Nathaniel Parke & Sarah Geer; 62-3 [parents of Alice & Nathaniel]).

45. JOSEPH HODGES CHOATE, 1832–1917, lawyer & diplomat; George Choate, Jr. & Margaret Manning Hodges, great-great-grandparents of Benjamin Crowninshield Bradlee, see 36 above.

46. (STEPHEN) GROVER CLEVELAND, 1837–1908, 22nd & 24th U.S. President; Richard Falley Cleveland & Anna Neal; William Cleveland & Margaret Falley; Aaron Cleveland IV & Abiah Hyde; Aaron Cleveland III & Susanna Porter; Aaron Porter & Susanna Sewall; Samuel Porter, Jr. & Joanna Cooke; Aaron Cooke III & Sarah Westwood; Aaron Cooke, Jr. & Mary Cooke; Aaron Cooke & 67 (parents of Aaron, Jr.).

47. SCHUYLER COLFAX (JR.), 1823–1885, U.S. Vice-President under Grant; Schuyler Colfax & Hannah Stryker; William Colfax & Hester Schuyler; George Colfax & Lucy Avery; Ebenezer Avery & Lucy Latham; William Latham & Hannah Morgan; James Morgan, Jr. & Mary Vine; 60-1.

48. SAMUEL COLT, 1814–1862, inventor & firearms manufacturer (of among other guns the "Colt 45"); Christopher Colt & Sarah Caldwell, great-grandparents of Russell Griswold Colt, husband of Ethel Barrymore, see 23 above.

49. ROSCOE CONKLING, 1829–1888, congressman, U.S. senator & New York Republican leader (wife, Julia Catherine Seymour; Henry Seymour & Mary Ledyard Forman; Moses Seymour & Mary Marsh, Jonathan Forman & Mary Ledyard; Ebenezer Marsh & Deborah Buell, Youngs Ledyard & Mary Avery; John Marsh III & Elizabeth Pitkin, Ebenezer Avery & Lucy Latham; John Marsh, Jr. & Sarah Lyman, William Latham & Hannah Morgan; Richard Lyman, Jr. & Hepzibah Ford, James Morgan, Jr. & Mary Vine; 66-7, 60-1).

50. (JOHN) CALVIN COOLIDGE (JR.), 1872–1933, 30th U.S. President; John Calvin Coolidge & Victoria Josephine Moor; Calvin Galusha Coolidge & Sarah Almeda Brewer; Israel C. Brewer & Sally Brown; Israel Putnam Brown & Sally Briggs; Asa Briggs & Elizabeth Paul; Silas Briggs & Esther Soper; Samuel Soper, Jr. & Esther Littlefield; Edmund Littlefield, Jr. & Bethiah Waldo; Daniel Waldo & Susanna Adams; Cornelius Waldo & Hannah Cogswell; 100-1.

51. (HAROLD) HART CRANE, 1899–1932, poet; Clarence Arthur Crane & Grace Hart; Clinton O. Hart & Elizabeth Belden; Joseph Chauncey Hart & Rosanna Goff; Gideon Baldwin Hart & Marilla Woodford; Gideon Hart & Elizabeth Hart, Joseph Woodford & Eunice Hart; Joseph Hart & Mary Bird (parents of Gideon), William Hart & Elizabeth Woodruff (parents of Elizabeth), Stephen Hart & Eunice Munson (parents of Eunice); Thomas Hart & Elizabeth Judd (parents of Joseph, William & Stephen); Stephen Hart, Jr. & Anne Fitch; 46-7.

52. JAMES DWIGHT DANA, 1813–1895, geologist; James Dana & Harriet Dwight; Seth Dwight & Hannah Strong; Joseph Dwight & Tabitha Bigelow, Joseph Strong III & Jane Gelston; Seth Dwight & Abigail Strong, 4-5; Ebenezer Strong, Jr. & Elizabeth Parsons (parents of Abigail); Ebenezer Strong & Hannah Clapp, Joseph Parsons, Jr., & Elizabeth Strong; 32-3 (parents of Ebenezer & Elizabeth).

53. CHARLES GATES DAWES, 1865–1951, U.S. Vice-President under Coolidge,

recipient of the Nobel Peace Prize for 1925; Rufus R. Dawes & Mary Beman Gates; Henry Dawes & Sarah Cutler, Beman Gates & Betsey Sibyl Shipman; Ephraim Cutler & Sally Parker, Charles Shipman & Joanna Herrick Bartlett; Manassah Cutler & Mary Balch, William Parker & Mary Warner, Joshua Shipman & Sibyl Chapman; Thomas Balch & Mary Sumner, Philemon Warner III & Elizabeth Woodward, Levi Chapman & Elizabeth Hull; Edward Sumner & Elizabeth Clapp, Philemon Warner, Jr. & Mary Prince, Joseph Hull & Sibylla Coe; Samuel Clapp & Hannah Leeds, Philemon Warner & Abigail Tuttle, John Coe & Hannah Parsons; Roger Clapp & Joanna Ford, Simon Tuttle & Sarah Cogswell, Samuel Parsons & Rhoda Taylor; 66-7, 100-1, John Taylor & Thankful Woodward; 42-3.

54. Clarence (Shepard) Day (Jr.), 1874–1935, author of *Life With Father;* Clarence Shepard Day & Lavinia Elizabeth Stockwell; Benjamin Henry Day & Evelina Shepard; Henry Day & Mary Ely, parents of Mrs. Moses Yale Beach, see 26 above.

55. Lee De Forest, 1873–1961, radio engineer and inventor (2nd wife, Nora Stanton Blatch; William Henry Blatch & Harriot Eaton Stanton; Henry Brewster Stanton & [Mrs.] Elizabeth [Smith] Cady Stanton, 203 below).

56. George Dewey, 1837–1917, admiral, captor of Manila in the Spanish-American War; Julius Yemans Dewey & Mary Perrin; Simeon Dewey & Prudence Yemans; William Dewey & Rebecca Carrier; Simeon Dewey & Anna Phelps; William Dewey & Mercy Saxton; Josiah Dewey, Jr. & Mehitable Miller, Joseph Saxton & Hannah Denison; Josiah Dewey & Hepzibah Lyman, George Denison & Bridget Thompson; Richard Lyman, Jr. & Hepzibah Ford, 126-7; 66-7.

57. John Dewey, 1859–1952, philosopher; Archibald Sprague Dewey & Lucina Artemisia Rich; Archibald Dewey & Jerusha Hopkins; Benjamin Hopkins & Zaresh Rudd; Zebulon Rudd & Jerusha Brewster; Nathaniel Rudd & Rebecca Waldo; John Waldo & Rebecca Adams; Cornelius Waldo & Hannah Cogswell; 100-1.

58. Thomas Edmund Dewey, 1902–1971, Governor of New York, Republican presidential candidate in 1944 & 1948; George Martin Dewey, Jr. & Annie Thomas; George Martin Dewey & Emma Bingham; Granville Dewey & Harriet B. Freeman; Martin Dewey & Hannah Waterman, Otis Freeman & Theoda Capron; Elijah Dewey & Abigail Martin, Benjamin Waterman & Experience Hyde, Edmund Freeman & Sarah Porter, ——— Capron & Amy Dewey; William Dewey & Mercy Saxton (see under 56 above); Daniel Waterman & Mary Gifford, John Porter & Abigail Arnold, Simeon Dewey & Anna Phelps (see under 56 above); Thomas Waterman, Jr. & Elizabeth Allyn, Samuel Gifford & Mary Calkins, Experience Porter & Abigail Williams; John Allyn & Elizabeth Gager, Stephen Gifford & Hannah Gore, Samuel Williams & Theoda Parke; 54-5, 110-1, William Parke & Martha Holgrave; 124-5.

59. Emily Elizabeth Dickinson, 1830–1886, poetess; Edward Dickinson & Emily Norcross; Joel Norcross & Betsy Fay; Jude Fay & Sarah Fairbanks; Eleazer Fairbanks III & Prudence Cary; Eleazer Fairbanks, Jr. & Martha Bullard; Eleazer Fairbanks & Martha Lovett; Daniel Lovett & Joanna Blott; 78-9.

60. Dorothea Lynde Dix, 1802–1887, humanitarian, prison & insane asylum reformer; Joseph Dix & Mary Bigelow; Elijah Dix & Dorothy Lynde; Joseph Lynde & Mary Lemmon; Nicholas Lynde & Dorothy Stanton; Thomas Stanton, Jr. & Sarah Denison; George Denison & Bridget Thompson; 126-7.

61. Neal Dow, 1804–1897, temperance reformer (wife, Maria Cornelia Durant Maynard; John Maynard & Mary Durant; Thomas Durant & Sally

Hallam; Edward Durant & Judith Waldo; Cornelius Waldo, Jr. & Faith Peck, Cornelius Waldo & Hannah Cogswell; 100-1).

62. EDWIN LAURENTINE DRAKE, 1819–1880, pioneer petroleum industrialist, 1st discoverer of underground oil (2nd wife, Laura Clarissa Dowd; Alfred Giles Dowd & Harriet Clarissa Scranton; Giles Dowd & Olive Brown; Didymus Dowd & Mercy Griswold; Giles Griswold & Mary Chatfield; Joseph Griswold & Temperance Lay; Robert Lay, Jr. & Mary Stanton; Thomas Stanton, Jr. & Sarah Denison; George Denison & Bridget Thompson; 126-7).

63. JOHN DAVID DRUMMOND, 17th Earl of Perth, b. 1907, British Colonial Secretary, 1957–1962 (wife, Nancy Seymour Fincke; Reginald Fincke & Edith Gilbert Clark; George Crawford Clark & Harriet Seymour Averell; Luther Clapp Clark & Julia Crawford; Bohan Clark & Mary White; Asahel Clark & Submit Clapp; Eliakim Clark & Esther Wright, Jonathan Clapp & Submit Strong; John Clark, Jr. & Elizabeth Cooke, Roger Clapp & Elizabeth Bartlett, Waitstill Strong & Mindwell Bartlett; John Clark & Mary Strong, Noah Cooke & Sarah Nash, Preserved Clapp & Sarah Newberry, 16-7 [parents of Waitstill]; 32-3 [parents of Mary], Aaron Cooke, Jr. & Joan Denslow, Roger Clapp & Joanna Ford; Aaron Cooke & 67 [parents of Aaron, Jr.], 66-7).

64. EDWIN FRANK "EDDIE" DUCHIN, 1909-1951, pianist & orchestra leader (1st wife, Marjorie Frances Marion Oelrichs; Charles DeLoosey Oelrichs & Marjorie Ramsey Turnbull; Charles May Oelrichs & Blanche DeLoosey, parents of Mrs. John Barrymore, see 24 above).

65-66. ALLEN WELSH DULLES, 1893–1969, director of the Central Intelligence Agency, 1953–1961, & JOHN FOSTER DULLES, 1888–1959, U.S. Secretary of State under Eisenhower; Allen Macy Dulles & Edith Foster; John Welsh Dulles & Harriet Lathrop Winslow; Miron Winslow & Harriet Wadsworth Lathrop; Charles Lathrop & Joanna Leffingwell; Christopher Leffingwell & Elizabeth Coit; Joseph Coit & Lydia Lathrop; Thomas Lathrop & Lydia Abell; Joshua Abell & Bethia Gager; 54-5.

67. TIMOTHY DWIGHT (IV), 1752–1817, president of Yale College, 1795–1817; Timothy Dwight III & Mary Edwards; Timothy Dwight II & Experience King; John King, Jr. & Mehitable Pomeroy; John King & Sarah Holton, Medad Pomeroy & Experience Woodward; 34-5, 42-3.

68. TIMOTHY DWIGHT (V), 1828–1916, president of Yale University, 1886–1899; James Dwight & Susan Breed; Timothy Dwight IV, 67 above, & Mary Woolsey.

69. (MRS.) AMELIA (MARY) EARHART (PUTNAM), 1898–1937, aviator (husband, George Palmer Putnam II; John Bishop Putnam & Frances Faulkner; George Palmer Putnam & Victorine Haven; Henry Putnam, Jr. & Catherine Hunt Palmer; Henry Putnam & Mary Hawkes; Adam Hawkes & Lydia Wiley; John Hawkes & Mary Whitford; Adam Hawkes & Elizabeth ———; John Hawkes & Sarah Cushman; 102-3).

70. RALPH WALDO EMERSON, 1803–1882, philosopher, essayist, & poet; William Emerson, Jr. & Ruth Haskins; William Emerson & Phebe Bliss; Joseph Emerson & Mary Moody; Edward Emerson & Rebecca Waldo; Cornelius Waldo & Hannah Cogswell; 100-1.

71. DAVID DUDLEY FIELD, 1805–1894, lawyer & law reformer (1st wife, Jane Lucinda Hopkins; John Sargeant Hopkins & Lucinda Fellowes; Mark Hopkins & Electa Sargeant, great-great-grandparents of Stanley Rossiter Benedict, husband of Mrs. Ruth Fulton Benedict, see 31 above).

72. MARSHALL FIELD (IV), 1916–1965, Chicago newspaper publisher (1st wife,

Joanne Bass; Robert Perkins Bass & Edith Harlan Bird; Perkins Bass & Clara Foster; Joel M. Bass & Katherine Wright Burnham; Joel Bass & Mary Martin, Walter Burnham, Jr. & Annis Crawford; Ebenezer Bass & Ruth Waldo, Walter Burnham & Submit Smith; Zaccheus Waldo & Tabitha Kingsbury, Benjamin Burnham, Jr. & Jemima Perkins; Edward Waldo & Thankful Dimmock, Benjamin Burnham & Mary Kinsman; John Waldo & Rebecca Adams, Thomas Burnham & 25; Cornelius Waldo & Hannah Cogswell; 100-1) (2nd wife, Katherine Miller Woodruff; Frederick William Woodruff, Jr. & Katherine Miller; Frederick William Woodruff & Nellie Davis; George Woodruff & Dorothy Smith; Frederick Woodruff & Lodema Andrews; Jonah Woodruff & Mary Olmsted; Benjamin Woodruff & Eunice Martin; Nathaniel Woodruff & Thankful Wright; Benjamin Wright & Thankful Taylor; John Taylor & Thankful Woodward; 42-3).

73. MARSHALL FIELD (V), b. 1941, Chicago newspaper publisher, son of 72 above & Joanne Bass.

74. MILLARD FILLMORE, 1800–1874, 13th U.S. President; Nathaniel Fillmore & Phoebe Millard; Abiathar Millard & Tabitha Hopkins, great-great-great-grandparents of Mrs. Alexander Calder, see 42 above.

75. HARVEY SAMUEL FIRESTONE, JR., 1898–1973, industrialist, president of Firestone Tire & Rubber Co., 1941–1948 (wife, Elizabeth Parke; Guy James Parke & Gertrude Newton Chambers; Virgil Hickox Parke & Ellen Elizabeth James; Elisha Parke & Abiah Hickox; Daniel Parke & Esther Ranney; Joseph Parke, Jr. & Amity Cady; Joseph Parke & Mary ———, Nathaniel Parke & Sarah Geer; 62-3).

76. F(RANCIS) SCOTT (KEY) FITZGERALD, 1896–1940, novelist (wife, Zelda Sayre; Anthony Dickerson Sayre & Minnie Buckner Machen; Daniel Sayre & Musidora Morgan; George Morgan & Frances Irby; Gideon Morgan & Patience Cogswell; Samuel Morgan & Rachel Kibbe, Emerson Cogswell & Mary Miles; James Morgan, Jr. & Mary Averill, Edward Cogswell & Hannah Brown; James Morgan & Bridget ———, William Cogswell, Jr. & Martha Emerson; John Morgan & Rachel Deming, 50-1; 60-1).

77. ARTHUR HENRY FLEMING, 1856–1940, lumber magnate, founder and benefactor of the California Institute of Technology (wife, Clara Huntington Fowler; Eldridge Merick Fowler & Mary Louise Skinner; Melzar Fowler & Clarissa Spicer; Silas Draper Spicer & Nancy Fish; Jason Fish & Jemima Williams; Samuel Williams & Mary Williams; Ebenezer Williams & Mary Wheeler [parents of Samuel], Eleazer Williams & Mary Hyde [parents of Mary]; Samuel Williams & Theoda Parke [parents of Ebenezer], Isaac Wheeler & Martha Parke, Isaac Williams & Martha Parke [parents of Eleazer]; William Parke & Martha Holgrave [parents of Theoda & Martha Williams], 62-3 [parents of Martha Wheeler]; 124-5 [parents of William Parke]).

78. WILLIAM FLOYD, 1734–1821, revolutionary patriot, signer of the Declaration of Independence (2nd wife, Joanna Strong; Benajah Strong & Martha Mills; Selah Strong & Abigail Terry; 16-7).

79. WILLIAM CLAY FORD, b. 1925, Ford Motor Company executive, brother of Henry Ford II (wife, Martha Parke Firestone, daughter of Harvey Samuel Firestone, Jr., 75 above, and Elizabeth Parke).

80. GEORGE HORACE GALLUP, b. 1901, pollster; George Henry Gallup & Nettie Quella Davenport; John Nelson Gallup & Happy Kinney Church; Nelson Gallup & Elizabeth Tanner; William Gallup & Amy Gallup; Isaac Gallup & Margaret Gallup (parents of William); John Gallup & Elizabeth Wheeler (parents of Isaac); Isaac Wheeler & Martha Parke; 62-3.

81. Erle Stanley Gardner, 1889–1970, detective novelist; Charles Walter Gardner & Grace Adelma Waugh; Walter Pinkham Gardner, Jr. & Olive Drake; Nathan Drake III & Sally Bird; Nathan Drake, Jr. & Jane Tolman, Abner Bird & Mary Gay; Johnson Tolman & Elizabeth Capen, Lemuel Gay & Abigail Davenport; Samuel Tolman & Experience Clapp, David Gay & Hannah Talbot; Desire Clapp & Sarah Pond, George Talbot & Mary Turell; Roger Clapp & Joanna Ford, Daniel Turell, Jr. & Hannah Barrell; 66-7, Daniel Turell & Lydia Blott; 78-9.

82. Mrs. Isabella Stewart Gardner, 1840–1924, Boston art collector & social leader, builder of Fenway Court; David Stewart & Adelia Smith; Selah Strong Smith & Anne Carpenter; James Smith & Hannah Strong; Thomas Strong & Susanna Thompson; Selah Strong & Abigail Terry; 16-7.

83. Charles Dana Gibson (II), 1867–1945, illustrator, creator of the "Gibson Girl"; Charles DeWolf Gibson & Josephine Elizabeth Lovett; Charles Dana Gibson & Abigail DeWolf; Thomas Gibson & Frances Maria Hastings; John Hastings & Lydia Dana; Jonathan Hastings, Jr. & Elizabeth Cotton; Jonathan Hastings & Sarah Sharp; Robert Sharp & Sarah Williams; Stephen Williams & Sarah Wise; Joseph Wise & Mary Thompson; 126-7.

84. Daniel Coit Gilman, 1831–1908, educator, president of the University of California and the Carnegie Institution, 1st president of Johns Hopkins University; William Charles Gilman & Eliza Coit; Daniel Lathrop Coit & Elizabeth Bill; Joseph Coit & Lydia Lathrop, Ephraim Bill & Lydia Huntington; Thomas Lathrop & Lydia Abell, Joshua Huntington & Hannah Perkins; Joshua Abell & Bethia Gager, Simon Huntington III & Lydia Gager; 54-5 (parents of Bethia & Lydia).

85-86. (Mrs.) Dorothy (Elizabeth) Gish (Rennie), 1898–1968, and Lillian (Diana) Gish, b. 1896, actresses & motion-picture pioneers; James Lee Gish & Mary Robinson McConnell; Henry C. McConnell & Elizabeth Ellen Robinson; Samuel H. Robinson & Emily Ward Barnard; Lemuel Barnard & Clorinda Taylor; Salah Barnard & Elizabeth Nims, Othniel Taylor, Jr. & Dorothy Wilder; Ebenezer Barnard & Elizabeth Foster, Othniel Taylor & Martha Arms; Joseph Barnard & Sarah Strong, Samuel Taylor & Mary Hitchcock; 32-3, John Taylor & Thankful Woodward; 42-3.

87. Bertram Grosvenor Goodhue, 1869–1924, neo-gothic architect (of West Point especially); Charles Wells Goodhue & Helen Grosvenor Eldredge; Edward Eldredge & Hannah Grosvenor; James Eldredge & Lucy Gallup; Charles Eldredge & Mary Starr, Joseph Gallup & Eunice Williams; Jonathan Starr & Elizabeth Morgan, John Williams & Martha Wheeler; James Morgan, Jr. & Mary Vine, Isaac Williams & Martha Parke, Isaac Wheeler & Martha Parke; 60-1, William Parke & Martha Holgrave (parents of Martha Williams), 62-3 (parents of Martha Wheeler); 124-5.

88. Mrs. Henrietta "Hetty" Howland Robinson Green, 1834–1916, Wall Street financier; Edward Mott Robinson & Abby Slocum Howland; Gideon Howland, Jr. & Mehitable Howland; Gideon Howland & Sarah Hicks (parents of Gideon, Jr.); Barnabas Howland & Rebecca Lapham; John Lapham, Jr. & Mary Russell; Joseph Russell & Elizabeth Fobes; 52-3.

89. Ernest (Henry) Gruening, 1887–1974, Alaskan statesman, governor & U.S. Senator (wife, Dorothy Elizabeth Smith; George Harding Smith & Laura Huntington Brown; Henry Sanders Brown & Lucretia Richardson Janes; Slade D. Brown & Laura Huntington Sanders; Daniel Clark Sanders & Anne Fitch; Jabez Fitch, Jr. & Lydia Huntington; Ebenezer Huntington & Sarah Leffingwell; Simon Huntington III & Lydia Gager; 54-5).

90. Arthur Twining Hadley, 1856–1930, economist, president of Yale University, 1899–1921; James Hadley & Anne Loring Twining; Stephen Twining & Almira Catlin; Alexander Catlin & Abigail Goodman; Timothy Goodman & Joanna Wadsworth; Joseph Wadsworth, Jr., & Joanna Hovey; Thomas Hovey & Sarah Cooke; Aaron Cooke III & Sarah Westwood; Aaron Cooke, Jr. & Mary Cooke; Aaron Cooke & 67 (parents of Aaron, Jr.).

91. Edward Everett Hale, 1822–1909, Unitarian clergyman, author of "The Man Without a Country"; Nathan Hale & Sarah Preston Everett; Enoch Hale & Octavia Throop; Richard Hale & Elizabeth Strong; 4-5.

92. Nathan Hale, 1755–1776, martyr spy of the American Revolution; Richard Hale & Elizabeth Strong; 4-5 (a 1st cousin 6 times removed of the Princess of Wales. her nearest kinsman among these 250).

93. G(ranville) Stanley Hall, 1844–1924, psychologist, philosopher, & educator; Granville Bascom Hall & Abigail Beals; Robert Beals & Abigail Vining; George Vining & Abigail Alden; Ezra Alden & Rebecca Keith; Ebenezer Alden & Anna Keith; Joseph Keith & Elizabeth Fobes; Edward Fobes & Elizabeth Howard; 52-3.

94. Marcus Alonzo "Mark" Hanna, 1837–1904, Cleveland businessman, politician & U.S. Senator; Leonard Hanna & Samantha Maria Converse; Porter Converse & Rhoda Howard; Israel Converse & Hannah Walbridge; Amos Walbridge, Jr. & Margaret ———; Amos Walbridge & Theoda Porter; Experience Porter & Abigail Williams; Samuel Williams & Theoda Parke; William Parke & Martha Holgrave; 124-5.

95. Lewis Harcourt, 1st Viscount Harcourt, 1863–1922, British Colonial Secretary, 1910–1915 (wife, Mary Ethel Burns; Walter Hayes Burns & Mary Lyman Morgan; Junius Spencer Morgan & Juliet Pierpont; Joseph Morgan, Jr. & Sally Spencer, John Pierpont & Mary Sheldon Lord; Joseph Morgan & Experience Smith, Lynde Lord, Jr. & Mary Lyman; David Smith & Experience Chapin, Joseph Lyman, Jr. & Mary Sheldon; Samuel Chapin & Hannah Sheldon, Joseph Lyman & Abigail Lewis, Benjamin Sheldon & Mary Strong; Isaac Sheldon & Mary Woodford [parents of Hannah & Thomas], Benjamin Lyman & Thankful Pomeroy, Thomas Sheldon [son of Isaac Sheldon & Mary Woodford] & Mary Hinsdale [parents of Benjamin], Ebenezer Strong, Jr. & Mary Holton; 38-9, Medad Pomeroy & Experience Woodward, Ebenezer Strong & Hannah Clapp, William Holton, Jr. & Sarah Marshfield; 42-3, 32-3, 34-5).

96. Sir William George Vernon Harcourt, 1827–1904, British Chancellor of the Exchequer, 1886 & 1892–1895 (2nd wife, Elizabeth Cabot Motley; John Lothrop Motley, 156 below, & Mary Elizabeth Benjamin).

97. John Marshall Harlan II, 1899–1971, jurist (wife, Ethel Andrews; Charles McLean Andrews & Evangeline Holcombe Walker; William Watson Andrews & Elizabeth Byrne Williams; John Williams & Mary Dyer; Ezekiel Williams & Prudence Stoddard; Solomon Williams & Mary Porter; William Williams & Christian Stoddard, Samuel Porter, Jr. & Joanna Cooke; Isaac Williams & Martha Parke, Aaron Cooke III & Sarah Westwood; William Parke & Martha Holgrave, Aaron Cooke, Jr. & Mary Cooke; 124-5, Aaron Cooke & 67 [parents of Aaron, Jr.]).

98. Mrs. Julia Ann Harris Julien Gurian, known as Julie Harris, b. 1925, actress; William Pickett Harris, Jr. & Elsie Stivers Smith; William Pickett Harris & Sarah Edma McGraw; Thomas McGraw & Sarah Edma Simpson; William Simpson & Ximena Haines; William Haines & Ximena Hart; John Hart, Jr. & Polly Smith; John Hart & Desire Palmer; Thomas, Hart, Jr. & Anna

Stanley; Thomas Hart & Elizabeth Judd; Stephen Hart, Jr. & Anne Fitch; 46-7.

99. RUTHERFORD BIRCHARD HAYES, 1822–1893, 19th U.S. President; Rutherford Hayes, Jr. & Sophia Birchard; Roger Birchard & Drusilla Austin; Daniel Austin & Abigail Phelps; Nathaniel Austin & Abigail Hovey; Thomas Hovey & Sarah Cooke; Aaron Cooke III & Sarah Westwood; Aaron Cooke, Jr. & Mary Cooke; Aaron Cooke & 67 (parents of Aaron, Jr.).

100. CHRISTIAN ARCHIBALD HERTER, 1895–1967, Governor of Massachusetts, U.S. Secretary of State under Eisenhower; Albert Herter & Adele McGinnis; Christian Herter & Mary Miles; Archibald Miles & Mary Treese; Erastus Miles & Sarah Fiske; Ichabod Ebenezer Fiske & Eleanor Roberts; Ebenezer Fiske & Sarah Newell; Samuel Newell, Jr. & Sarah Norton; Samuel Newell & Mary Hart; Thomas Hart & Ruth Hawkins; 46-7.

101. HENRY LEE HIGGINSON, 1834–1919, banker, founder of the Boston Symphony Orchestra, Harvard benefactor; George Higginson, Jr. & Mary Cabot Lee; George Higginson & Martha Hubbard Babcock; Stephen Higginson, Jr. & Susanna Cleveland; Aaron Cleveland III & Susanna Porter, great-great-grandparents of (Stephen) Grover Cleveland, see 46 above.

102. THOMAS WENTWORTH HIGGINSON, 1823–1911, reformer, essayist, colonel of the 1st black Union regiment; Stephen Higginson III & Louisa Storrow; Stephen Higginson, Jr. & Susanna Cleveland, great-grandparents of Henry Lee Higginson, see 101 immediately above.

103. ETHAN ALLEN HITCHCOCK, 1835–1909, businessman, diplomat, U.S. Secretary of the Interior; Henry Hitchcock & Anne Erwin; Samuel Hitchcock & Lucy Caroline Allen; Ethan Allen, 12 above, & Mary Bronson.

104. OLIVER WENDELL HOLMES, 1809–1894, physician, poet, novelist, author of *The Autocrat at the Breakfast Table;* Abiel Holmes & Sarah Wendell; David Holmes & Temperance Bishop; John Bishop & Temperance Lathrop; 24-5.

105. OLIVER WENDELL HOLMES, JR., 1841–1935, jurist, son of 104 above & Amelia Lee Jackson.

106. MARK HOPKINS, 1802–1887, educator, president of Williams College, 1836–1872; Archibald Hopkins & Mary Curtis; Mark Hopkins & Electa Sargeant, great-great-grandparents of Stanley Rossiter Benedict, husband of Mrs. Ruth Fulton Benedict, see 31 above.

107. H(AROLDSON) L(AFAYETTE) HUNT (JR.), 1889–1974, Texas oil magnate (1st wife, Lyda Bunker; Nelson Waldo Bunker & Sarah Rebecca Hunnicutt; Charles Waldo Bunker & Lydia Starbuck; Andrew Bunker & Nancy Colesworthy; Jonathan Waldo Colesworthy & Hepzibah Gardner; Gilbert Colesworthy & Mary Waldo: Jonathan Waldo, Jr. & Susanna Blaque; Jonathan Waldo & Hannah Mason; Cornelius Waldo & Hannah Cogswell; 100-1).

108-110. LAMAR HUNT, b. 1932; NELSON BUNKER HUNT, b. 1926; & WILLIAM HERBERT HUNT, b. 1929, oilmen – sons of 107 above & Lyda Bunker.

111. RICHARD MORRIS HUNT, 1828–1895, architect (wife, Catherine Clinton Howland; Samuel Shaw Howland & Joanna Hone, great-great-grandparents of Louis Stanton Auchincloss, see 17 above).

112. CHARLES EDWARD IVES, 1874–1954, composer; George Edward Ives & Mary Elizabeth Parmelee; George White Ives & Sarah Hotchkiss Wilcox; Isaac Ives & Sarah Amelia White; John Ives, Jr. & Mary Hall; John Ives & Hannah Royce; Joseph Royce & Mary Porter; Nehemiah Royce & Hannah Morgan; 60-1.

113. (MRS.) HELEN (MARIA FISKE) HUNT JACKSON, 1830–1885, authoress of *Ramona* (1st husband, Edward Bissell Hunt; Sanford Hunt & Fanny Rose; Gad Hunt & Elizabeth Woodward, Samuel Rose & Elizabeth Hale; Simeon Hunt & Hannah Lyman, Richard Hale & Elizabeth Strong; Ebenezer Hunt & Hannah

Clark, Jonathan Lyman & Lydia Loomis, 4-5; William Clark, Jr. & Hannah Strong; Richard Lyman III & Elizabeth Cowles; 32-3, Richard Lyman, Jr. & Hepzibah Ford; 66-7).

114. DONALD LINES JACOBUS, 1887-1970, genealogist; John Ira Jacobus & Ida Wilmot Lines; Henry Lines & Mary Anne Wilmot; David Harpin Lines & Julia Anne Morse; Street Hall Morse & Martha Bartholomew; Joel Morse & Hannah Hall; Street Hall & Hannah Fowler; Josiah Fowler & Hannah Baldwin; Jonathan Baldwin & Thankful Strong; 32-3.

115. (JOHN) ROBINSON JEFFERS, 1887–1962, poet; William Hamilton Jeffers & Annie Robinson Tuttle; Edwin Rush Tuttle & Mary Evelyn Sherwood; Benjamin Royce Tuttle & Mary Anne Robinson; Amos Tuttle & Sarah Richards; Timothy Tuttle & Mehitable Royce; Phineas Royce & Thankful Merriman; Nehemiah Royce, Jr. & Kezia Hall; Nehemiah Royce & Hannah Morgan; 60-1.

116. DAVID STARR JORDAN, 1851–1932, botanist, peace advocate, 1st president of Stanford University, 1891–1913; Hiram Jordan & Huldah Lake Hawley; David Hawley & Anna Waldo; John Elderkin Waldo & Beulah Foster; Zachariah Waldo & Elizabeth Wight; Edward Waldo, Jr. & Abigail Elderkin; Edward Waldo & Thankful Dimmock; John Waldo & Rebecca Adams; Cornelius Waldo & Hannah Cogswell; 100-1.

117. GEORGE FROST KENNAN, b. 1904, diplomat, Soviet affairs expert; Kossuth Kent Kennan & Florence James; Thomas Lathrop Kennan & Loa Brown; George Kennan & Mary Tullar, Jedediah Brown & Eunice Branch; Thomas Kennan & Sarah Lathrop, Walter Branch & Eunice Shaw; Denison Lathrop & Sarah Hubbard Harris, Samuel Branch & Hannah Witter; Elisha Lathrop & Hannah Hough, Joseph Witter & Elizabeth Gore; Samuel Lathrop & Elizabeth Waterman, Ebenezer Witter & Dorothy Morgan; Thomas Waterman, Jr. & Elizabeth Allyn, 30-1; John Allyn & Elizabeth Gager; 54-5.

118. SPENCER WOOLLEY KIMBALL, b. 1895, president of the Mormon Church since 1973; Andrew Kimball & Olive Woolley; Heber Chase Kimball & Ann Alice Gheen; Solomon Farnham Kimball & Anna Spalding; Charles Spalding & Abigail Gates; Thomas Gates & Abigail Coit; Joseph Coit, Jr. & Experience Wheeler; Isaac Wheeler & Martha Parke; 62-3.

119. JOHN THORNTON KIRKLAND, 1770–1840, president of Harvard College, 1810–1828; Samuel Kirkland & Jerusha Bingham, great-great-great-great-grandparents of Mrs. McGeorge Bundy, see 40 above.

120. HENRY KNOX, 1750–1806, revolutionary general & 1st U.S. Secretary of War (wife, Lucy Flucker; Thomas Flucker & Hannah Waldo; Samuel Waldo & Lucy Wainwright; Jonathan Waldo & Hannah Mason; Cornelius Waldo & Hannah Cogswell; 100-1).

121. SAMUEL PIERPONT LANGLEY, 1834–1906, astronomer, aeronautics pioneer, 3rd secretary of the Smithsonian Institution; Samuel Langley III & Mary Sumner Williams; John Williams, Jr. & Nancy Dowse; John Williams & Mary Sumner; Joseph Williams, Jr. & Martha Howell (great-grandparents of Mrs. Amos Bronson Alcott, see 8 above), Samuel Sumner & Abigail Mather; Edward Sumner & Elizabeth Clapp, great-great-great-great-grandparents of Charles Gates Dawes, see 53 above.

122. ROBERT LANSING, 1864–1928, U.S. Secretary of State under Wilson; John Lansing & Maria Lay Dodge; Edwin Dodge & Jerusha Lay Sterling; William Sterling, Jr. & Jerusha Ely; Robert Ely & Jerusha Lay; Christopher Lay & Mary ———; Robert Lay III & Mary Grinnell; Robert Lay, Jr. & Mary Stanton; Thomas Stanton, Jr. & Sarah Denison; George Denison & Bridget Thompson; 126-7.

123. Gilbert Newton Lewis, 1875–1946, physical chemist, co-inventor of the cyclotron (wife, Mary Hinckley Sheldon; Edward Stevens Sheldon & Katherine Hamlin Hinckley; Barney Hinckley & Malvina Hamlin Wheeler; Seth Hinckley & Anstis Ross Gorham; Barnabas Hinckley & Mary Billings; Daniel Billings & Mary Ruggles; Benjamin Ruggles & Alice Merrick; Timothy Ruggles & Mary White; Benjamin White & Susanna Cogswell; 50-1).

124. Henry Cabot Lodge, 1850–1924, U.S. Senator & Republican party leader (wife, Anna Cabot Mills Davis; Charles Henry Davis & Harriette Blake Mills; Elijah Hunt Mills & Harriette Blake; Benjamin Mills & Mary Hunt; Jonathan Hunt III & Thankful Strong; Jonathan Hunt, Jr. & Martha Williams, Jerijah Strong & Thankful Stebbins; Samuel Williams & Theoda Parke, 32-3; William Parke & Martha Holgrave; 124-5).

125. Henry Cabot Lodge II, b. 1902, U.S. Senator, Vice-Presidential candidate in 1960, Ambassador to the United Nations; George Cabot Lodge & Matilda Elizabeth Frelinghuysen Davis; 124 above & Anna Cabot Mills Davis.

126. Henry Wadsworth Longfellow, 1807–1882, poet (2nd wife, Frances Elizabeth Appleton; Nathan Appleton & Maria Theresa Gold; Thomas Gold & Martha Marsh; Perez Marsh & Sarah Williams; Job Marsh & Mehitable Porter, Israel Williams & Sarah Chester; Samuel Porter, Jr. & Joanna Cooke, William Williams & Christian Stoddard – both couples great-great-great-great-grandparents of Mrs. John Marshall Harlan II, see 97 above).

127. Seth Low, 1850–1916, Mayor of New York City, president of Columbia University, 1890–1901; Abiel Abbot Low & Ellen Almira Dow; Seth Low & Mary Porter; David Low IV & Hannah Haskell; David Low III & Abigail Choate, Nathaniel Haskell & Hannah White; David Low, Jr. & Susanna Low, John White & Lucy Wise; David Low & Mary Lamb (parents of David, Jr.), John Wise & Abigail Gardner; Caleb Lamb & Mary Wise, Joseph Wise & Mary Thompson (parents of John & Mary); 126-7.

128. A(bbott) Lawrence Lowell, 1856–1943, president of Harvard University, 1909–1933 (wife, Anna Parker Lowell; George Gardner Lowell & Mary Ellen Parker; James Parker & Anne Tucker; Richard Dalton Tucker & Sally Chandler; Nathaniel Tucker, Jr. & Anna Dalton; Nathaniel Tucker & ———; Samuel Tucker & Rebecca Leeds; Joseph Leeds & Miriam Cooke; Aaron Cooke, Jr. & Mary Cooke; Aaron Cooke & 67 [parents of Aaron, Jr.]).

129. Guy Lowell, 1870–1927, architect; Edward Jackson Lowell & Mary Wolcott Goodrich; Samuel Griswold Goodrich & Mary Boott; Samuel Goodrich & Elizabeth Ely; Elizur Goodrich & Catherine Chauncey, John Ely & Sarah Worthington; Elihu Chauncey & Mary Griswold, William Worthington & Temperance Gallup (great-great-great-great-grandparents of Mrs. Louis Bromfield, see 38 above); Nathaniel Chauncey, Jr. & Sarah Judson; Nathaniel Chauncey & Abigail Strong; 32-3.

130-131. Henry Robinson Luce, 1898–1967, publisher, founder of *Time, Fortune, Life & Sports Illustrated* magazines, whose 2nd wife was Mrs. Clare Boothe (Brokaw) Luce, b. 1903, playwright, congresswoman, & diplomat; Henry Winters Luce & Elizabeth Middleton Root; Lynott Bloodgood Root & Anna Robbins; Philander Sheldon Root & Elizabeth Bloodgood; Elihu Root & Achsah Pomeroy; James Root & Nannie Rob, Eliakim Pomeroy & Sarah Sheldon; Hewit Root & Experience Pomeroy, Noah Pomeroy & Abigail Remington; Medad Pomeroy & Hannah Trumbull (parents of Experience), Joseph Pomeroy & Hannah Seymour (parents of Noah & Medad); Medad Pomeroy & Experience Woodward (parents of Joseph); 42-3.

132. Sidney Lumet, b. 1924, film director (2nd wife, Gloria Morgan Vander-

bilt, previously married to Leopold A. S. B. Stokowski, 208 below; Reginald Claypoole Vanderbilt & Gloria Morgan; Cornelius Vanderbilt II, 222 below, & Alice Claypoole Gwynne).

133. EDWARD ALEXANDER MACDOWELL, 1861–1908, composer (wife, Marian Griswold Nevins; David Henry Nevins & Cornelia Leonard Perkins; Thomas Shaw Perkins & Marian Griswold; Elias Perkins & Lucretia Shaw Woodbridge; Joseph Perkins III & Joanna Burnham, Ephraim Woodbridge & Mary Shaw; Joseph Perkins, Jr. & Mary Bushnell, Benjamin Burnham & Mary Kinsman, Paul Woodbridge & Sarah Goodridge; Joseph Perkins & Martha Morgan, Thomas Burnham & 25, Ephraim Woodbridge & Hannah Morgan; 30-1 [parents of Martha], John Morgan & Rachel Deming [parents of Hannah]; 60-1).

134. ARCHIBALD MACLEISH, 1892–1982, poet & playwright; Andrew MacLeish & Martha Hillard; Elias Brewster Hillard & Julia Whittlesey; Moses Hillard & Patty Brewster; Elias Brewster & Margery Morgan; Simon Brewster & Anne Andrus, James Morgan & Grace Smith; Benjamin Brewster & Elizabeth Witter, Samuel Morgan & Elizabeth Forsyth; Ebenezer Witter & Dorothy Morgan, James Morgan & Bridget ———; 30-1 (parents of Dorothy), John Morgan & Rachel Deming (parents of James); 60-1.

135. JOHN PHILLIPS MARQUAND (II), 1893–1960, novelist; Philip Marquand & Margaret Fuller; John Phillips Marquand & Margaret Searle Curzon; Joseph Marquand & Sarah Winslow Tyng; Dudley Atkins Tyng & Sarah Higginson; Stephen Higginson, Jr. & Susanna Cleveland, grandparents of Thomas Wentworth Higginson & great-grandparents of Henry Lee Higginson, see 101 and 102 above.

136. JOHN LOUDON MCADAM, 1756–1836, British road engineer (1st wife, Gloriana Margaretta Nicoll; William Nicoll & Joanna D'Honneur; Samuel D'Honneur & Rachel Strong; Selah Strong & Abigail Terry; 16-7).

137. WILLIAM GIBBS MCADOO, 1863–1941, U.S. Senator & Secretary of the Treasury (2nd wife, Eleanor Randolph Wilson; [Thomas] Woodrow Wilson, 245 below & Ellen Louise Axson).

138. GEORGE BRINTON MCCLELLAN, 1826–1885, Union general, Democratic Presidential candidate in 1864, Governor of New Jersey; George McClellan & Elizabeth Sophia Brinton; James McClellan & Eunice Eldredge; James Eldredge & Lucy Gallup, great-grandparents of Bertram Grosvenor Goodhue, see 87 above.

139. CYRUS HALL MCCORMICK, 1809–1884, farm machinery manufacturer, inventor of the reaper (wife, Nancy Maria Fowler; Melzar Fowler & Clarissa Spicer, grandparents of Mrs. Arthur Henry Fleming, see 77 above).

140. (MRS.) MARGARET MEAD (CROSSMAN FORTUNE BATESON), 1901–1978, anthropologist; Edward Sherwood Mead & Emily Fogg; James Leland Fogg & Elizabeth Bogart Lockwood; James Pecker Fogg & Emily Ware; Josiah Fogg & Hannah Pecker, Orlando Ware & Deborah Starr; James Pecker, Jr. & Hannah Dalton, John Ware, Jr. & Hannah Leland; James Pecker & Susanna Cogswell, Caleb Leland & Judith Morse; John Cogswell, Jr. & Susanna Low, Ebenezer Leland & Martha Fairbanks; John Cogswell & Hannah Goodhue, Eleazer Fairbanks & Martha Lovett; 50-1, Daniel Lovett & Joanna Blott; 78-9.

141. GEORGE GORDON MEADE, 1815–1872, Union general (wife, Margaretta Sergeant; John Sergeant & Margaretta Watmough; James Horatio Watmough & Maria Carmick; Edward Watmough & Maria Ellis; Edward Ellis & Mary Willard; Robert Ellis & Elizabeth Pemberton; Edward Ellis & Sarah Blott; 78-9).

142. PAUL MELLON, b. 1907, philanthropist & art collector (2nd wife, Rachel

Lowe Lambert; Gerard Barnes Lambert & Rachel Parkhill Lowe; Arthur Houghton Lowe & Anne Elizabeth Parkhill; John Lowe & Sarah Mead; David Lowe & Louisa Adeline Messenger; Joseph Low, Jr. & Mary Sawyer; Joseph Low & Abigail Low; David Low, Jr. & Susanna Low [parents of Joseph], Caleb Low & Abigail Varney [parents of Abigail]; David Low & Mary Lamb [parents of David, Jr. & Caleb]; Caleb Lamb & Mary Wise; Joseph Wise & Mary Thompson; 126-7).

143-144. MRS. NEDENIA HUTTON RUMBOUGH ROBERTSON, known as DINA MERRILL, b. 1925, actress, whose 2nd husband is CLIFF(ORD) (PARKER) ROBERTSON (III), b. 1925, actor; Edward Francis Hutton & (Mrs.) Marjorie Merriweather Post (Close Hutton Davies May), 174 below.

145. WILLIAM LENDRUM "BILLY" MITCHELL, 1879–1936, army officer & aviator (1st wife, Caroline Stoddard; Enoch Vine Stoddard, Jr. & Caroline Sarah Butts; Enoch Vine Stoddard & Mary Smith Allen; Vine Stoddard & Prudence Morgan, Lewis Allen & Mary Denison Smith; Joseph Morgan, Jr. & Prudence Avery, Denison Smith & Waity Smith; Joseph Morgan & Dorothy Avery, James Avery & Elizabeth Smith, Oliver Smith & Mary Denison [parents of Denison], Jabez Smith & Waity Burrows [parents of Waity]; William Morgan & Margaret Avery, Ebenezer Avery & Dorothy Parke [parents of Dorothy], Nehemiah Smith III & Dorothy Wheeler [parents of Elizabeth & Nathan], Nathan Smith & Mary Denison [parents of Oliver & Jabez]; James Morgan, Jr. & Mary Vine, John Parke & Mary Witter, Isaac Wheeler & Martha Parke; 60-1, 62-3 [parents of John & Martha]) (2nd wife, Elizabeth Trumbull Miller; Sidney Trowbridge Miller & Lucy Trumbull Robinson; Henry Cornelius Robinson & Eliza Niles Trumbull; David Franklin Robinson & Anne Seymour, John F. Trumbull & Ann Eliza Smith; Asa Seymour & Elizabeth Denison, Joseph Smith III & Nancy Eells; Thomas Denison & Catherine Starr, Joseph Smith, Jr. & Hannah Hewitt, Joseph Eells & Anna Stanton; Daniel Denison & Rachel Starr, Samuel Starr & Anne Bushnell, Charles Hewitt & Hannah Stanton, Thomas Stanton & Elizabeth Bell; Thomas Starr & Mary Morgan [parents of Rachel], Jonathan Starr & Elizabeth Morgan [parents of Samuel], Joseph Stanton, Jr. & Anna Wheeler [parents of Hannah], William Stanton & Anna Stanton [parents of Thomas]; James Morgan, Jr. & Mary Vine [parents of Mary & Elizabeth], Joseph Stanton & Margaret Chesebrough [parents of Joseph, Jr.], William Wheeler & Hannah Gallup, Thomas Stanton, Jr. & Sarah Denison [parents of William]; 60-1, Nathaniel Chesebrough & Hannah Denison, Isaac Wheeler & Martha Parke, George Denison & Bridget Thompson [parents of Sarah & Hannah]; 62-3, 126-7).

146. HARRIET (STONE) MONROE, 1860–1936, poetess, editor, patroness; Henry Stanton Monroe & Martha Mitchell; Henry Monroe & Sylvia Thomas; Gaius Thomas & Elizabeth Stanton; Phineas Stanton, Jr. & Esther Gallup; Elisha Gallup & Mercy Denison; Joseph Gallup & Eunice Williams, great-great-grandparents of Bertram Grosvenor Goodhue, see 87 above.

147. DWIGHT LYMAN MOODY, 1837–1899, evangelist, founder of the Chicago (later Moody) Bible Institute; Edwin Moody & Betsey Holton; Luther Holton & Betsey Hodges; Lemuel Holton & Lydia Shattuck; William Holton, Jr. & Bethiah Hall; William Holton & Abigail Edwards; John Holton & Abigail Fisher; 34-5.

148. JOHN PIERPONT MORGAN, 1837–1913, banker, art & book collector; Junius Spencer Morgan & Juliet Pierpont, grandparents of Lady Lewis Harcourt, Viscountess Harcourt, see 95 above.

149. JOHN PIERPONT MORGAN, JR., 1867–1943, banker; John Pierpont Morgan, 148 above, & Frances Louise Tracy; Charles Tracy & Louisa Kirkland; Joseph

Kirkland, Jr. & Sarah Backus; Joseph Kirkland & Hannah Perkins; Daniel Kirkland & Mary Perkins, Matthew Perkins & Hannah Bishop; Joseph Perkins & Martha Morgan (parents of Mary & Matthew), 12-3; 30-1.

150. LEWIS HENRY MORGAN, 1818–1881, ethnologist & anthropologist; Jedediah Morgan & Harriet Steele; Thomas Morgan & Sarah Leeds, Lemuel Steele & Mary Clapp; John Morgan III & Sarah Cobb, Elijah Clapp & Mary Benton; John Morgan, Jr. & Ruth Shapley, Thomas Clapp & Mary King; John Morgan & Rachel Deming, Preserved Clapp & Sarah Newberry, Thomas King & Mary Webster; 60-1, Roger Clapp & Joanna Ford, John King & Sarah Holton; 66-7, 34-5.

151. THOMAS HUNT MORGAN, 1866–1945, biologist, recipient of the Nobel Prize in physiology & medicine in 1933; Charlton Hunt Morgan & Ellen Key Howard; Calvin Cogswell Morgan & Henrietta Hunt; Luther Morgan & Anne Cameron Dold; Gideon Morgan & Patience Cogswell, great-great-grandparents of Mrs. F(rancis) Scott (Key) Fitzgerald, see 76 above.

152. SAMUEL ELIOT MORISON, 1887–1976, historian (1st wife, Elizabeth Shaw Greene; William Batchelder Greene, Jr. & Sarah Ellery Sargent Austin; Ivers James Austin & Elizabeth Turner Amory; James Trecothick Austin & Catherine Gerry; Jonathan Loring Austin & Hannah Ivers; Benjamin Austin & Elizabeth Waldo; Cornelius Waldo III & Faith Savage; Cornelius Waldo, Jr. & Faith Peck; Cornelius Waldo & Hannah Cogswell; 100-1) (2nd wife, Priscilla Randolph Barton; Randolph Barton, Jr. & Eleanor Addison Morison; Robert Brown Morison & Elizabeth Hawkins Williams; George Hawkins Williams & Eleanor Addison Gittings; George Williams & Elizabeth Bordley Hawkins; Joseph Williams III & Susanna May, great-grandparents of Charles Joseph Bonaparte, see 35 above).

153. SAMUEL FINLEY BREESE MORSE, 1791–1872, artist, inventor of the telegraph (2nd wife, Sarah Elizabeth Griswold; Samuel Birdsall Griswold & Catherine Walker Breese; Edmund Griswold & Martha Birdsall; Jedediah Griswold & Patience Bates; Joseph Griswold & Temperance Lay, great-great-great-grandparents of Mrs. Edwin Laurentine Drake, see 62 above).

154. LEVI PARSONS MORTON, 1824–1920, congressman, diplomat, Governor of New York, U.S. Vice-President under B. Harrison; Daniel Oliver Morton & Lucretia Parsons; Justin Parsons & Electa Frary; Benjamin Parsons & Rebecca Sheldon, Nathan Frary & Elizabeth Barnard; Ebenezer Parsons & Mercy Stebbins, Benjamin Sheldon & Mary Strong, Ebenezer Barnard & Elizabeth Foster; Joseph Parsons, Jr. & Elizabeth Strong, Thomas Sheldon & Mary Hinsdale, Ebenezer Strong, Jr. & Mary Holton, Joseph Barnard & Sarah Strong; 32-3 (parents of Elizabeth, Ebenezer, & Sarah), Isaac Sheldon & Mary Woodford, Ebenezer Strong & Hannah Clapp, William Holton, Jr. & Sarah Marshfield; 38-9, 34-5.

155. WILLIAM THOMAS GREEN MORTON, 1819–1868, discoverer of ether as an anaesthetic (wife, Elizabeth Whitman; Edward Whitman & Almira Olmsted; Francis Flowers Olmsted & Nancy Judd; Jesse Judd & Mary Buell; William Judd & Ruth Lee; John Lee,. Jr. & Elizabeth Loomis; 22-3).

156. JOHN LOTHROP MOTLEY, 1814–1877, historian, diplomat (wife, Mary Elizabeth Benjamin; Park Benjamin & Mary Judith Gall, great-grandparents of Mrs. Enrico Caruso, see 44 above).

157. EDWARD ROSCOE MURROW, 1908–1965, radio & television commentator, head of the U.S. Information Agency (wife, Janet Huntington Brewster; Charles Huntington Brewster & Jennie Johnson; Charles Kingman Brewster & Celina Sophia Baldwin, grandparents of Kingman Brewster, Jr., see 37 above).

158. Walter Loomis Newberry, 1805–1868, merchant, banker, philanthropist, founder of the Newberry Library in Chicago; Amasa Newberry & Ruth Warner; John Warner & Margaret Loomis; Jonathan Loomis & Sarah Higley; John Higley & Sarah Strong; Return Strong & Sarah Warham; 32-3.

159. (Benjamin) Frank(lin) Norris (Jr.), 1870–1902, novelist & "muckraker"; Benjamin Franklin Norris & Gertrude Glorvina Doggett; Simeon Wales Doggett & Harriet Wotton; Simeon Doggett & Anonima "Nancy" Fobes; Perez Fobes & Prudence Wales; Josiah Fobes & Freelove Edson; John Fobes & Abigail Robinson; Edward Fobes & Elizabeth Howard; 52-3.

160. Frederick Law Olmsted, 1822–1903, landscape architect & author, designer of Central Park in New York City; John Olmsted & Charlotte Law Hull; Benjamin Olmsted & Content Pitkin, Samuel Hull & Abigail Doolittle; Jonathan Olmsted & Hannah Meakins, Amos Doolittle & Abigail Ives; Joseph Olmsted & Hannah Marsh, Jotham Ives & Abigail Burroughs; John Marsh, Jr. & Sarah Lyman, Gideon Ives & Mary Royce, Edward Burroughs & Abigail Chauncey; Richard Lyman, Jr. & Hepzibah Ford, Joseph Royce & Mary Porter, Nathaniel Chauncey & Abigail Strong; 66-7, Nehemiah Royce & Hannah Morgan, 32-3; 60-1.

161. Thomas Nelson Page, 1853–1922, novelist & diplomat, author of *In Ole Virginia* (2nd wife, Florence Wentworth Lathrop; Jedediah Hyde Lathrop & Mariana Bryan; Samuel Lathrop & Lois Huntington; Elisha Lathrop & Hannah Hough [great-great-great-great-grandparents of George Frost Kennan, see 117 above], Theophilus Huntington & Lois Gifford; Samuel Gifford, Jr. & Experience Hyde; Samuel Gifford & Mary Calkins; Stephen Gifford & Hannah Gore; 110-1).

162. Potter Palmer, 1826–1902, Chicago merchant & real estate promoter, builder of the Palmer House Hotel; Benjamin Palmer & Rebecca Potter; Samuel Palmer & Hannah Eells; Thomas Palmer & Priscilla Chesebrough; Nehemiah Palmer, Jr. & Jerusha Saxton, Samuel Chesebrough (half-brother of Jerusha Saxton) & Priscilla Alden; Joseph Saxton & Hannah Denison, Nathaniel Chesebrough & Hannah Denison (same Hannah); George Denison & Bridget Thompson; 126-7.

163. Talcott Parsons, 1902–1979, sociologist; Edward Smith Parsons & Mary Augusta Ingersoll; George Lyman Ingersoll & Catherine L. Talcott; Alvan Hyde Ingersoll & Hannah Lyman; David Ingersoll & Sarah Parsons, Caleb Lyman & Delight Wilson; Elihu Parsons & Sarah Edwards, Ebenezer Lyman, Jr. & Elizabeth Seward; Ebenezer Parsons & Mercy Stebbins, Ebenezer Lyman & Experience Pomeroy (great-grandparents of Lyman Beecher, see 28 above); Joseph Parsons, Jr. & Elizabeth Strong; 32-3.

164. George Smith Patton (III), 1885–1945, World War II army commander (wife, Beatrice Banning Ayer; Frederick Ayer, Jr. & Ellen Banning; Frederick Ayer & Persis Cook; Elisha Ayer & Hope Fanning; Thomas Fanning & Elizabeth Capron; John Fanning & Deborah Parke; William Parke & Hannah Frink; 62-3).

165. Benjamin Peirce, 1809–1880, mathematician & astronomer (wife, Sarah Hunt Mills; Elijah Hunt Mills & Harriette Blake, grandparents of Mrs. Henry Cabot Lodge, see 124 above).

166. Charles Sanders Peirce, 1839–1914, Pragmatist philosopher, son of 165 above & Sarah Hunt Mills.

167. Anthony Perkins, b. 1932, actor; (James Ripley) Osgood Perkins & Janet Esselstyn Rane; Henry Phelps Perkins, Jr. & Helen Virginia Anthony; Henry Phelps Perkins & Stella L. Burnham; Walter Burnham, Jr. & Annis Crawford, great-great-grandparents of the 1st Mrs. Marshall Field (IV), see 72 above.

168. JOHN JOSEPH PERSHING, 1860–1948, World War I army commander (wife, Helen Frances Warren; Francis Emroy Warren & Helen Maria Smith; Joseph Spencer Warren & Cynthia Estella Abbott; Joseph Warren & Susan Willey; Ezra Warren & Rebecca Dean; Joseph Warren & Eunice Hyde; Ezra Hyde & Elizabeth Leffingwell; John Leffingwell & Sarah Abell; Joshua Abell & Bethia Gager; 54-5).

169. WILLIAM LYON PHELPS, 1865–1943, literary critic & teacher; Sylvanus Dryden Phelps & Sophia Emilia Lyon Linsley; James Harvey Linsley & Sophia Brainerd Lyon; James Linsley & Sarah Maltby; Benjamin Maltby & Elizabeth Fowler; Josiah Fowler & Hannah Baldwin; Jonathan Baldwin & Thankful Strong; 32-3.

170. PHILIP WINSTON PILLSBURY, b. 1903, president & chairman of the Board, Pillsbury (Flour) Co.; Charles Stinson Pillsbury & Helen Pendleton Winston; Philip Bickerton Winston & Katharine Deborah Stevens; John Harrington Stevens & Frances Helen Miller; Abner Miller & Sally Lyman; Giles Miller, Jr. & Janet McCollum, David Lyman & Sarah Comstock; Giles Miller & Elizabeth Parsons, John Lyman & Hope Hawley (grandparents of Lyman Beecher, see 28 above); Moses Parsons & Abigail Ball; Joseph Parsons, Jr. & Elizabeth Strong; 32-3.

171. (MRS.) LYDIA (ESTES) PINKHAM, 1819–1883, reformer, patent medicine manufacturer (husband, Isaac Pinkham; Daniel Pinkham & Nabby Hawkes; Matthew Hawkes & Ruth Collins; Samuel Hawkes & Philadelphia Estes; Ebenezer Hawkes & Elizabeth Cogswell; John Hawkes & Sarah Cushman, John Cogswell III & Margaret Gifford; 102-3, John Cogswell, Jr. & ———; 100-1).

172. WILLIAM SYDNEY PORTER (O. HENRY), 1862–1910, short story writer; Algernon Sydney Porter & Mary Jane Virginia Swaim; Sidney Porter & Ruth Coffin Worth; Eleazer Williams Porter & Sarah Keyes; Eleazer Porter, Jr. & Susanna Edwards; Eleazer Porter & Sarah Pitkin; Samuel Porter, Jr. & Joanna Cooke; Aaron Cooke III & Sarah Westwood; Aaron Cooke, Jr. & Mary Cooke; Aaron Cooke & 67 (parents of Aaron, Jr.).

173. CHARLES WILLIAM POST, 1854–1914, breakfast food manufacturer, pioneer of the prepared food industry; Charles Rollin Post & Caroline Cushman Lathrop; Erastus Lathrop & Sarah Bailey; Azel Lathrop & Elizabeth Hyde; John Lathrop & Elizabeth Abell; Joshua Abell & Bethia Gager; 54-5.

174. (MRS.) MARJORIE MERRIWEATHER POST (CLOSE HUTTON DAVIES MAY), 1887–1973, society leader, founder of General Foods, Inc., daughter of 173 above & Ella Letitia Merriweather.

175. WILLIAM HICKLING PRESCOTT, 1796–1859, historian; William Prescott, Jr. & Catharine Greene Hickling; William Prescott & Abigail Hale; Jonathan Hale & Susanna Tuttle; John Tuttle & Martha Ward; Simon Tuttle & Sarah Cogswell; 100-1.

176. (EDWARD) WILLIAM PROXMIRE, b. 1915, U.S. Senator (1st wife, Elsie Rockefeller; William Avery Rockefeller & Florence Lincoln; William Goodsell Rockefeller & Sarah Elsie Stillman; William Rockefeller, 180 below & Almira Geraldine Goodsell).

177. MRS. LEA ANN REMICK COLLERAN GOWANS, known as LEE REMICK, b. 1935, actress; Frank E. Remick & Gertrude Margaret Waldo; Lewis Howell Waldo & Gertrude Duffield; John Bruce Waldo & Helen Brett; William Besley Waldo & Jane Anne Bruce; Charles Waldo & Elizabeth Besley; Jesse Waldo & Bridget Thompson; Shubael Waldo & Abigail Allen; Edward Waldo & Thankful Dimmock; John Waldo & Rebecca Adams; Cornelius Waldo & Hannah Cogswell; 100-1.

178. FREDERIC(K) (SACKRIDER) REMINGTON, 1861-1909, western painter & sculptor; Seth Pierrepont Remington & Clara Bascomb Sackrider; Seth Williston Remington & Maria Pickering; Thomas Remington, Jr. & Olive Nelson; Thomas Remington & Mary Remington; Daniel Remington & Sarah Winchell (parents of Thomas); Jonathan Winchell & Sarah Hovey; Thomas Hovey & Sarah Cooke; Aaron Cooke III & Sarah Westwood; Aaron Cooke, Jr. & Mary Cooke; Aaron Cooke & 67 (parents of Aaron, Jr.).
179-180. JOHN DAVISON ROCKEFELLER, 1839-1937, oil tycoon & philanthropist, founder of Standard Oil Co., the University of Chicago, the Rockefeller Institute for Medical Research & the Rockefeller Foundation, & WILLIAM ROCKEFELLER, 1841-1922, financier & industrialist; William Avery Rockefeller & Eliza Davison; Godfrey Rockefeller & Lucy Avery; Miles Avery & Malinda Pixley; Solomon Avery & Hannah Punderson; Humphrey Avery & Jerusha Morgan; William Morgan & Margaret Avery; James Morgan, Jr. & Mary Vine; 60-1.
181. JOHN DAVISON ROCKEFELLER, JR., 1874-1960, philanthropist & builder of Rockefeller Center, son of 179 above & Laura Celestia Spelman.
182-184. JOHN DAVISON ROCKEFELLER III, 1906-1978, philanthropist (founder of the Population Council, president of Lincoln Center, Inc.), NELSON ALDRICH ROCKEFELLER, 1908-1978, Governor of New York, U.S. Vice-President under Ford, art collector & patron, & DAVID ROCKEFELLER, b. 1915, president & chief executive officer, Chase Manhattan Bank; John Davison Rockefeller, Jr., 181 above, & Abby Greene Aldrich; Nelson Wilmarth Aldrich, 10 above & Abby Pearce Truman Chapman.
185. GEORGE WILCKEN ROMNEY, b. 1907, president of American Motors, Governor of Michigan, U.S. Secretary of Housing & Urban Development (wife, Lenore LaFaunt; Harold Arundle LaFaunt & Alma Luella Robison; Charles Edward Robison & Rosetta Mary Berry; Robert Berry, Jr. & Elvira Lucretia Warner; Robert Berry & Nancy Russell, Luther Warner & Permelia Stanton; Oliver Russell & Nancy Newton, David C. Warner & Mary Russell; Ellis Russell & Jane Catherine Wolcott [parents of Oliver & Mary]; Ebenezer Russell & Deborah Hibbard; Samuel Hibbard & Mary Bond; 56-7).
186-187. FRANKLIN DELANO ROOSEVELT, 1882-1945, 32nd U.S. President, husband of (MRS. ANNA) ELEANOR (ROOSEVELT) ROOSEVELT, 1884-1962, humanitarian & reformer; James Roosevelt & Sara Delano; Isaac Roosevelt & Mary Rebecca Aspinwall, Warren Delano & Catherine Robbins Lyman; John Aspinwall & Susan Howland, Joseph Lyman III & Anne Jean Robbins; Joseph Howland & Lydia Bill (great-great-great-grandparents of Louis Stanton Auchincloss, see 17 above), Joseph Lyman, Jr. & Mary Sheldon (great-great-great-grandparents of Lady Lewis Harcourt, Viscountess Harcourt, see 95 above).
188. THEODORE ROOSEVELT (JR.), 1858-1919, 26th U.S. President (2nd wife, Edith Kermit Carow; Charles Carow & Gertrude Elizabeth Tyler; Daniel Tyler IV & Emily Lee; Daniel Tyler III & Sarah Edwards; Daniel Tyler, Jr. & Mehitable Shurtleff; Daniel Tyler & Anna Geer; Hopestill Tyler & Mary Lovett; Daniel Lovett & Joanna Blott; 78-9).
189. ELIHU ROOT, 1845-1937, lawyer, U.S. Senator, Secretary of War, & Secretary of State; Oren Root & Nancy Whitney Buttrick; Elihu Root & Achsah Pomeroy, great-great-grandparents of Henry Robinson Luce, see 130 above.
190. JOHN WELLBORN ROOT, 1850-1891, architect, designer of the Columbian Exposition (2nd wife, Dora Louise Monroe, sister of Harriet Stone Monroe, 146 above).
191. HENRY AUGUSTUS ROWLAND (III), 1848-1901, physicist; Henry Augustus

Rowland, Jr. & Harriet Heyer; Henry Augustus Rowland & Frances Bliss; Moses Bliss & Abigail Metcalf; Jedediah Bliss & Rachel Sheldon; Joseph Sheldon & Mary Whiting; Isaac Sheldon & Mary Woodford; 38-9.

192. JOSIAH ROYCE, 1855–1916, philosopher (wife, Katherine Head; Edward Francis Head & Eliza Ann Clements; Charles Head & Sarah Winslow Tyng, later Mrs. Joseph Marquand, great-grandmother of John Phillips Marquand II, see 135 above).

193. BERTRAND ARTHUR WILLIAM RUSSELL, 3rd Earl Russell, 1872–1970, British philosopher & mathematician (4th wife, Edith Finch; Edward Bronson Finch & Delia Brodhead Gardner; Peter Voorhees Finch & Harriet Anna Bronson; Thomas Bronson & Cynthia Elizabeth Bartlett; Cyrus McCall Bartlett & Betsey McCall; Hobart McCall & Lucy Strong; Archippus McCall & Deborah Marsh, Daniel Strong & Esther Chappell; Ebenezer Marsh & Deborah Buell, Stephen Strong & Abigail Buell; John Marsh III & Elizabeth Pitkin, Jedediah Strong, Jr. & Abiah Ingersoll; John Marsh, Jr. & Sarah Lyman, 20-1; Richard Lyman, Jr. & Hepzibah Ford; 66-7).

194. THOMAS FORTUNE RYAN, 1851–1928, financier & traction magnate (2nd wife, Mary Townsend Nicoll; Solomon Townsend Nicoll & Charlotte Anne Nicoll; Samuel Benjamin Nicoll, Jr. & Sarah Brown Payne [parents of Charlotte Anne]; Samuel Benjamin Nicoll & Anna Willett Floyd; William Nicoll & Joanna D'Honneur, parents also of Mrs. John Loudon McAdam, see 136 above).

195. ARTHUR MEIER SCHLESINGER, JR., b. 1917, historian & presidential advisor (2nd wife, Alexandra Temple Emmet; William Temple Emmet, Jr. & Lily Dulany Cushing; Howard Gardiner Cushing & Ethel Cochrane; Robert Maynard Cushing & Olivia Donaldson Dulany [grandparents of Mrs. Alexander Calder, see 42 above], Alexander Cochrane, Jr. & Mary Lynde Sullivan; John Langdon Sullivan & Mary Eliza Lynde; Thomas Russell Sullivan & Charlotte Caldwell Blake; Francis Blake & Elizabeth Augusta Chandler; Gardiner Chandler & Elizabeth Ruggles; Timothy Ruggles, Jr. & Bathsheba Bourne; Timothy Ruggles & Mary White; Benjamin White & Susanna Cogswell; 50-1).

196. CHARLES SCRIBNER, JR., 1854–1930, publisher (wife, Louisa Flagg; Jared Bradley Flagg & Louisa Hart; Henry Collins Flagg, Jr. & Martha Whiting, Samuel Hart & Orpha North; William Joseph Whiting & Martha Lyman, Elijah Hart III & Anna Andrews; Medad Lyman & Mary Bassett, Elijah Hart, Jr. & Sarah Gilbert [great-great-grandparents of Walter Chauncey Camp, see 43 above]; Benjamin Lyman & Thankful Pomeroy; Medad Pomeroy & Experience Woodward; 42-3.).

197. CHARLES SEYMOUR, 1885–1963, historian, president of Yale University, 1937–1951; Thomas Day Seymour & Sarah Melissa Hitchcock; Nathan Perkins Seymour & Elizabeth Day; Charles Seymour, Jr. & Catherine Perkins, Thomas Day & Sarah Coit; Nathan Perkins & Catherine Pitkin, Wheeler Coit & Sybil Tracy; Matthew Perkins & Hannah Bishop, Samuel Coit & Sarah Spalding; Joseph Perkins & Martha Morgan, 12-13, Joseph Coit, Jr. & Experience Wheeler; 30-1, Isaac Wheeler & Martha Parke; 62-3.

198. HORATIO SEYMOUR, 1810–1886, Governor of New York, Democratic Party leader, brother of Mrs. Roscoe Conkling, see 49 above.

199. JAMES SCHOOLCRAFT SHERMAN, 1855–1912, lawyer, businessman, congressman & U.S. Vice President under Taft (wife, Carrie Babcock; Lewis Hamilton Babcock & Ellen Catherine Sherrill; Albert Franklin Babcock & Ann Almira Crandall; Joshua Babcock & Clarissa Crandall, Erastus Crandall & Nancy Ann Rhodes; Joseph Babcock & Sarah Babcock, Archibald Crandall &

Susanna Maxson [parents of Clarissa & Erastus]; Christopher Babcock & Mehitable Chalker [parents of Sarah], William Maxson & Lucy Minor; William Babcock & Sarah Denison, Simeon Minor & Hannah Wheeler; Samuel Denison & Mary Lay, William Wheeler & Hannah Gallup; Robert Lay, Jr. & Mary Stanton, Isaac Wheeler & Martha Parke; Thomas Stanton, Jr. & Sarah Denison, 62-3; George Denison & Bridget Thompson; 126-7).

200. William Sowden Sims, 1858–1936, naval officer, reformer, & World War I commander (wife, Anne Erwin Hitchcock; Ethan Allen Hitchcock, 103 above, & Margaret Dwight Collier; George Collier & Sarah Ann Bell; William Bell, Jr. & Margaret Van Horn Dwight; Maurice William Dwight & Margaret Dewitt; Timothy Dwight III & Mary Edwards, parents of Timothy Dwight IV, see 67 above).

201. Theobald Smith, 1859–1934, pathologist (wife, Lilian Hillyer Egleston; Nathaniel Hillyer Egleston & Sarah Anne Winship; Nathaniel Egleston & Emily Hillyer; Samuel Egleston & Dorcas Loomis; Stephen Loomis & Grace Loomis; Aaron Loomis & Deborah Egleston [parents of Grace]; David Loomis & Lydia Marsh; John Marsh & Hepzibah Ford; 66-7).

202. Benjamin (McLane) Spock, b. 1903, pediatrician, author & peace advocate (1st wife, Jane Davenport Cheney; John Davenport Cheney & Mary Wilcox Russell; Frank Woodbridge Cheney & Mary Bushnell; Charles Cheney & Waitstill Dexter Shaw; George Cheney & Electa Woodbridge; Deodatus Woodbridge & Esther Welles; Russell Woodbridge & Anna Olmsted; Joseph Olmsted & Hannah Marsh; John Marsh, Jr. & Sarah Lyman; Richard Lyman, Jr. & Hepzibah Ford; 66-7).

203. (Mrs.) Elizabeth (Smith) Cady Stanton, 1815–1902, feminist & reformer (husband, Henry Brewster Stanton; Joseph Stanton & Susan M. Brewster; Simon Brewster, Jr. & Mehitable Belcher; Simon Brewster & Anne Andrus [great-great-great-grandparents of Archibald MacLeish, see 134 above], William Belcher & Desire Morgan; Daniel Morgan & Elizabeth Gates; James Morgan & Bridget ———; John Morgan & Rachel Deming; 60-1).

204. Adlai Ewing Stevenson II, 1900–1965, Governor of Illinois, Democratic presidential candidate in 1952 & 1956, Ambassador to the United Nations (wife, Ellen Borden; John Borden & Ellen Waller; William Borden & Mary DeGama Whiting; John Talman Whiting & Mary Sophia Hill; John Leffingwell Whiting & Harriet C. Talman; John Whiting & Lydia Leffingwell; Christopher Leffingwell & Elizabeth Coit, great-great-great-grandparents of Allen Welsh Dulles & John Foster Dulles, see 65 & 66 above).

205. Henry Lewis Stimson, 1867–1950, lawyer, diplomat, U.S. Secretary of War & Secretary of State (wife, Mabel Wellington White; Charles Atwood White & Frances Spencer Eaton; Henry White & Martha Sherman; Roger Sherman, Jr. & Susanna Staples; John Staples & Susanna Perkins; Matthew Perkins & Hannah Bishop, great-great-great-grandparents of Charles Seymour, see 197 above).

206. Joseph Story, 1779–1845, jurist (1st wife, Mary Lynde Oliver; Thomas Fitch Oliver & Sarah Pynchon; William Pynchon, Jr. & Catherine Sewall; William Pynchon & Catherine Brewer; Daniel Brewer & Catherine Chauncey; Nathaniel Chauncey & Abigail Strong; 32-3) (2nd wife, Sarah Waldo Wetmore; William Wetmore & Sarah Waldo; Samuel Waldo, Jr. & Sarah Erving; Samuel Waldo & Lucy Wainwright, grandparents of Mrs. Henry Knox, see 120 above).

207. (Mrs.) Harriet (Elizabeth) Beecher Stowe, 1811–1896, abolitionist, authoress of *Uncle Tom's Cabin,* daughter of Lyman Beecher, 28 above & Roxana Foote.

208. Leopold (Antoni Stanislaw Boleslawowicz) Stokowski, 1882–1977, conductor (3rd wife, Gloria Morgan Vanderbilt, later married to Sidney Lumet, 132 above).
209. Jack Isidor Straus, b. 1900, president & chief executive officer, Macy's Department Store (1st wife, Margaret Shelton Hollister; Frederick Kellogg Hollister & Harriet May Shelton; George Gregory Shelton & Ida Elizabeth Sherman; George Wellington Shelton & Margaret Gray Atwood; George Shelton & Betsey Wooster; William Shelton & Susanna Strong; Thomas Strong & Susanna Thompson; Selah Strong & Abigail Terry; 16-7).
210. Caleb Strong (Jr.), 1745–1819, Federalist statesman, lawyer, U.S. Senator & Governor of Massachusetts; Caleb Strong & Phebe Lyman; Jonathan Strong & Mehitable Stebbins; Ebenezer Strong & Hannah Clapp; 32-3.
211. (William) Stuart Symington (Jr.), b. 1901, U.S. Senator from Missouri, Secretary of the Air Force (1st wife, Evelyn Wadsworth; James Wolcott Wadsworth, Jr. & Alice Hay; James Wolcott Wadsworth & Louisa Travers; James Samuel Wadsworth & Mary Craig Wharton; James Wadsworth & Naomi Wolcott; Samuel Wolcott & Jerusha Wolcott; Gideon Wolcott & Naomi Olmsted [parents of Samuel]; Joseph Olmsted & Hannah Marsh; John Marsh, Jr. & Sarah Lyman; Richard Lyman, Jr. & Hepzibah Ford; 66-7).
212. Robert Alphonso Taft, 1889–1953, U.S. Senator, Republican leader (wife, Martha Wheaton Bowers; Lloyd Wheaton Bowers & Louise Bennett Wilson; Samuel Dwight Bowers & Martha Wheaton Dowd; William Bowers & Almira Bailey; Nathaniel Bowers & Phebe Clark; Benjamin Clark & Abiah Hall; Daniel Hall, Jr. & Mary Dwight; Samuel Dwight & Mary Lyman; John Lyman, Jr. & Mindwell Sheldon; Isaac Sheldon & Mary Woodford; 38-9).
213. Yves Tanguy, 1900–1955, surrealist painter (wife, Katherine "Kay" Linn Sage; Henry Manning Sage & Anna Wheeler Ward; Samuel Baldwin Ward & Cornelia Wheeler; Lebbeus Baldwin Ward & Abigail Dwight Partridge; Cotton Partridge & Hannah Lyman; Samuel Partridge & Abigail Dwight, Joseph Lyman & Hannah Huntington; Cotton Partridge & Margaret Cooke, Seth Dwight & Abigail Strong [great-great-grandparents of James Dwight Dana, see 52 above], Jonathan Lyman, Jr. & Bethiah Clark, Simon Huntington & Sarah Huntington [great-great-great-great-grandparents of Kingman Brewster, Jr., see 37 above]; Moses Cooke & Mary Barnard, Jonathan Lyman & Lydia Loomis [great-great-grandparents-in-law of Mrs. Helen Maria Fiske Hunt Jackson, see 113 above], William Clark III & Bethiah Williams; Aaron Cooke III & Sarah Westwood, William Clark, Jr. & Hannah Strong; Aaron Cooke, Jr. & Mary Cooke, 32-3; Aaron Cooke & 67 [parents of Aaron, Jr.]).
214. (Mrs.) Shirley (Jane) Temple (Agar Black), b. 1928, actress, diplomat (2nd husband, Charles Alden Black; James Byers Black & Katharine McElrath; John Edgar McElrath & Elsie Anne Alden; Solomon Ellsworth Alden & Ann Edwards Cornwall; Darius Alden & Marilla Ellsworth, Asa Cornwall & Anna Ellsworth; Solomon Ellsworth & Mary Moseley [parents of Marilla & Anna]; Abner Moseley & Elizabeth Lyman; John Lyman, Jr. & Mindwell Sheldon; Isaac Sheldon & Mary Woodford; 38-9).
215. Lowell (Jackson) Thomas, 1892–1981, travel author, radio & television commentator; Harry George Thomas & Harriet May Wagner; David Randall Thomas & Pheriba Anne Jackson; Charles W. Thomas & Mercy Sackett; Cyrus Sackett & Nancy Stapleton; Reuben Sackett & Mercy Finney; Jonathan Sackett & Anne Filer; Samuel Filer & Abigail ———; Zerubbabel Filer & Experience Strong; 32-3.
216. Louis Comfort Tiffany, 1848–1933, art patron, glassmaker & designer of

the "Tiffany Lamp" (1st wife, Mary Woodbridge Goddard; Levi Hart Goddard & Mary Woodbridge Perkins; Calvin Goddard & Alice Cogswell Hart, Henry Perkins & Mary Woodbridge; Levi Hart & Rebecca Bellamy, Elisha Perkins & Sarah Douglas, Nathaniel Shaw Woodbridge & Elizabeth Mumford; Thomas Hart, Jr. & Anna Stanley, Joseph Perkins, Jr. & Mary Bushnell [great-great-great-grandparents of Mrs. Edward Alexander MacDowell, see 133 above], Ephraim Woodbridge & Mary Shaw [great-great-grandparents of Mrs. MacDowell]; Thomas Hart & Elizabeth Judd; Stephen Hart, Jr. & Anne Fitch; 46-7).

217. SPENCER TRACY, 1900–1967, actor (wife, Louise Ten Broeck Treadwell; Alliene Wetmore Treadwell & Bright Smith; George Edwards Treadwell & Caroline Tudor Wetmore; Oliver Wetmore Treadwell & Anna Helena Kramer; John Pomeroy Treadwell & Hannah Edwards Wetmore; John Treadwell & Dorothy Pomeroy; Josiah Pomeroy & Lydia Ashley; Ebenezer Pomeroy & Sarah King; Medad Pomeroy & Experience Woodward, John King & Sarah Holton; 42-3, 34-5).

218. HARRY S TRUMAN, 1884–1972, 33rd U.S. President (wife, Elizabeth Virginia "Bess" Wallace; David Willock Wallace & Margaret "Madge" Gates; George Porterfield Gates & Elizabeth Emery; George Williams Gates & Sarah D. Todd; Samuel Gates, Jr. & Jerusha Clark; Ebenezer Clark III & Eunice Pomeroy; Ebenezer Clark, Jr. & Jerusha Russell, Ebenezer Pomeroy III & Mindwell Lyman; Ebenezer Clark & Abigail Parsons, Ebenezer Pomeroy, Jr. & Elizabeth Hunt, John Lyman III & Abigail Moseley; John Clark & Mary Strong, Joseph Parsons, Jr. & Elizabeth Strong, Ebenezer Pomeroy & Sarah King, Jonathan Hunt, Jr. & Martha Williams, John Lyman, Jr. & Mindwell Sheldon; 32-3 [parents of Mary & Elizabeth], Medad Pomeroy & Experience Woodward, John King & Sarah Holton, Samuel Williams & Theoda Parke, Isaac Sheldon & Mary Woodford; 42-3, 34-5, William Parke & Martha Holgrave, 38-9; 124-5).

219. JAMES JOSEPH "GENE" TUNNEY, 1898–1978, boxer, world heavyweight champion, 1926–1928 (wife, Mary Josephine Lauder; George Lauder, Jr. & Katherine Morgan Rowland; George Rowland & Maria Townsend Durfee; James Edward Rowland & Catherine A. Morgan; Jasper Morgan & Catherine Copp; William Morgan III & Lydia Smith, Joseph Copp & Rachel Denison; William Morgan, Jr. & Temperance Avery, Jonathan Copp & Margaret Stanton, Daniel Denison & Rachel Starr; William Morgan & Mary Avery, Joseph Stanton & Margaret Chesebrough, Thomas Starr & Mary Morgan; John Morgan & Elizabeth Jones [parents of William], Nathaniel Chesebrough & Hannah Denison, James Morgan, Jr. & Mary Vine [parents of Mary]; 60-1 [parents of John & James], George Denison & Bridget Thompson; 126-7).

220. RUDOLPH VALENTINO (Rodolfo Alfonzo Raffaelo Pierre Filibert Guglielmi Di Valentina d'Antonguolla), 1895–1926, movie idol (2nd wife, Natacha Rambova, originally Winifred Shaughnessy; Michael Shaughnessy & Winifred Kimball; Heber Parley Kimball & Phebe Theresa Judd; Heber Chase Kimball [grandfather of Spencer Woolley Kimball, see 118 above] & Vilatte Murray).

221. CYRUS ROBERTS VANCE, b. 1917, lawyer, diplomat, U.S. Secretary of State under Carter (wife, Grace Elsie Sloane; John Sloane & Elsie Nicoll; Benjamin Nicoll & Grace Davison Lord; Solomon Townsend Nicoll & Charlotte Anne Nicoll [parents of Mrs. Thomas Fortune Ryan, see 194 above], James Cooper Lord & Margaretta Hunter Brown; Daniel Lord III & Susan DeForest; Daniel Lord, Jr. & Phebe Crary; Peter Crary, Jr. & Lucretia Palmer; Peter Crary & Dorothy Copp; Jonathan Copp & Margaret Stanton, great-great-great-great-grandparents of Mrs. James Joseph "Gene" Tunney, see 219 above).

222. CORNELIUS VANDERBILT II, 1843–1899, financier & philanthropist (wife,

Alice Claypoole Gwynne; Abraham Evan Gwynne & Rachel "Cettie" Moore Flagg; Henry Collins Flagg, Jr. & Martha Whiting, grandparents of Mrs. Charles Scribner, Jr., see 196 above).

223. THORSTEIN BUNDE VEBLEN, 1857-1929, economist & social theorist (1st wife, Ellen May Rolfe; Charles G. Rolfe & Ellen Sylvia Strong; Elijah Gridley Strong & Sarah Ashley Partridge; Elijah Strong & Sylvia Gridley; Elisha Strong & Sarah Lewis; Jonathan Strong & Mehitable Stebbins [grandparents of Caleb Strong, Jr., see 210 above], Daniel Lewis & Mary Strong; Asahel Strong & Margaret Hart [parents of Mary]; 16 & Mary Hewett, Thomas Hart & Ruth Hawkins; 46-7).

224. JOSEPH WARREN (III), 1741-1775, physician, revolutionary patriot, hero of Bunker Hill; Joseph Warren, Jr. & Mary Stevens; Joseph Warren & Deborah Williams; Samuel Williams & Theoda Parke; William Parke & Martha Holgrave; 124-5.

225. ROBERT PENN WARREN, b. 1905, novelist & man of letters (2nd wife, Eleanor Clark; Frederick Huntington Clark & Eleanor Phelps; John Bates Clark & Myra Almeda Smith, Charles Henry Phelps & Mary Booth; John Hezekiah Clark & Charlotte Stoddard Huntington, Charles William Phelps & Mary Wilson Smith; Thomas Huntington & Elizabeth Colfax, Joseph Smith, Jr. & Sophia Smith; Jedediah Huntington & Anne Moore, George Colfax, Jr. & Mary Robbins, Joseph Smith & Eunice Goodman [parents of Joseph, Jr.], Caleb Smith & Olive Hibbard [parents of Sophia]; Jabez Huntington & Elizabeth Backus, George Colfax & Lucy Avery [great-grandparents of Schuyler Colfax, Jr., see 47 above], Alexander Smith & Rebecca Warriner [parents of Joseph], Benjamin Smith & ——— [parents of Caleb], George Hibbard & Lydia Allen; Joshua Huntington & Hannah Perkins, Joseph Smith III & Sarah Alexander [parents of Alexander], John Smith, Jr. & Mary ——— [parents of Benjamin], Joseph Hibbard, Jr. & Martha Smith, John Allen & Miriam Clark; Simon Huntington III & Lydia Gager, Nathaniel Alexander & Hannah Allen, John Smith & Elizabeth Hovey [parents of John, Jr.], Joseph Hibbard & Abigail Lyndon, Benoni Clark & Hannah Root; 54-5, Samuel Allen, Jr. & Hannah Woodford, Thomas Hovey & Sarah Cooke, 28-9, William Clark, Jr. & Hannah Strong; 36-7, 38-9, Aaron Cooke III & Sarah Westwood, 32-3; Aaron Cooke, Jr. & Mary Cooke; Aaron Cooke & 67 [parents of Aaron, Jr.]).

226-229. CADWALLADER COLDEN WASHBURN, 1818-1882, industrialist, congressman & Governor of Wisconsin, ISRAEL WASHBURN (V), 1813-1883, congressman & Governor of Maine, WILLIAM DREW WASHBURN, 1831-1912, millowner, Minnesota congressman & U.S. Senator, & ELIHU BENJAMIN WASHBURNE, 1816-1887, diplomat, Illinois congressman & U.S. Secretary of State under Grant; Israel Washburn IV & Martha Benjamin; Israel Washburn III & Abiah King; Israel Washburn, Jr. & Leah Fobes; Joshua Fobes & Abigail Dunbar; Edward Fobes & Elizabeth Howard; 52-3.

230. NOAH WEBSTER (JR.), 1758-1843, lexicographer; Noah Webster & Mercy Steele; Daniel Webster & Miriam Cooke; Noah Cooke & Sarah Nash; Aaron Cooke, Jr. & Joan Denslow; Aaron Cooke & 67 (parents of Aaron, Jr.).

231-232. THEODORE DWIGHT WELD, 1803-1895, abolitionist, whose wife was ANGELINA EMILY GRIMKÉ, 1805-1879, abolitionist & feminist; Ludovicus Weld & Elizabeth Clark; Ezra Weld & Anna Weld; John Weld & Esther Waldo (parents of Ezra); Daniel Waldo & Susanna Adams; Cornelius Waldo & Hannah Cogswell; 100-1.

233-234. (GEORGE) ORSON WELLES, b. 1915, actor, motion picture director & producer, whose 2nd wife was RITA HAYWORTH, originally Margarita Carmen

Cansino, b. 1918, actress; Richard Head Welles & Beatrice Ives; Richard Jones Welles & Mary Blanche Head; Orson Sherman Head & Mary Jane Treadwell; Jonathan Head, Jr. & Hepzibah Livermore; Jonathan Head & Ruth Little; Fobes Little & Sarah Baker; John Little & Constant Fobes; William Fobes & Martha Pabodie; 52-3.

235. Barrett Wendell, 1855–1921, teacher & man of letters; Jacob Wendell, Jr. & Mary Bertodi Barrett; Jacob Wendell & Mehitable Rindge Rogers; John Wendell, Jr. & Dorothy Sherburne; Henry Sherburne, Jr. & Sarah Warner; Daniel Warner & Sarah Hill; Philemon Warner & Abigail Tuttle; Simon Tuttle & Sarah Cogswell; 100-1.

236. Byron Raymond White, b. 1917, jurist (wife, Marion Lloyd Stearns; Robert Lawrence Stearns & Amy Pitkin; Robert James Pitkin & Amy Moore; Frederick Walker Pitkin & Fidelia M. James; Eli Pitkin & Hannah Miller Torrey; Eleazur Pitkin & Mehitable Cone; Stephen Cone III & Thankful Strong; David Strong & Thankful Loomis; John Strong III & Mary Pinney; John Strong, Jr. & Elizabeth Warriner; 32 & Marjorie Dean).

237. Paul Dudley White, 1886–1973, physician, heart specialist; Herbert Warren White & Elizabeth Abigail Dudley; Ephraim Mann White & Mary Frances Niles; John Niles & Mary Jane Thayer; Joshua Niles & Kezia Howard; John Howard & Abigail Hudson; Robert Howard & Abigail Keith; Joseph Keith & Elizabeth Fobes; Edward Fobes & Elizabeth Howard; 52-3.

238. Mrs. Gertrude Vanderbilt Whitney, 1872–1942, sculptress, founder of the Whitney Museum of American Art in New York City; Cornelius Vanderbilt II, 222 above, & Alice Claypoole Gwynne.

239. William Collins Whitney, 1841–1904, financier, sportsman & U.S. Secretary of the Navy (2nd wife, Edith Sibyl May; John Frederick May & Sarah Maria Mills; Frederick May & Julia Matilda Slocum, great-grandparents of Mrs. John Barrymore, see 24 above).

240. Ray Lyman Wilbur, 1875–1949, U.S. Secretary of the Interior, president of Stanford University, 1916–1943; Dwight Locke Wilbur & Edna Maria Lyman; Elias Lyman & Hannah Cogswell Fiske; Joel Lyman & Achsah Parsons; Elias Lyman & Anne Phelps, Isaac Parsons & Lucina Strong; Moses Lyman, Jr. & Mindwell Sheldon, Josiah Parsons & Sarah Sheldon, Jonathan Strong & Mehitable Stebbins; Isaac Sheldon, Jr. & Sarah Warner (parents of Mindwell & Sarah), Joseph Parsons, Jr. & Elizabeth Strong, Ebenezer Strong & Hannah Clapp; Isaac Sheldon & Mary Woodford, 32-3 (parents of Elizabeth & Ebenezer); 38-9.

241. Mrs. Emma Hart Willard, 1787–1870, educator; Samuel Hart, Jr. & Lydia Hinsdale; Samuel Hart & Mary Hooker; John Hart, Jr. & Mary Moore; John Hart & Sarah ———; 46-7.

242. Elisha Williams, 1694–1755, Congregational clergyman, legislator, jurist, rector (president) of Yale College, 1726–1739; William Williams & Elizabeth Cotton, great-great-great-great-great-great-grandparents of Mrs. McGeorge Bundy, see 40 above.

243. William Williams, 1731–1811, revolutionary patriot, signer of the Declaration of Independence; Solomon Williams & Mary Porter, great-great-great-grandparents of Mrs. John Marshall Harlan II, see 97 above.

244. H(enry) Parker Willis, 1874–1937, economist, editor, educator, 1st Secretary of the Federal Reserve Board; John Henry Willis & Olympia Brown; Asa Briggs Brown & Lephia Olympia Brown; Israel Putnam Brown & Sally Briggs (parents of Asa Briggs Brown), great-great-grandparents of (John) Calvin Coolidge (Jr.), see 50 above.

245. (THOMAS) WOODROW WILSON, 1856–1924, 28th U.S. President, Governor of New Jersey, president of Princeton University (1st wife, Ellen Louise Axson; Samuel Edward Axson & Margaret Jane Hoyt; Nathan Hoyt & Margaret Bliss; Alexander Bliss & Abigail Williams; Thomas Williams & Abigail Williams; Eleazer Williams & Sarah Tileston [parents of Thomas], Elijah Williams & Lydia Dwight [parents of Abigail]; Samuel Williams, Jr. & Sarah May [parents of Eleazer], John Williams & Abigail Allen [parents of Elijah]; Samuel Williams & Theoda Parke [parents of Samuel, Jr. & John]; William Parke & Martha Holgrave; 124-5).
246. HENRY ALEXANDER WISE, 1806–1876, congressman, diplomat, Governor of Virginia, Confederate general (2nd wife, Sarah Sergeant, sister of Mrs. George Gordon Meade, see 141 above).
247. THEODORE DWIGHT WOOLSEY, 1801–1889, political scientist, president of Yale University, 1846–1871; William Walton Woolsey & Elizabeth Dwight; Timothy Dwight III & Mary Edwards, parents of Timothy Dwight (IV), see 67 above.
248-249. WILBUR WRIGHT, 1867–1912, & ORVILLE WRIGHT, 1871–1948, inventors of the airplane, aviation industry pioneers; Milton Wright & Susan Catharine Koerner; Dan Wright, Jr. & Catherine Reeder; Dan Wright & Sarah Freeman; Edmund Freeman & Sarah Porter, great-great-great-grandparents of Thomas Edmund Dewey, see 58 above.
250. BRIGHAM YOUNG, 1801–1877, Mormon leader & colonizer of Utah (3 of the 16 wives by whom he left issue):
1) Lucy Bigelow; Nahum Bigelow & Mary Gibbs; Benjamin Gibbs & Adah Hubbard; Truman Gibbs & Anne Barnes; Benjamin Gibbs & Dinah Woodruff; Nathaniel Woodruff & Thankful Wright; Benjamin Wright & Thankful Taylor; John Taylor & Thankful Woodward; 42-3.
2) Zina Diantha Huntington; William Huntington, Jr. & Zina Baker; William Huntington & Presinda Lathrop; John Huntington III & Mehitable Steele; Stephen Steele & Ruth Porter; Samuel Porter, Jr. & Joanna Cooke; Aaron Cooke III & Sarah Westwood; Aaron Cooke, Jr. & Mary Cooke; Aaron Cooke & 67 (parents of Aaron, Jr.).
3) Emily Dow Partridge; Edward Partridge & Lydia Clisbee; William Partridge & Jemima Bidwell; Oliver Partridge & Anna Williams; Edward Partridge & Martha Williams (sister of William, Jr.), William Williams, Jr. & Hannah Stoddard, great-great-great-great-great-grandparents of Mrs. McGeorge Bundy, see 40 above.

So far I have found only two major American figures linked to the Princess of Wales through Frank Work's Boude ancestors, originally of Boston and Marblehead. Both married descendants of Grimstone Boude (d. 1716) of Boston and Philadelphia, as follows:

1. ALFRED IRENEE DUPONT, 1864-1935, early 20th century head of E. I. duPont de Nemours (1st wife, Bessie Gardner; Dorsey Gardner & Margaretta Sherman Potts; Charles Cazenove Gardner & Maria Ridgely Dorsey; John Syng Dorsey & Maria Ralston; Robert Ralston & Sarah Clarkson; Matthew Clarkson III & Mary Boude; Thomas Boude & Sarah Newbold, great-grandparents of Frank Work).
2. MICHAEL HILLEGAS, 1729–1804, revolutionary patriot & 1st Treasurer of the U.S. (wife, Henrietta Boude; Samuel Boude & Deborah Cox; Grimstone Boude & Mary ———, great-great-grandparents of Frank Work).

Chapter Two

FIFTY ADDITIONAL NOTABLE DISTANT KINSMEN OF DR. JOSEPH STRONG AND H.R.H. THE PRINCESS OF WALES*

Outlined below are all recently discovered New England-derived kinships between various noted Americans, plus one Canadian figure, and H.R.H. The Princess of Wales. Some of the following additional lines and kinsmen were first traced by Mr. William Addams Reitwiesner. Others were developed from sources I found initially at the library of the Genealogical Society of the Church of Jesus Christ of Latter-day Saints in Salt Lake City. Several were taken largely from Jane Erickson Hutchinson, *The Descendants of Thomas Hutchinson of Southold, New York, 1666–1982* (Baltimore, 1982), a work that treats the full known progeny of a half-brother of Mrs. Susanna Hawkes Cogswell; another 1982 work, *The Search for a Heritage,* by Alan and Mickey Cogswell, privately printed, covers many English and English-speaking Cogswells in great detail. Also included below, although excluded earlier, are notable descendants of Experience Mitchell of Bridgewater, about whose wives and children see the *Register*, 127 (1973): 94-95, *The Mayflower Quarterly*, 49 (1983): 130-134, and *The American Genealogist*, 59 (1983): 28-31, the very likely brother of Mrs. Constant Mitchell Fobes (Mrs. Cogswell and Mrs. Fobes are respectively #s 51 and 53 in the ancestor table of Dr. Joseph Strong). The lines for Mrs. Samuel Langhorne Clemens, Mrs. Anthony Crosland, Martha Graham, Mrs. William McChesney Martin, Mrs. George McGovern, and Bart Saxbe were submitted or suggested by correspondents, to whom I am most grateful. The line for Nancy Reagan was widely reported in the press and national media.

The "Additional Lines and Kinsmen" treated below cover, firstly, further ancestors shared by Dr. Joseph Strong, the Princess of Wales, and fifteen of the already treated 250 notable distant kinsmen, including additional wives for three of them. Also listed are two presidential wives, Frances Cleveland and Grace Coolidge, who were spouses of such kinsmen but shared ancestry with Dr. Strong themselves as well. Included secondly are lines for Richard Morris Hunt, James Schoolcraft Sherman,

*An earlier version of this chapter was published as "A Supplement to the New England Ancestry of H.R.H. The Princess of Wales" in *Genealogies of Connecticut Families from The New England Historical and Genealogical Register*, 3 (Baltimore, 1983): 676-680.

and Robert Alphonso Taft, #s 111, 199, and 212 among the 250 but previously listed only as husbands of distant kinsmen, not as such kinsmen themselves. William Morris Hunt, R. M. Hunt's brother, is listed as #251.

The remainder of the "Additional Lines and Kinsmen" section, the bulk of this chapter, treats forty-nine further notable distant kinsmen of Dr. Strong, for a total of 300. These forty-nine include members of various "tycoon" families (Astor, duPont, Flagler, Moore, Paley, and Woolworth), at least three more nineteenth-century literary leaders (W. C. Bryant, J. F. Cooper, and Mark Twain), several additional twentieth-century figures active in entertainment, media, sports, or the arts (Alistair Cooke, Elsie de Wolfe, Martha Graham, Cary Grant, Sonja Henie, W. S. Paley, and Brooke Shields), an eleventh and a twelfth U.S. president (Taft and Reagan), a sixth and seventh vice-president (Hobart and Wallace), a ninth and tenth secretary of state (Evarts and Colby), a third president of Harvard (Eliot), an eighth president of Yale (Angell), and two foreign heads of state or government (E. H. Childers of Ireland and Sir Charles Tupper, 1st Baronet, of Canada). Also covered by this study, although not counted in their own right among the 300, are six American "first ladies"—Frances Cleveland, Edith Roosevelt, Ellen Wilson, Grace Coolidge, Bess Truman, and Nancy Reagan; a seventh, Eleanor Roosevelt, the spouse of a kinsman of Dr. Strong but not a kinswoman herself, is #187. Of the seventy U.S. presidents and vice-presidents to date, the Princess of Wales can be genealogically linked through various New England forebears to nineteen. A likely twentieth connection, through the Claytons of New Jersey to Nixon, is treated in the next chapter.

The format for these forty-nine additional kinsmen is exactly that followed in the preceding chapter. For those among the first 250 figures for whom the following outlines merely a single additional line, I have, however, indicated only that figure's number and name, then the last already listed couple through one of whom the new line derives, and finally the line itself.

Additional Lines and Kinsmen

40. MRS. MCGEORGE BUNDY: Joseph Buckminster, Jr. & Mary Lyman; Isaac Lyman & Ruth Plummer; Moses Lyman, Jr. & Mindwell Sheldon; Isaac Sheldon, Jr. & Sarah Warner; Isaac Sheldon & Mary Woodford; 38-9.

41. MRS. RICHARD EVELYN BYRD, JR.: Daniel Ames & Hannah Keith; John Ames, Jr. & Sarah Washburn; John Washburn, Jr. & Elizabeth Mitchell; Experience Mitchell & ———; 106-7.

46. (STEPHEN) GROVER CLEVELAND (wife, Frances Folsom; Oscar Folsom & Emma Cornelia Harmon; Elisha Harmon & Ruth Hayward Rogers; Rawson Harmon & Lydia Murdock; Anan Harmon & Sarah Rawson; Nathaniel Harmon & Elizabeth Bridgeman; James Bridgeman & Elizabeth Allis; John Bridgeman & Mary Sheldon; Isaac Sheldon & Mary Woodford; 38-9).

50. (JOHN) CALVIN COOLIDGE (JR.) (wife, Grace Anna Goodhue; Andrew Issachar Goodhue & Lemira A. Barrett; Benjamin Goodhue & Caroline Andrews; Issachar Andrews & Abigail Manning; Joseph Andrews IV & Margaret Ober; Joseph Andrews III & Rachel Burnham; Thomas Burnham & Hannah Cogswell; John Cogswell & Hannah Goodhue; 50-1).

63. Nancy Seymour Fincke, wife of JOHN DAVID DRUMMOND, 17th Earl of Perth; Bohan Clark & Mary White; Enoch White & Susanna Goodman; Jonathan White & Lydia Rugg; Nathaniel White, Jr. & Esther Strong; Samuel Strong & Esther Clapp; 32-3.

136. JOHN LOUDON MCADAM (2nd wife, Anna Charlotte De Lancey; John Peter De Lancey & Elizabeth Floyd; Richard Floyd III & Arabella Jones; Richard Floyd, Jr. & Elizabeth Hutchinson; Matthias Hutchinson & Mary Fanieul; Thomas Hutchinson & Martha Corwin; [Thomas?] Hutchinson & 103).

193. Edith Finch, 4th wife of BERTRAND ARTHUR WILLIAM RUSSELL, 3rd Earl Russell: Thomas Bronson & Cynthia Elizabeth Bartlett; Bennett Bronson & Anna Smith; Stephen Bronson & Sarah Humiston; Thomas Bronson, Jr. & Susanna Southmayd; Thomas Bronson & Elizabeth Upson; Stephen Upson & Mary Lee; 22-3.

194, 221. MRS. THOMAS FORTUNE RYAN & MRS. CYRUS ROBERTS VANCE: Samuel Benjamin Nicoll & Anna Willett Floyd; Richard Floyd III & Arabella Jones, grandparents of Mrs. John Loudon McAdam, see the addition to 136 above.

195. ARTHUR MEIER SCHLESINGER, JR. (1st wife, Marian Cannon; Walter Bradford Cannon & Cornelia James; Henry Clay James & Frances Linda Haynes; Francis Greenleaf Haynes & Harriet King Williams; Seth Williams III & Hannah Waters; Seth Williams, Jr. & Zilpha Ingraham; Seth Williams & Susanna Fobes; William Fobes & Thankful Dwelly; Edward Fobes & Elizabeth Howard; 52-3).

195. MRS. ARTHUR MEIER SCHLESINGER, JR.: Thomas Russell Sullivan & Charlotte Caldwell Blake; John Langdon Sullivan & Elizabeth Russell; James Sullivan & Mehitable Odiorne; William Odiorne & Avis Adams; Hugh Adams & Susanna Winborne; John Winborne & Elizabeth Hart; Isaac Hart & Elizabeth Hutchinson; (Thomas?) Hutchinson & 103.

210. CALEB STRONG (JR.): Caleb Strong & Phebe Lyman; Moses Lyman, Jr. & Mindwell Sheldon, see the addition to 40 above.

211. MRS. (WILLIAM) STUART SYMINGTON (JR.): James Wadsworth & Naomi Wolcott; John Noyes Wadsworth & Esther Parsons; Timothy Parsons & Mary Robinson; Samuel Parsons & Rhoda Taylor; John Taylor & Thankful Woodward; 42-3.
226-229. CADWALLADER COLDEN WASHBURN, ISRAEL WASHBURN (V), WILLIAM DREW WASHBURN, & ELIHU BENJAMIN WASHBURNE: Israel Washburn, Jr. & Leah Fobes; Israel Washburn & Waitstill Sumner; Samuel Washburn & Deborah Packard; John Washburn, Jr. & Elizabeth Mitchell; Experience Mitchell & ———; 106-7.
250. MRS. BRIGHAM YOUNG (Louisa Beeman, another of the sixteen wives by whom the Mormon leader left issue; Alvah Beeman & Sally Burtts; Reuben Beeman & Meriam ———; Ebenezer Beeman & Rachel Tracy; Thomas Beeman & Phebe Parke; Nathaniel Parke & Sarah Geer; 62-3).

111, 251. RICHARD MORRIS HUNT, 1828-1895, architect, and WILLIAM MORRIS HUNT, 1824-1879, artist; Jonathan Hunt, Jr. & Jane Maria Leavitt; Jonathan Hunt & Lavinia Swan; Samuel Hunt & Anna Ellsworth; Jonathan Hunt, Jr. & Martha Williams; Samuel Williams & Theoda Parke; William Parke & Martha Holgrave; 124-5.

199. JAMES SCHOOLCRAFT SHERMAN, 1855–1912, lawyer, businessman, congressman, and U.S. Vice-President under Taft; Richard Updike Sherman & Mary Frances Sherman; Richard Winslow Sherman & Frances Lucretia Williams (parents of Mary Frances); Stalham Williams & Mary Augusta Barron; William Williams & Dorothy Ashley; Israel Williams & Sarah Chester, Jonathan Ashley, Jr. & Dorothy Williams; William Williams & Christian Stoddard (parents of Israel & Dorothy), great-great-great-great-grandparents of Mrs. John Marshall Harlan II, see 97 above.

212. ROBERT ALPHONSO TAFT, 1889–1953, U.S. Senator, Republican leader; William Howard Taft, 294 below, & Helen Herron.
252. JAMES ROWLAND ANGELL, 1869–1949, psychologist, president of Yale University, 1921–1937 (1st wife, Marion Isabel Watrous; Charles Leach Watrous & Sophia Glover; Joseph Watrous & Lydia Emerson Leach; Jonathan Leach, Jr. & Lydia Emerson Pettingell; Jonathan Leach & Abigail Leach; Timothy Leach & Sarah Leach [parents of Jonathan]; Benjamin Leach & Hepzibah Washburn [parents of Sarah]; [almost certainly] Joseph Washburn & Hannah Latham; John Washburn, Jr. & Elizabeth Mitchell; Experience Mitchell & ———; 106-7).
253. (WILLIAM) VINCENT ASTOR, 1891–1959, financier, philanthropist, twentieth-century head of the American Astor family (2nd wife, Mary Benedict Cushing; Harvey Williams Cushing, 264 below, & Katharine Stone Crowell).
254. JACQUES BARZUN, b. 1907, philosopher & critic (wife, Mariana Lowell; Frederick Eldridge Lowell & Isabel Pelham Shaw; Edward Jackson Lowell & Mary Wolcott Goodrich, parents of Guy Lowell, see 129 above).
255. WILLIAM CULLEN BRYANT, 1794–1878, poet & newspaper editor; Peter Bryant & Sarah Snell; Philip Bryant & Silence Howard, Ebenezer Snell & Sarah Packard; Abiel Howard & Silence Washburn, Zachariah Snell & Abigail Hayward, Abiel Packard & Sarah Ames; Nehemiah Washburn & Jane Howard, Joseph Hayward & Hannah Mitchell, John Ames, Jr. & Sarah Washburn; Samuel Washburn & Deborah Packard (parents of Nehemiah), Experience Mitchell & ——— (parents of Hannah & Elizabeth), John Washburn, Jr. & Elizabeth Mitchell (parents of Sarah & Samuel); 106-7.

256. Erskine Hamilton Childers, 1905–1974, President of Ireland, 1973–1974; (Robert) Erskine Childers, 257 below, & Mary Alden Osgood.
257. (Robert) Erskine Childers, 1870–1922, Irish nationalist (wife, Mary Alden Osgood; Hamilton Osgood & Margaret Cushing Pearmain; John H. Osgood & Adeline Stevens; John Osgood & Patty Fletcher; Benjamin Osgood & Tryphena Cummings; Thomas Cummings & Lucy Lawrence; Eleazer Lawrence, Jr. & Lucy Tuttle; Simon Tuttle, Jr. & Mary Rogers; Simon Tuttle & Sarah Cogswell; 100-1).
258. Samuel Langhorne Clemens (Mark Twain), 1835–1910, novelist, humorist, & man of letters (wife, Olivia Langdon; Jervis Langdon & Olivia Lewis; Edward Lewis & Olive Barnard; Moses Barnard & Hannah Barnard; Francis Barnard & Lucretia Pinney [parents of Moses], Edward Barnard & Mabel Pinney [parents of Hannah]; Joseph Barnard, Jr. & Abigail Griswold [parents of Francis & Edward]; Joseph Barnard & Sarah Strong; 32-3).
259. Bainbridge Colby, 1869–1950, lawyer, U.S. Secretary of State under Wilson (1st wife, Nathalie Sedgwick Washburn; William Tucker Washburn & Katherine Sedgwick; William Rounsevill Peirce Washburn & Susan Ellen Tucker; Abiel Washburn & Elizabeth Peirce; Edward Washburn, Jr. & Phoebe Smith; Edward Washburn & Elizabeth Richmond; James Washburn & Mary Bowden; John Washburn, Jr. & Elizabeth Mitchell; Experience Mitchell & ———; 106-7).
260. (Alfred) Alistair Cooke, b. 1908, journalist, broadcaster (1st wife, Ruth Emerson; Haven Emerson & Grace Parrish; John Haven Emerson & Susan Tompkins; William Emerson III & Susan Woodward Haven; William Emerson, Jr. & Ruth Haskins, parents of Ralph Waldo Emerson, see 70 above).
261. James Fenimore Cooper, 1789–1851, novelist & man of letters (wife, Susan Augusta De Lancey; John Peter De Lancey & Elizabeth Floyd, parents of Mrs. John Loudon McAdam, see the addition to 136 above).
262. Archibald Cox (Jr.), b. 1912, lawyer, educator, U.S. Solicitor General, & Watergate prosecutor; Archibald Cox & Frances Bruen Perkins; Edward Clifford Perkins & Elizabeth Hoar Evarts; William Maxwell Evarts, 269 below, & Helen Minerva Wardner.
263. (Charles) Anthony (Raven) Crosland, 1918–1977, British M.P. & cabinet official, Foreign Secretary, 1976–1977 (2nd wife, Susan Barnes Watson; Mark Skinner Watson & Susan Owens; Winslow Charles Watson & Ella S. Barnes; Winslow Cossoul Watson & Susan Pierpont Skinner; Richard Skinner & Fanny Pierpont; Timothy Skinner & Susanna Marsh; Gideon Skinner & Dorothy Strong, Isaac Marsh & Susanna Pratt; Josiah Strong & Joanna Gillette, John Marsh III & Elizabeth Pitkin; John Strong, Jr. & Elizabeth Warriner, John Marsh, Jr. & Sarah Lyman; 32 & Marjorie Dean, Richard Lyman, Jr. & Hepzibah Ford; 66-7).
264. Harvey Williams Cushing, 1869–1939, neurological surgeon; Henry Kirke Cushing & Betsey Maria Williams; William Williams & Lucy Fitch; Zalmon Fitch & Betsey Mygatt; Comfort Starr Mygatt & Lucy Knapp; Eli Mygatt & Abigail Starr; Joseph Mygatt III & Elizabeth Starr; Joseph Mygatt, Jr. & Elizabeth Taylor; John Taylor & Thankful Woodward; 42-3.
265. Ella Anderson de Wolfe, Lady (Charles) Mendl, known as Elsie de Wolfe, 1865–1950, actress, socialite, pioneer interior decorator; Stephen de Wolfe & Georgina Watt Copeland; Stephen Brown de Wolfe & Harriette Ruggles; Timothy Ruggles III & Sarah Dwight; Timothy Ruggles, Jr. & Bathsheba Bourne [ancestors of Mrs. Arthur Meier Schlesinger, Jr., see 195 above], Simeon Dwight & Sybil Dwight; Samuel Dwight & Mary Lyman (parents of Sybil), great-

great-great-great-great-grandparents of Mrs. Robert Alphonso Taft, see 212 above.

266. Andrew Jackson Downing, 1815–1852, landscape gardener, architect, horticulturist (wife, Caroline Elizabeth de Windt; John Peter de Windt & Caroline Amelia Smith; William Stephens Smith & Abigail Amelia Adams; John Adams, Jr., 2nd U.S. President, 4 above, & Abigail Smith).

267. Pierre Samuel duPont IV, b. 1935, congressman & Governor of Delaware; Pierre Samuel duPont III & Jane Holcomb; Frederick Wainwright Holcomb & Dorothy Doolittle; Edgar Jared Doolittle, Jr. & Martha Warner Couch; Edgar Jared Doolittle & Jane Elizabeth Sage; Jared Doolittle & Anna Jones; Joseph Doolittle III & Sarah Hart, Nicholas Jones & Elizabeth Hall; Nathaniel Hart, Jr. & Alice Hall, Isaac Hall & Esther Moseley; Nathaniel Hart & Martha Lee, Abner Moseley & Elizabeth Lyman; Hawkins Hart & Sarah Royce, Stephen Lee & Elizabeth Royce, John Lyman, Jr. & Mindwell Sheldon; Thomas Hart & Ruth Hawkins, 22-3, Isaac Sheldon & Mary Woodford; 46-7, 38-9.

268. Charles William Eliot, 1834–1926, president of Harvard University, 1869–1909; Samuel Atkins Eliot & Mary Lyman; Theodore Lyman & Lydia Williams; Isaac Lyman & Ruth Plummer, see the addition to 40 above.

269. William Maxwell Evarts, 1818–1901, lawyer, diplomat, U.S. Senator, Attorney General, & Secretary of State under Hayes (wife, Helen Minerva Wardner; Allen Wardner & Minerva Bingham; Frederick Wardner & Rebecca Waldo; Shubael Waldo & Abigail Allen, great-great-great-great-great-grandparents of Lee Remick, see 177 above).

270. Philo Taylor Farnsworth, 1906–1971, television, radar & electronics engineer (wife, Elma Gardner; Bernard Edward Gardner & Alice Maria Mecham; Ira Walter Gardner & Alice Snow; Walter Elias Gardner & Martha Ann Tuttle; Edward Tuttle & Catherine Vannever Geyer; Joseph Tuttle & Elizabeth Pratt; Benjamin Tuttle & Mary Turell; Joseph Turell & Joanna Ward; Daniel Turell, Jr. & Hannah Barrell; Daniel Turell & Lydia Blott; 78-9).

271. George Washington Gale Ferris, Jr., 1859–1896, civil engineer, inventor of the Ferris Wheel; George Washington Gale Ferris & Martha Edgerton Hyde; Jabez Perkins Hyde & Martha Edgerton; Jedediah Hyde, Jr. & Elizabeth Brown; Jedediah Hyde & Jerusha Perkins; Joseph Perkins & Martha Morgan; 30-1.

272. Henry Morrison Flagler, 1830–1913, capitalist & Florida developer (1st wife, Mary Harkness; Lamon Gray Harkness & Julia Follett; Eliphalet Follett, Jr. & Tryphena Dimock; Abel Dimock & Theoda Burbank; John Burbank & Rachel Austin; Nathaniel Austin & Abigail Hovey, great-great-grandparents of Rutherford Birchard Hayes, see 99 above).

273. George Franklin Gilder, b. 1939, economist, author of *Wealth and Poverty*; Richard Watson Gilder & Anne Spring Alsop; Reese Denny Alsop & Julia Sanford Chapin; Reese Fell Alsop & Mary Lee Spring; James Walton Spring & Mary O'Hara Denny; Gardiner Spring & Susan Barney; Samuel Spring & Hannah Hopkins; Samuel Hopkins, Jr. & Sarah Porter; Samuel Hopkins & Esther Edwards, Eleazer Porter & Sarah Pitkin (great-great-great-grandparents of William Sydney Porter, "O. Henry," see 172 above); John Hopkins & Hannah Strong; John Strong, Jr. & Mary Clark; 32 & Marjorie Dean.

274. Martha Graham, b. 1893, dancer, teacher, choreographer of modern dance; George G. Graham & Jane Beers; John Beers & Mary Hamilton; William Hamilton & Frances Staples; Job Staples & Susanna Hayes; John Staples &

Frank Work (1819-1911), great-great-grandfather of the Princess of Wales *(New-York Daily Tribune, 17 March 1911)*

Mrs. Frances Burke Roche (1857-1947), great-grandmother of the Princess of Wales
(New-York Tribune, 29 April 1911)

Edmund Maurice Burke Roche, 4th Baron Fermoy (1885-1955), maternal grandfather of the Princess of Wales

The Princess's mother, Frances Ruth Burke Roche, now Mrs. Shand Kydd

Susanna Perkins, great-great-grandparents of Mrs. Henry Lewis Stimson, see 205 above.

275. ARCHIBALD ALEXANDER LEACH, known as CARY GRANT, b. 1904, actor (2nd wife, Barbara Hutton; Franklin Laws Hutton & Edna Woolworth; Frank Winfield Woolworth, 300 below, & Jennie Creighton).

276. (MRS.) SONJA HENIE (TOPPING GARDINER ONSTAD), 1912–1969, ice skating champion & actress (2nd husband, Winthrop Gardiner, Jr.; Winthrop Gardiner & Isabel Lemmon; John Lyon Gardiner & Elizabeth Coralie Jones; Samuel Buell Gardiner & Mary Gardiner Thompson; John Lyon Gardiner & Sarah Griswold; David Gardiner & Jerusha Buell; Samuel Buell & Jerusha Meacham; Joseph Meacham & Esther Williams; John Williams & Eunice Mather; Samuel Williams & Theoda Parke; William Parke & Martha Holgrave; 124-5).

277. GARRET AUGUSTUS HOBART, 1844–1899, U.S. Vice-President under McKinley (wife, Hester Jane Tuttle; Socrates Tuttle & Jane Winters; Horatio Tuttle & Betsey Thomas; Jonathan Tuttle & Katherine Gray; John Tuttle & Sarah Robbins; Simon Tuttle, Jr. & Mary Rogers; Simon Tuttle & Sarah Cogswell; 100-1).

278. HAROLD LECLAIR ICKES, 1874–1952, journalist, author, U.S. Secretary of the Interior (1st wife, Anna Hawes Wilmarth; Henry Martin Wilmarth & Mary Jane Hawes; Jonathan Munroe Wilmarth & Lucy Cheney; Joseph Cheney & Susanna Wadsworth; John Wadsworth & Jerusha White; Benjamin White & Sarah Talbot; George Talbot & Mary Turell; Daniel Turell, Jr. & Hannah Barrell; Daniel Turell & Lydia Blott; 78-9).

279. AMOS ADAMS LAWRENCE, 1814–1886, merchant, philanthropist, founder of Lawrence University, treasurer of the Emigrant Aid Society; Amos Lawrence & Sarah Richards; Giles Richards & Sarah Adams; Abijah Richards & Huldah Hopkins; Thomas Richards & Hannah Upson, Timothy Hopkins & Mary Judd; Stephen Upson & Mary Lee, John Hopkins & Hannah Strong; 22-3, John Strong, Jr. & Mary Clark; 32 & Marjorie Dean.

280. WILLIAM LAWRENCE, 1850–1941, Episcopal Bishop of Massachusetts, 1893–1927; Amos Adams Lawrence, 279 above, & Sarah Elizabeth Appleton; William Appleton & Mary Ann Cutler; James Cutler & Mehitable Sullivan; James Sullivan & Mehitable Odiorne, see the addition to 195 above.

281. WILLIAM MCCHESNEY MARTIN, JR., b. 1906, chairman of the Federal Reserve Board, 1951–1970 (wife, Cynthia Davis; Dwight Filley Davis & Helen Brooks; John Tilden Davis & Maria Jeanette Filley; Samuel Craft Davis & Caroline Tilden; Robert Sharp Davis & Lucy Stearns; Ebenezer Davis & Lucy Sharp; Robert Sharp III & Sarah Payson; Robert Sharp, Jr. & Susanna White; Robert Sharp & Sarah Williams, Benjamin White & Susanna Cogswell [great-grandparents of John Adams, Jr., see 3 above]; Stephen Williams & Sarah Wise; Joseph Wise & Mary Thompson; 126-7).

282. GEORGE STANLEY MCGOVERN, b. 1922, U.S. Senator from South Dakota, Democratic presidential candidate in 1972 (wife, Eleanor Faye Stegeberg; Earl Stegeberg & Marion Faye Payne; Seward Quincy Payne, Jr. & Edna May Wright; Charles Wright & Adeline Hollister; Sidney H. Wright & Mabel Fenn; John Wright IV & Seloma Gillette; Nathan Gillette & Lucy Harrison; Zaccheus Gillette & Ruth Phelps; Isaac Gillette & Elizabeth Griswold; Benjamin Griswold & Elizabeth Cooke; Moses Cooke & Elizabeth Clark; Aaron Cooke, Jr. & Mary Cooke; Aaron Cooke & 67 [parents of Aaron, Jr.]).

283. CHARLES FOLLEN MCKIM, 1847–1909, architect, partner in McKim, Mead,

& White (wife, Julia Amory Appleton; Charles Hook Appleton & Isabella Mason; William Appleton & Mary Ann Cutler, grandparents of William Lawrence, see 280 above).

284. Paul Moore, Jr., b. 1919, Episcopal Bishop of New York since 1972; Paul Moore & Fanny Weber Hanna; William Henry Moore, 285 below, & Ada Waterman Small, Leonard Cotton Hanna & Fanny Wilson Mann; Edward Alonzo Small & Mary Caroline Roberts, Leonard Hanna & Samantha Maria Converse (parents of Marcus Alonzo "Mark" Hanna, see 94 above); Edward Small, Jr. & Rebecca Pratt; Edward Small & Sarah Mitchell; Seth Mitchell & Deborah Andrews; Jacob Mitchell, Jr. & Rebecca Cushman; Jacob Mitchell & Susanna Pope; Experience Mitchell & ———; 106-7.

285. William Henry Moore, 1848–1923, lawyer, capitalist, trust promoter; Nathaniel Ford Moore & Rachel Arvilla Beckwith; George Beckwith III & Mary Bradley; George Beckwith, Jr. & Rachel Marsh; John Marsh IV & Sarah Webster; John Marsh III & Elizabeth Pitkin; John Marsh, Jr. & Sarah Lyman; Richard Lyman, Jr. & Hepzibah Ford; 66-7.

286. William Samuel Paley, b. 1901, founder and president of Columbia Broadcasting System (CBS) (2nd wife, Barbara Cushing; Harvey Williams Cushing, 264 above, & Katharine Stone Crowell).

287. Max(well Evarts) Perkins, 1884–1947, editor, man of letters; Edward Clifford Perkins & Elizabeth Hoar Evarts, grandparents of Archibald Cox (Jr.), see 262 above.

288. John Pope, 1822–1892, Union general (wife, Clara Pomeroy Horton; Valentine Baxter Horton & Clara Alsop Pomeroy; Samuel Wyllys Pomeroy & Clarissa Alsop; Eleazer Pomeroy & Mary Wyllys, great-great-great-great-grandparents of J. W. Alsop V & S. J. O. Alsop, see 13-14 above).

289. Ronald Wilson Reagan, b. 1911, actor, Governor of California, 40th U.S. President (2nd wife, Nancy Davis, born Anne Francis Robbins; Kenneth Seymour Robbins & Edith Luckett; John Newell Robbins & Anne Ayers Francis; Frederick Augustus Francis & Jessie Ann Stevens; Manning Francis & Elizabeth Robbins Root; George Bridges Rodney Root & Honor Robbins; Ezekiel Root & Ruth Noble; Asa Noble & Bethia Noble; Luke Noble & Ruth Wright [parents of Asa]; Joseph Wright & Ruth Sheldon; Isaac Sheldon & Mary Woodford; 38-9).

290. John Davison Rockefeller IV, b. 1937, Governor of West Virginia; John Davison Rockefeller III, 182 above, & Blanchette Ferry Hooker; Elon Huntington Hooker & Blanche Ferry; Horace B. Hooker & Susan Pamelia Huntington; Horace Hooker & Helen Wolcott; Erastus Wolcott & Chloe Bissell; Aaron Bissell & Dorothy Stoughton; Ebenezer Bissell & ———; Thomas Bissell, Jr. & Hester Strong; 32-3.

291. William Bart Saxbe, b. 1916, U.S. Senator & Attorney General, diplomat; Bart Rockwell Saxbe & Faye Henry Carey; Henry Clay Carey & Elizabeth Letitia Henry; William Allen Carey & Catherine Vandemark; Cephas Cary & Jane Williamson; Ezra Cary, Jr. & Lydia Thompson; Ezra Cary & Mary Holman; Ephraim Cary & Hannah Waldo; Daniel Waldo & Susanna Adams; Cornelius Waldo & Hannah Cogswell; 100-1.

292. John Sedgwick, 1813–1864, Union general; Benjamin Sedgwick & Olive Collins; Philo Collins & Olive Foote; Cyprian Collins & Azuba Gibbs; Benjamin Gibbs & Dinah Woodruff, great-great-grandparents of Lucy Bigelow, Mrs. Brigham Young, see 250 above.

293. (Christa) Brooke (Camille) Shields, b. 1965, model and actress; Francis

Alexander Shields & Teri Schmon; Francis Xavier Shields & Marina, Princess Torlonia; Marino Torlonia, 4th Prince of Civitella-Cesi, & Mary Elsie Moore; Charles Arthur Moore & Mary Campbell; John Keyes Campbell & Betsey Sheffield; George Sheffield & Thirza Baker; John Baker & Susanna Strong; Ozias Strong & Susanna West; Phineas Strong & Mary Parker; 8-9.

294. WILLIAM HOWARD TAFT, 1857–1930, 27th U.S. President & 10th Chief Justice; Alphonso Taft & Louisa Maria Torrey; Peter Rawson Taft & Sylvia Howard; Aaron Taft & Rhoda Rawson; Abner Rawson & Mary Allen; Edmund Rawson & Elizabeth Hayward; John Hayward & Sarah Mitchell; Experience Mitchell & ———; 106-7.

295. SIR CHARLES TUPPER, 1st Bt., 1821–1915, Canadian statesman, Prime Minister from 27 April until 8 July 1896 (wife, Frances Amelia Morse; Silas Hibbert Morse & Elizabeth Stewart; Alpheus Morse & Theodory Crane; Silas Crane & Lucy Waterman; Jonathan Crane, Jr. & Mary Hibbard, [probably] Thomas Waterman III & Martha ———; 28-9, Thomas Waterman, Jr. & Elizabeth Allyn; John Allyn & Elizabeth Gager; 54-5).

296. HENRY AGARD WALLACE, 1888–1965, U.S. Secretary of Agriculture & Commerce, Vice-President under F. D. Roosevelt; Henry Cantwell Wallace & Carrie May Brodhead; John Avery Brodhead & Mary Ann Matilda White; James Howell White & Emmeline Guiteau; John White & Matilda Leavens; John Leavens & Esther Williams; Isaac Williams & Elizabeth Sabin; John Williams & Mary Goad; Isaac Williams, Jr. & Elizabeth Hyde; Isaac Williams & Martha Parke; William Parke & Martha Holgrave; 124-5.

297. MALCOLM WALLOP, b. 1933, U.S. Senator from Wyoming; Hon. Oliver Malcolm Wallop & Jean Moore; Edward Small Moore & Jean Ray McGinley; William Henry Moore, 285 above, & Ada Waterman Small, grandparents of Paul Moore, Jr., see 284 above.

298. JULIAN ALDEN WEIR, 1852–1919, painter (both wives, sisters Anna Dwight Baker & Ella Baker; Charles Taintor Baker & Anna Bartlett Dwight; Jonathan Dwight III & Ann Bartlett; Jonathan Dwight, Jr. & Sarah Shepard, parents of Mrs. George Bancroft, see 20 above).

299. JOHN HAY WHITNEY, 1904–1982, financier, philanthropist, & diplomat (2nd wife, Betsey Cushing; Harvey Williams Cushing, 264 above, & Katharine Stone Crowell).

300. FRANK WINFIELD WOOLWORTH, 1852–1919, founder of the F. W. Woolworth department store chain; John Hubbell Woolworth & Fanny McBrier; Jasper Woolworth & Elizabeth G. Buel; Phineas Woolworth & Mercy Sheldon; Simeon Sheldon & Grace Phelps; Thomas Sheldon, Jr. & Mary Smith; Thomas Sheldon & Mary Hinsdale; Isaac Sheldon & Mary Woodford; 38-9.

Addendum

After the production of this volume was well underway, two further—and quite surprising—notable distant kinsmen of Dr. Joseph Strong and H.R.H. The Princess of Wales were noticed and brought to the attention of the authors by Mr. Joseph Paul Mazza of Washington, D.C. As one of these was the wife of a third foreign head of state or government (in addition to E. H. Childers and Sir Charles Tupper, 1st Baronet) related to the Princess through her New England forebears, an addendum seems merited. The kinships may be outlined as follows:

1. JAN GARRIGUE MASARYK, 1886–1948, diplomat, Foreign Minister of Czechoslovakia; Tomas Garrigue Masaryk & Charlotte Garrigue, below.

2. Tomas Jan Masaryk, later TOMAS GARRIGUE MASARYK, 1850–1937, philosopher, Czechoslovak patriot, President of Czechoslovakia, 1918–1935 (Charlotte Garrigue; Rudolph Garrigue & Charlotte Lydia Whiting; William Loring Whiting & Mary E. Starr; John Whiting & Lydia Leffingwell [great-great-great-grandparents of Mrs. Adlai Ewing Stevenson II, see 204, chapter 1, above], Joshua Starr, Jr. & Lucy Colfax; George Colfax, Jr. & Mary Robbins, great-great-great-grandparents of Mrs. Robert Penn Warren, see 225, chapter 1, above).

Chapter Three

THE MID-ATLANTIC ANCESTRY OF H.R.H. THE PRINCESS OF WALES

I

The Maryland, Philadelphia, and New Jersey ancestry of the Princess of Wales, and of her son, H.R.H. Prince William Arthur Philip Louis, is derived through both a great-great-great- and a great-great-great-great-grandmother of the Princess, Mrs. Sarah Duncan Boude Work and Mrs. Rebecca Young Strong Gardiner respectively. However, the father of Mrs. Gardiner (wife firstly of the Connecticut-born Dr. Joseph Strong) was almost certainly a native of Scotland; her mother's maiden surname is unknown, and none of her siblings left traceable issue. Thus this chapter is concerned solely with the ancestry and kinsmen of Mrs. Work. The generations between this last and Prince William, all fully documented in the chapter on the Princess's New England ancestry, may be outlined as follows: 1) Sarah Duncan Boude (1790–1860) & John Work (1781–1823); 2) Frank(lin H.) Work (1819–1911) & Ellen Wood (1831–1877); 3) Frances Eleanor (Ellen) Work (1857–1947) & James Boothby Burke Roche, 3rd Baron Fermoy (1851–1920); 4) Edmund Maurice Burke Roche, 4th Baron Fermoy (1885–1955) & Ruth Sylvia Gill (b. 1908); 5) the Hon. Frances Ruth Burke Roche (b. 1936) & Edward John Spencer, 8th Earl Spencer (b. 1924); 6) Lady Diana Frances Spencer, now H.R.H. The Princess of Wales (b. 1961) & H.R.H. Prince Charles Philip Arthur George, Prince of Wales (b. 1948); and 7) H.R.H. Prince William Arthur Philip Louis of Wales (b. 1982).

Although born twenty years after Dr. Joseph Strong, the Princess's "gateway" ancestor to New England, Sarah Duncan Boude is only a partially comparable forebear for the mid-Atlantic region, for several reasons. The Maryland ancestry of Sarah's mother, Barbara Black, daughter of a William Black of Anne Arundel County whose 1771 will names a wife Catharine, is unknown beyond these parents. Grimstone Boude, Sarah's great-grandfather, the son almost certainly of an innkeeper of Marblehead, Massachusetts, arrived in Philadelphia only about 1700; the maiden surname of Mary, his second wife and Sarah's great-grandmother, is unknown. Thus Sarah Duncan Boude has no as yet known seventeenth-century forebears in either Maryland or Pennsylvania. I cannot readily trace any notable kinsmen through the Blacks, and only two major such kinsmen, or their spouses, through the Boudes. Sarah's paternal grandmother, Sarah Newbold (1700–1780) of Burlington County, New Jersey, is indeed a "gateway" ancestress of sorts, and nine of the ten major notable mid-Atlantic-derived kinsmen of the Princess of Wales who are listed below are descendants of Sarah Newbold, her siblings, aunts or uncles. But Sarah Newbold was herself the granddaughter of immigrants to New Jersey in the late 1670s. Her maternal grandparents, John Clayton and Alice Myres, were Quakers, and some of their descendants followed the usual Quaker migration patterns, as is suggested by their being likely forebears of President Richard M. Nixon. Sarah Newbold's paternal grandparents, Michael Newbold, Sr. and Anne ———, also of Burlington County, left a progeny largely concentrated in Philadelphia and environs, where it is socially and civically prominent. In addition to the six Newbold descendants listed below and Mrs. A. I. duPont, this progeny includes various later Lippincotts and Noyeses listed in *Who's Who* and associated with J. B. Lippincott & Co. or the Washington *Star*, several Gummeres (one a president of Haverford College) and Janviers active in Philadelphia literary or academic life, a William Romaine Newbold (the family's major genealogist) and George Newbold Lawrence treated in the *Dictionary of American Biography*, a Newbold Morris among civic leaders of New York City, the wives of John Syng Dorsey and FitzWilliam Sargent among Philadelphia surgeons, George Wood among noted New Jersey lawyers, and the wife of Henry Howard Houston among Pennsylvania railroad tycoons. As has been well argued by E. Digby Baltzell in *Puritan Boston and Quaker Philadelphia: Two Protestant Ethics and the Spirit of Class Authority and Leadership* (New York, 1979) and *Philadelphia Gentlemen: The Making of a National Upper Class* (New York, 1958), and by Nathaniel Burt in *The Perennial Philadelphians: The Anatomy of an American Aristocracy* (Boston, 1963), whereas Boston and New England have produced numerous nationally prominent figures, Philadelphia has produced mostly local leaders, largely in business or the professions. Additionally, of course, the mid-Atlantic region was settled, on average, fifty years or more after New England, by a population that was much larger, immigrated over several generations, and consisted in sizable part of several distinct ethnic or religious groups (Dutch, Germans, Quakers, Scotch-Irish Presbyterians, etc.) that often did not readily intermarry.

With no known seventeenth-century Maryland or Pennsylvania ancestors, no known Dutch, German, or Scotch-Irish forebears, only one pair of seventeenth-century Quaker ancestors, and descent from only one family widely represented in the Philadelphia patriciate, Sarah Duncan Boude then is hardly comparable to Dr. Joseph Strong as a regional "gateway" ancestor. Note too that her Quaker forebears lived in New

Jersey, not Pennsylvania, and that the city to whose later, largely Episcopal, upper class she has genealogical links is not New York but Philadelphia. Nonetheless, the ancestry and major notable kinsmen of Sarah Duncan Boude are of considerable historical interest. They link the Princess of Wales and likely future sovereigns to another American region, and when added to the Princess's New England forebears through Dr. Strong and the Virginia ancestry of H.M. Queen Elizabeth The Queen Mother through Robert Porteus, Jr., give Prince William and any siblings ancestral associations with six of the thirteen American colonies—Massachusetts, Connecticut, New Jersey, Pennsylvania, Maryland, and Virginia. If we recall the later residence of various of the Princess's forebears in what is now West Virginia, in Kentucky, in Ohio, and in New York City and Newport, the full extent of these state and regional associations becomes apparent. Moreover, the number of living descendants of Joseph Boude (Grimstone's father, and including his New England progeny also), Michael Newbold, Sr., John Clayton, and William Black is probably several hundred thousand. This total is calculated by assuming three children and thirty years per generation, eleven generations of progeny, three now living, for Boude, Newbold, and Clayton, and nine generations for Black, and considerable overlap and cousin intermarriage; the figure is less, however, than the likely progeny for any one of the twenty-three Great Migration New England forebears of Dr. Strong. Fully acknowledging the small number of Sarah Duncan Boude's known immigrant ancestors, their later arrival and thus much reduced progeny to date, and the lesser national role played by Philadelphia and the mid-Atlantic region generally, the number of the Princess's traceable distant mid-Atlantic-derived notable kinsmen is still startling. Through Dr. Strong's New England forebears I can trace 300; through Sarah Duncan Boude's mid-Atlantic forebears, only ten. This enormous contraction not only highlights the relative contribution of both regions; it suggests much as well about their overall genealogical scholarship.

This last statement and the generally mediocre genealogical coverage of the mid-Atlantic colonial population notwithstanding, printed and typescript sources for the Princess's Boude, Newbold, and Clayton forebears are good. The parents, grandparents, and patrilineal great- and great-great-grandparents of Sarah Duncan Boude are, with one exception (that of the Blacks), definitively covered by Francis James Dallett in "The Inter-Colonial Grimstone Boude and His Family," *The Genealogist* (New York), 2 (1981): 74-114, 257. Newbold genealogies include William Romaine Newbold and Rev. E. Boudinot Stockton, "Newbold Family and Connections: Ancestors and Descendants of Michael and Anne Newbold of Burlington County, N.J.," 4 vols., 1928, a typescript in the collections of the Genealogical Society of Pennsylvania; and Charles Platt, Jr., *Newbold Genealogy in America: The Line of Michael Newbold, Who Arrived in Burlington County, New Jersey, About 1680, and Other Newbold Lines, Including That of Thomas Newbold, Who Arrived in Somerset County, Maryland, About 1665* (New Hope, Pa., 1964). Both Newbolds and Claytons are treated in George Norwood Comly, *Comly Family in America: Descendants of Henry and John Comly Who Came to America in 1682 from Bedminster, Somersetshire, England, with Short Accounts of the Ancestors of Charles and Debby Ann (Newbold) Comly* (Philadelphia, 1939), pp. 791-793 and 937-951. The marriage of John Clayton & Alice Myres and the birth records of three children were discovered by Mary Ann Nicholson and published in *The American Genealogist*, 58 (1982): 115, to which I added a note entitled "Clayton of New Jersey to Prince William of Wales" (pp. 242 and 246). Other Clayton material, compiled by Dr. Raymond Martin Bell and including some speculative connections to Rhode Island and other New England Claytons, appeared in *The Quaker Yeomen*, 7 (1980): 1-7 and *Some New Jersey Families: Bunn, Burdg, Clayton, Inskeep, Malmsbury, Trimmer, Vankirk* (Washington, Pa., 1983), 8-13.

The remainder of this chapter consists of an ancestor table for Sarah Duncan Boude and a listing of her ten major notable kinsmen, in the same format used for similar coverage of Dr. Joseph Strong. Sources other than the above are listed in the text; for the ancestor table I am especially indebted to the "Ancestors of Joseph Boude" section of "The American Ancestors and Relatives of Her Royal Highness The Princess of Wales," draft copy, 1982, privately distributed by William Addams Reitwiesner, a section *not* incorporated into chapter five below.

II

An Ancestor Table of Mrs. Sarah Duncan Boude Work

1. SARAH DUNCAN BOUDE, b. Elkridge Landing, Maryland 15 Dec. 1790, d. Columbus, Ohio 17 Dec. 1860, m. Baltimore Co., Md. (license 2 Feb. 1808) John Work or Wark, almost certainly the John, son of John and Sarah Work or Wark, b. Plymouth, Devon, England 28 Oct. 1781 and bp. 8 Nov. 1781 at Batter Street Presbyterian Church, Plymouth, d. Chillicothe, Ohio 16 Apr. 1823 "aged 40." The middle name and birth and death dates of Sarah Duncan Boude, and the death date of John Work are taken from a Work genealogy whose compiler is unknown, prepared probably for James Henry Work, their grandson, between 1908 and 1912. Copies of a seventy-five-page typescript version of this study, apparently never published, and of an outline chart of it, were sent to W. A. Reitwiesner by Mrs. Nancy E. Swan and Mrs. Howard Slade respectively. The ancestry therein claimed for the two John Works seems suspect and has not been confirmed. The immigrant John Work (Jr.) is said to have been a civil engineer. His parents were Scottish; their place of origin, as suggested by the above-mentioned anonymous genealogy, may be Stranraer, Wigtonshire.

2. JOSEPH BOUDE, bp. Christ Church, Philadelphia 29 Dec. 1740, aged 2 weeks and 2 days, d. post 1793/4 (after the birth of his youngest child), attended the academy of Philadelphia (a preparatory school for, and part of, the College of Philadelphia, later the University of Pennsylvania), 1751–4, and was said by a grandson to have been a revolutionary soldier (an assertion not yet proved), m. Baltimore Co., Md. (license 11 Dec. 1781)

3. BARBARA BLACK, mentioned, along with siblings John, Christopher, Rudolph (after whom she named a son, Rudolph Thomas Clarkson Boude), and Elizabeth Black, in the will of her father.

4. THOMAS BOUDE, b. ca. 1700 probably in Perth Amboy, N.J., d. Philadelphia 11 Sept. 1781, bricklayer (for the central block, 1731), contractor (for the two wings, 1733–6) of Independence Hall, earlier involved in the construction of Christ Church, Coroner of Philadelphia, 1754–7, m. ca. 1722

5. SARAH NEWBOLD, b. Springfield Township, Burlington Co., N.J. 29 Nov. 1700, bur. Christ Church, Philadelphia 11 Apr. 1780.

6. WILLIAM BLACK of Anne Arundel Co., Md., whose will was dated 8 Jan. 1771 and proved 21 Apr. 1771, m.

7. (probably) CATHARINE ———, mentioned in William Black's will, who m. 2) before 9 Sept. 1772 Stephen Muntchell. Much further Maryland research on the Blacks is required.

8. GRIMSTONE BOUDE, b. ca. 1660/1, probably in Boston, Mass., will dated 3 Feb. 1715/6 and proved in Philadelphia 3 Apr. 1716, a cordwainer in Boston 1678–95, then "merchant" (probably shopkeeper) in Perth Amboy and after 1700 an innkeeper in Philadelphia, m. 1) probably in Boston ca. 1680–2 Elizabeth ———, whose first and last children were born in Boston 22 Aug. 1683 & 13 Aug. 1688 respectively, and 2) by 1698

9. MARY ———, probably considerably younger than her 1st husband, bur. Christ Church, Philadelphia 15 June 1744, m. 2) ante May 1721 George Campion, also bur. at Christ Church, 6 Dec. 1731, "aged 40."

10. MICHAEL NEWBOLD, JR., bp. Eckington, Yorkshire, England 3 Oct. 1667, d. Chesterfield Township, Burlington Co., N.J. 1 Dec. 1721, Justice of the Peace for Burlington Co., m. probably in Chesterfield Township 24 Feb. 1697

11. RACHEL CLAYTON, b. Shrewsbury, Monmouth Co., N.J. 16 June 1677, d. Burlington Co. shortly after 17 Apr. 1712, a Quakeress.

12-15. ———

16. (almost certainly) JOSEPH BOUDE, innkeeper & distiller, of Boston, 1653–60, & Marblehead, Mass., 1663–71, d. ante Nov. 1683, m. probably in Boston ante 20 Aug. 1657

17. (almost certainly) ELIZABETH ———, d. Marblehead, Mass. 1670.

18-19. ———

20. MICHAEL NEWBOLD, b. Hansworth Woodhouse, Yorkshire, England 1 July 1623, will dated 19 May 1690, proved Burlington Co., N.J. 25 Feb. 1692/3, an immigrant from Sheffield, Yorkshire to Burlington Co. ca. 1680. He was a son, according to the notes of William Romaine Newbold, of Thomas Newbold of Hansworth Woodhouse, d. 1652, and Jane or Joanna Syms (bp. 11 Feb. 1588, m. 18 Feb. 1616, d. 10 Feb. 1625, presumably all at Hansworth Woodhouse), a grandson of John Newbold, yeoman, of Hackenthorpe, Derbyshire, d. 7 May 1610, and Isabel, his wife, d. 1614, and of Matthew Syms, and a great-grandson of Thomas Newbold of Hackenthorpe, d. 1562/3. Earlier Newbolds of Hackenthorpe include at least two Johns (living 1486–8 and 1523–43 respectively) and Thomas (fined in 1451) and his wife Margaret. The immigrant Michael Newbold m. probably in Yorkshire ante 1653

21. ANNE ———, mentioned in her husband's will, d. post 1692/3.

22. JOHN CLAYTON, will dated 16 May 1704, proved 2 June 1704, Burlington Co., N.J., an immigrant to Shrewsbury, Monmouth Co., N.J. ca. 1677, later of Chesterfield Township, Burlington Co., Quaker, m. Swarthmoor, Lancashire, England monthly meeting (in whose records other Claytons and Myreses appear as well) 11 10th mo. 1661.

23. ALICE MYRES, possibly related to the Myres family of Beakcliffe, Adingham, Lancashire, d. N.J. post 1678, not mentioned in her husband's will.

24-31. ———.

III

Ten Notable Distant Kinsmen of Mrs. Sarah Duncan Boude Work and H.R.H. The Princess of Wales

1 & 2. Mrs. Alfred Irénée duPont & Mrs. Michael Hillegas — see p. 60 (covered in the chapter treating the Princess's New England ancestors as descendants of Grimstone Boude).

3. Irving Fisher, 1867–1947, economist (wife, Margaret Hazard; Rowland Hazard & Margaret Ann Rood; Rowland Gibson Hazard & Caroline Newbold; John Newbold & Elizabeth Lawrie; William Newbold & Susanna Stevenson; Thomas Newbold & Edith Coate; 10-11).

4. Joshua Ballinger Lippincott, 1813–1886, publisher, founder of J. B. Lippincott & Co.; Jacob Wills Lippincott & Sarah Ballinger; Levi Lippincott & Lettice Wills; Micajah Wills & Rebecca Hewlings; James Wills & Elizabeth Woolston; Daniel Wills & Margaret Newbold, John Woolston & Lettice Newbold; 20-1 (parents of Margaret & Lettice).

5. Richard Milhous Nixon, b. 1913, 37th U.S. President; Francis Anthony Nixon & Hannah Milhous; Samuel Brady Nixon & Sarah Ann Wadsworth; Thomas Wiley Wadsworth & Mary Louise Moore; Joseph Dickinson Moore & Jane Brown; Isaac Brown & Mary Clayton; Thomas Clayton (Jr.) & Mary ———; (probably, unproved) Thomas Clayton & Hannah ———; Zebulon Clayton & Mary Hartshorne; 22-3.

6. Frank Brett Noyes, 1863–1948, newspaper publisher, president of the Associated Press (wife, Janet Thruston Newbold; Charles Ross Newbold & Frances Kemper Lowe; Thomas Ross Newbold & Julia Sarah Fleming; Caleb Newbold & Elizabeth Ross; Daniel Newbold & Rachel Newbold; Caleb Newbold & Sarah Haines [parents of Daniel], John Newbold & Mary Coles [parents of Rachel]; Thomas Newbold & Edith Coate [parents of Caleb], Michael Newbold III & Susanna Scholey [parents of John]; 10-11 [parents of Thomas & Michael III]).

7. Philip Syng Physick, 1768–1837, surgeon & surgical inventor (wife, Elizabeth Emlen; Samuel Emlen & Sarah Mott; Asher Mott & Deborah Tallman; Gershom Mott & Sarah Clayton; 22-3).

8. Elliot Lee Richardson, b. 1920, cabinet official (Secretary of Health, Education & Welfare, of Defense, and of Commerce, U.S. Attorney General), diplomat (wife, Anne Francis Hazard; Thomas Pierrepont Hazard & Anne Francis Cope; Rowland Gibson Hazard & Mary Pierrepont Bushnell; Rowland Hazard & Margaret Ann Rood, parents of Mrs. Irving Fisher, see 3 above).

9. John Singer Sargent, 1856–1925, artist; FitzWilliam Sargent & Mary Newbold Singer; John Singer & Mary B. Newbold; William Newbold, Jr. & Mary Smith; William Newbold & Susanna Stevenson; Thomas Newbold & Edith Coate; 10-11.

10. Frederick Winslow Taylor, 1856–1915, mechanical engineer, inventor

& efficiency expert, founder of "scientific management;" Franklin Taylor & Emily Annette Winslow; Anthony Taylor, Jr. & Mary Newbold; Anthony Taylor & Anne Newbold, Caleb Newbold & Sarah Haines; Michael Newbold III & Susanna Scholey (parents of Anne), Thomas Newbold & Edith Coate (parents of Caleb); 10-11 (parents of Michael III & Thomas).

For Mrs. duPont and Mrs. Hillegas see the Boude article by F. J. Dallett listed above and J. Robert T. Craine and Harry W. Hazard, *The Ancestry and Posterity of Matthew Clarkson (1664–1702)* (n.p., 1971): 18, 19, 28, 46, 47, 89, 170, and 281; for Mrs. Noyes, Sargent, and Taylor see the Newbold genealogies cited above and various biographical dictionaries; for Nixon see Raymond Martin Bell, *The Ancestry of Richard Milhous Nixon* (Washington, Pa., 1972, revised, 1976); for Lippincott, Mrs. Fisher, and Mrs. Richardson see, in addition to the cited Newbold genealogies, George and Richard Haines, *Ancestry of the Haines, Sharp, Collins, Wills, Gardiner, Prickitt, Eves, Evans, Moore, Troth, Borton and Engle Families* (Camden, N.J., 1902): 277, 279, 282, Judith M. Olsen, *Lippincott: Five Generations of the Descendants of Richard and Abigail Lippincott* (Woodbury, N.J., 1982): 224, Caroline E. Robinson, *The Hazard Family of Rhode Island, 1635–1894* (Boston, 1895): 122, 123, 198-200, and 248, and *Who Was Who in America, 5 (1969–1973)* (Chicago, 1973): 319; and for Mrs. Physick see John Edwin Stillwell, *Historical and Genealogical Miscellany: Early Settlers of New Jersey*, 4 (New York, 1916. Reprint. Baltimore, 1970): 76-80, 90, 99.

Addendum

Another notable distant kinsman of Mrs. Sarah Duncan Boude Work and H.R.H. The Princess of Wales was Mary Wistar Wheeler, whose descent from Michael and Rachel (Clayton) Newbold (numbers 10 and 11 in the above ancestor table of Mrs. Sarah Duncan Boude Work) is as follows: Mary Wistar Wheeler; Charles Wheeler & Susan Farnum; John Farnum & Elizabeth Davis; Isaac Davis & Mary Wistar; John Wistar & Charlotte Newbold; Clayton Newbold & Mary Foster; Michael Newbold III & Susanna Scholey; 10-11.

Mary Wistar Wheeler was born in Pembroke, Pa. on 13 Feb. 1872. She married, Philadelphia, Pa., 30 Apr. 1890, *Maximilian* Albrecht Friedrich Karl Ludwig Haupt, Graf und Herr zu Pappenheim, b. at Pappenheim 15 Feb. 1860, d. Oberkirch 12 Aug. 1920, who was, at the time of his marriage, the Head of the Mediatized Countly House of Pappenheim. According to the House Laws of this House, a Miss Wheeler of Philadelphia did not possess Ebenbürtigheit (equality of birth), which means, in effect, that a descendant of Michael and Rachel (Clayton) Newbold was not of sufficiently high rank to marry a Pappenheim. As a result of his marriage, Maximilian was obliged to renounce, as of 13 Jan. 1891, his title of Graf und Herr zu Pappenheim, his position of Head of the Mediatized Countly House of Pappenheim, and to take the title of Graf von Pappenheim. See *Genealogisches Handbuch des Adels,* 75 (*Genealogisches Handbuch der Fürstlichen Häuser*, XI, 1980), 202, and *Genealogisches Handbuch des Adels*, 28 (*Genealogisches Handbuch der Gräflichen Häuser*, A IV, 1962), 358. See also Henry W. Fischer, *Secret Memoirs* (New York, 1912), 257, 258. Happily, the House Laws of the United Kingdom of Great Britain and Northern Ireland are not as strict as the House Laws of the Mediatized Countly House of Pappenheim, and so the Prince of Wales could, without renouncing his rights, marry Lady Diana Frances Spencer, a descendant of Michael and Rachel (Clayton) Newbold.

Chapter Four

THE VIRGINIA ANCESTRY OF H.R.H. PRINCE WILLIAM OF WALES: A POSTSCRIPT

I

In addition to third or fourth great-grandparents born in Connecticut and Maryland who provide considerable New England and some mid-Atlantic colonial ancestry, the Princess of Wales also has a great-great-great-grandfather born in Virginia. He is John Wood (1785–1848), a native probably of Shepherdstown (or environs), Berkeley County, now Jefferson County, West Virginia, who died in Chillicothe, Ohio and whose parents, George Wood and Elizabeth Conner, died respectively in Kentucky and near Columbus, Ohio. Everything known about John Wood, his parents, and their progeny—information which unfortunately does not include the ancestry, parentage or origin of George Wood and Elizabeth Conner—is outlined in the second section of the chapter on the Princess's New England ancestry, and in the following chapter on the Princess's near American relatives. I have found a few Conners in neighboring Virginia counties, but research commissioned in Martinsburg, West Virginia in the 1930s and 1940s by Capt. Gerard Hadden Wood, although undertaken with care, produced meager results. Given the history of that part of Virginia, moreover, the Woods and Conners may have been either mid-Atlantic rather than Tidewater in origin, or eighteenth- rather than seventeenth-century immigrants, or both.

Nonetheless, the present British royal family, including Prince William, the Prince of Wales, H. M. The Queen, and H. M. Queen Elizabeth The Queen Mother, has a major "gateway" ancestor to colonial Tidewater Virginia in one of the Queen Mother's ancestors, Robert Porteus, Jr. (ca. 1705–1754), who returned to England with his father in 1720, received a bachelor of arts degree from Peterhouse, Cambridge, in 1730, and became rector of Cockayne Hatley, Bedfordshire. Porteus's father was the son of Edward Porteus, a likely immigrant, and ———, his wife; no further paternal ancestry is known. The Tidewater forebears of 1) Mildred Smith of Purton, Gloucester County, Virginia, first wife of Robert Porteus, Sr. and mother of the Bedfordshire rector, can be listed as follows. She was the daughter of 2) John Smith, Jr. of Purton and 3) Mary Warner of Warner Hall (also in Gloucester County); granddaughter of 4) John Smith, Sr. of Purton and 5) Anne Bernard, and of 6) Augustine Warner, Jr. of Warner Hall and 7) Mildred Reade; and great-granddaughter of 8) Thomas Smith, another likely immigrant, and 9) ———, an unknown wife, of 10) Richard Bernard and 11) Anna Cordray, of 12) Augustine Warner, Sr. and 13) Mary Towneley, and of 14) George Reade and 15) Elizabeth Martiau, this last a daughter of the Huguenot immigrant Nicholas Martiau and Jane ———, his wife. Richard Bernard (ca. 1608–ante 1652), his wife Anna Cordray (ca. 1608–ca. 1670), Mrs. Mary Towneley Warner (1614–1662), and George Reade (1608–1670/1, usually called "Colonel," as are the two Augustine Warners and William Bernard below) were all gentle-born immigrants with royal descents; Richard Bernard was a double first cousin, moreover, of the immigrant William Bernard of Nansemond and Isle of Wight counties, Virginia; Mrs. Anna Cordray Bernard was an aunt of Francis and William Ironmonger, immigrant brothers, also of Gloucester County; and Mrs. Mary Towneley Warner was an aunt of the immigrants Lawrence Towneley, also her son-in-law, and (almost certainly) Maj. Lawrence Smith of Gloucester and York counties. For further details and documentation see Sir Anthony Richard Wagner, "The Queen of England's American Ancestry and Cousinship to Washington and Lee," *The New York Genealogical and Biographical Record*, 70 (1939): 201-206 (reprinted with a slightly different title in *Genealogists' Magazine*, 8 [1939]: 368-375); Gerald Paget, *The Lineage and Ancestry of H.R.H. Prince Charles, Prince of Wales*, 2 (Edinburgh, London, and Baltimore, 1977), #H219, p. 9, etc.; my own review and general essay on this last work, in *The Genealogist* (New York), 1 (1980): 106-127 (especially p. 113, item #3, and sources listed in the accompanying footnotes), 2 (1981): 244-257; and, for the Reades, Warners, and Towneleys, York Lowry Wilson, *A Carolina-Virginia Genealogy* (Aldershot, Hants., England, 1962): 253-335 (Reade), and two superb articles by Mary Burton Derrickson McCurdy, "A Discovery Concerning the Towneley and Warner Families of Virginia" and "The Towneleys and Warners of Virginia and Their English Connections," in *The Virginia Magazine of History and Biography*, 77 (1969): 473-476; 81 (1973): 319-367 (reprinted in *Genealogies of Virginia Families from The Virginia Magazine of History and Biography*, 5 [Baltimore, 1981]: 538-590).

Except for Nicholas Martiau all of the Queen Mother's Virginia immigrant ancestors were post-Jamestown "cavalier" founders of the Tidewater plantation aristocracy. Arriving mostly in the 1630s, 40s, or 50s, they were quickly absorbed into the ruling oligarchy of other second or third generation Virginia immigrants—Carters, Lees, and Randolphs especially. These nine ancestors and kinsmen—Edward Porteus, Thomas Smith, Richard Bernard, Augustine Warner, Sr., Nicholas Martiau, William Bernard, Francis Ironmonger, William Ironmonger, and

Lawrence Smith (the descendants of Lawrence Towneley and George Reade are absorbed by those of Warner and Martiau respectively), like the New England forebears of the Princess of Wales, also left a sizable progeny that has long played a major part in American history. Once again assuming three children and thirty years per generation, considerable overlap and cousin intermarriage, and thirteen generations of descendants, three now living, for Thomas Smith, the two Bernards, Warner and Martiau—but only twelve for Porteus, the two Ironmongers, and Lawrence Smith—the total number of living Americans who share Virginia ancestors with the Queen Mother might well be five million. Since the Tidewater aristocracy was highly insular, so that progeny overlap among immigrants and cousin intermarriage are even more extensive than usual, this figure should probably be much reduced. Also worth noting is the greater difficulty, relative to New England research, of tracing southern descents generally. Still, numerous Americans can prove Virginia-derived kinship to the Queen Mother. Prince William, then, has both a sizable number of ancestors from all three of the major geographical sections of the American colonies, and at least many thousands of southern, as well as millions of northern, American kinsmen.

"The Mowbray Connection," my life's work, contains extensive material on notable descendants of Richard Bernard, Mrs. Anna Cordray Bernard, Mrs. Mary Towneley Warner, George Reade, William Bernard, Francis Ironmonger, William Ironmonger, Lawrence Towneley, and Lawrence Smith. Major descendants of Mrs. Warner, Reade, Towneley, and Smith, moreover, are charted in my manuscript monograph, "Some Notable Kinsmen of Presidents Washington, Jefferson, Madison, the Two Harrisons, Tyler, Taylor, and/or the Second Mrs. Woodrow Wilson ..." at the Virginia State Library in Richmond. All of this data may eventually be culled for a separate volume on the Virginia ancestry and southern kin of the British royal family. Listed below, however, are fifty notable distant kinsmen of Robert Porteus, Jr., the Queen Mother, and Prince William of Wales. As in the lists of notable New England or mid-Atlantic-derived kinsmen of the Princess of Wales, each figure's name is followed by his or her birth and death years, a word or phrase that denotes the area of achievement, and parenthesis and the name of a wife or husband if the spouse, not the figure himself, is the cousin of the Queen Mother. Following this information, in parenthesis if the kinsman is the figure himself, after semi-colons within a parenthesis if the kinship is to a spouse, are listed not all generations between the figure and the ancestor shared by Porteus, but only the common forebear or immigrant kinsman. Parents, grandparents, and great-grandparents of Mrs. Mildred Smith Porteus are indicated by their above-designated number; immigrant near kinsmen of these ancestors are named. Ten of these fifty figures are derived through lines that lack absolute proof: two notes indicate the areas of possible doubt.

Over thirty of these fifty Virginia-derived notable kinsmen of Prince

William, reflecting the overall contribution of the Tidewater aristocracy to American history generally, were statesmen (especially of the revolutionary and early national period), soldiers (of the Revolution, the Confederacy, and both world wars), or explorers. The statesmen include one president (Washington), one vice-president (Stevenson), one secretary of state (Stettinius), and governors, senators, or public officials of Virginia, Kentucky, Missouri, South Carolina, Georgia, Illinois, California, the Republic of Texas, and New York City. Some post-Civil War migration and inter-marriage with notable northerners are suggested by #s 2, 4, 10, 12, 22, 25, 32, 37, 39, 40, 41, 43, 48, and 49; #s 9, 25, 30, 31, 32, 41, 42, 48, and 49, or their wives, are also among the 300 notable kinsmen of Dr. Joseph Strong and the Princess of Wales; and #s 38 and 45—William Glover Stanard and Lyon Gardiner Tyler—were two of Virginia's greatest genealogists.

II

Fifty Notable Distant Kinsmen of Robert Porteus, Jr., H.M. Queen Elizabeth The Queen Mother, and H.R.H. Prince William of Wales

1. Thomas Hart Benton, 1782-1858, statesman, U.S. Senator from Missouri (wife, Elizabeth McDowell; Lawrence Smith).

2. Irving Berlin (born Israel Baline), b. 1888, composer (2nd wife, Ellin Mackay; William Bernard).

3-4. David Kirkpatrick Este Bruce, 1898-1977, diplomat (14-15 & William Bernard, through Clement Read, however; this latter's parentage requires further research) & his 1st wife, Mrs. Ailsa Mellon Bruce, 1901-1969, philanthropist & art patron.

5-6. Simon Bolivar Buckner, 1823-1914, Confederate general, newspaper editor, Governor of Kentucky (wife, Delia Hayes Claiborne; 6-7) & his son, Simon Bolivar Buckner, Jr., 1886-1945, World War II army commander, commandant of the U.S. Military Academy (West Point) (6-7).

7. William Christian Bullitt (III), 1891-1967, diplomat, 1st U.S. Ambassador to the U.S.S.R. (Lawrence Smith).

8-9. Harry Flood Byrd, 1887-1966, newspaper publisher, U.S. Senator & Governor of Virginia, & Richard Evelyn Byrd (Jr.), 1888-1957, naval officer & explorer, discoverer of the South Pole, brothers (William Bernard).

10. Henry Clews, 1834-1923, Civil War financier (wife, Lucy Madison Worthington; Lawrence Smith).

11. Howell Cobb, 1815-1868, Governor of Georgia, U.S. Secretary of the Treasury, Speaker of the House of Representatives (2-3, William Bernard, Lawrence Smith).

12. Ralph Adams Cram, 1863-1942, architect (wife, Elizabeth Carrington Read; 14-15 & William Bernard through Clement Read, see 3 above).

13. John Buchanan Floyd, 1806-1863, Governor of Virginia, U.S. Secretary of War, Confederate soldier (Lawrence Smith).

14. John Charles Fremont, 1813-1890, explorer & soldier, U.S. Senator from California, Republican presidential candidate in 1856 (wife, Jessie Benton, daughter of 1 above; Lawrence Smith).

15. Wade Hampton, 1818-1902, Confederate general, U.S. Senator, Governor of South Carolina (1st wife, Margaret Preston; Lawrence Smith).

16. Albert Sidney Johnston, 1803-1862, Confederate general, Secretary of War of the Republic of Texas (1st wife, Henrietta Preston; Lawrence Smith. Mrs. Benton, J. B. Floyd, Mrs. Hampton & Mrs. Johnston were all 1st cousins. Their mutual grandmother, Mrs. Susanna Smith Preston, daughter of Francis Smith & Elizabeth Waddy, was probably a granddaughter of William Smith—son of the immigrant Lawrence Smith—& Elizabeth Ballard. Final proof of this Francis Smith's parentage remains elusive).

17. Helen (Adams) Keller, 1880-1968, humanitarian, benefactor of the blind and deaf (William Bernard).

18-20. HENRY "LIGHT HORSE HARRY" LEE (III), 1756–1818, revolutionary officer, Governor of Virginia (12-13, Lawrence Towneley); his son, ROBERT EDWARD LEE, 1807–1870, Confederate commander (12-13, Lawrence Towneley, William Bernard); and this latter's nephew, FITZHUGH LEE, 1835–1905, Confederate general, Governor of Virginia (12-13, Lawrence Towneley, William Bernard).

21. MERIWETHER LEWIS, 1774–1809, explorer & soldier, commander of the Lewis & Clark expedition (6-7, Lawrence Smith).

22. JOHN VLIET LINDSAY, b. 1921, congressman, mayor of New York City, urban spokesman (wife, Mary Anne Harrison; 12-13, Lawrence Towneley).

23. GEORGE CATLETT MARSHALL, JR., 1880–1959, World War II army commander (U.S. Chief of Staff), U.S. Secretary of State & Defense, author of the "Marshall Plan," recipient of the Nobel Peace Prize, 1953 (Lawrence Smith).

24. ROBERT MILLS, 1781–1855, architect (of, among other structures, the Washington Monument) (wife, Eliza Barnwell Smith; 2-3).

25. SAMUEL ELIOT MORISON, 1887–1976, historian (2nd wife, Priscilla Randolph Barton; 6-7, Lawrence Smith).

26-27. ROGERS CLARK BALLARD MORTON, 1914–1979, congressman, U.S. Secretary of the Interior, & THRUSTON BALLARD MORTON, 1907–1982, U.S. Senator from Kentucky, brothers (Lawrence Smith).

28. (CHARLES LOUIS NAPOLEON) ACHILLE, 2ND PRINCE MURAT, sometime Crown Prince of Naples, 1801–1847, author & nephew of Napoleon I, Emperor of the French (wife, Catherine Daingerfield Willis; 6-7).

29-30. THOMAS NELSON, 1738–1789, signer of the Declaration of Independence, Governor of Virginia (14-15), & his great-grandson, THOMAS NELSON PAGE, 1852–1922, novelist & diplomat, author of *In Ole Virginia* (12-13, 14-15, Lawrence Towneley).

31. GEORGE SMITH PATTON (III), 1885–1945, World War II army commander (6-7, William Bernard, Lawrence Smith).

32. PHILIP WINSTON PILLSBURY, b. 1903, president & chairman of the Board, Pillsbury (Flour) Co. (William Bernard).

33. WILLIAM CABELL RIVES, 1793–1868, diplomat, U.S. Senator from Virginia (wife, Judith Page Walker; 14-15, Lawrence Smith).

34. RANDOLPH (CRANE) SCOTT, b. 1898, "cowboy" actor (William Ironmonger).

35. HOKE SMITH, 1855–1931, newspaper publisher, U.S. Senator & Secretary of the Interior, Governor of Georgia (1st wife, Birdie Cobb, niece of 11 above; 2-3, William Bernard, Lawrence Smith).

36. JAMES SPEED, 1812–1887, U.S. Attorney General under Lincoln (Lawrence Smith).

37. JAMES JOSEPH SPEYER, 1861–1941, banker, philanthropist (wife, Ellin Leslie Prince; William Bernard).

38. WILLIAM GLOVER STANARD, 1858–1933, genealogist, editor of *The Virginia Magazine of History and Biography* (14-15, William Bernard, William Ironmonger).

39. EDWARD RILEY STETTINIUS, JR., 1900–1949, industrialist, U.S. Secretary of State, 1st U.S. Ambassador to the United Nations (14-15 & William Bernard through Clement Read, see 3 above).

40-41. ADLAI EWING STEVENSON, 1835–1914, congressman, Vice-President under Cleveland (wife, Letitia Green; Lawrence Smith) & his grandson, ADLAI

EWING STEVENSON II, 1900–1965, Governor of Illinois, Democratic presidential candidate in 1952 & 1956, Ambassador to the United Nations (Lawrence Smith).

42. (WILLIAM) STUART SYMINGTON (JR.), b. 1901, U.S. Senator from Missouri, Secretary of the Air Force (1st wife, Evelyn Wadsworth; William Bernard).

43. JUAN TERRY TRIPPE, 1899–1981, founder and president, Pan American World Airways (wife, Elizabeth Stettinius, sister of 39 above; 14-15 & William Bernard through Clement Read, see 3 above).

44. GEORGE TUCKER, 1775–1861, historian & political economist (1st wife, Maria Ball Carter; 6-7).

45. LYON GARDINER TYLER, 1853–1935, president of the College of William and Mary, historian, founder & editor of *The William and Mary College Quarterly Historical Magazine & Tyler's Quarterly Historical and Genealogical Magazine* (1st wife, Annie Baker Tucker, Lawrence Smith; 2nd wife, Sue Ruffin, 2-3).

46-47. GEORGE WASHINGTON, 1732–1799, American revolutionary commander, 1st U.S. President, the "Father of His Country," & his nephew, BUSHROD WASHINGTON, 1762–1829, jurist (6-7).

48. BYRON RAYMOND WHITE, b. 1917, jurist (wife, Marion Lloyd Stearns; 12-13, Lawrence Towneley).

49. HENRY PARKER WILLIS, 1874–1937, economist, editor, educator, 1st Secretary of the Federal Reserve Board (wife, Rosa Johnston Brooke; 14-15).

50. WILLIAM WIRT, 1772–1834, U.S. Attorney General, anti-Masonite presidential candidate in 1832, author of *Letters of the British Spy* (1st wife, Mildred Gilmer; Lawrence Smith).

Chapter Five

THE AMERICAN RELATIVES OF H.R.H. THE PRINCESS OF WALES

Introductory Note

This chapter traces all of the known American relatives of the Princess of Wales as far as fifth cousins. It is divided into eight parts. Each part contains information on the descendants of a specific set of the Princess's American ancestors, treated in genealogical order (see the following chart outlining the immediate ancestry of Frances Eleanor Work, Mrs. Burke Roche, the Princess's American great-grandmother). This data is arranged as a series of descendant lists and written in standard "Register" style—a couple, their children (listed in strict birth order when known), then grandchildren, then great-grandchildren, etc., with continued offspring numbered sequentially. All descendants—daughters of daughters of daughters as well as sons of sons of sons—are covered. The information given includes names, titles, occupations (of deceased relatives), dates and locations of birth, marriage and death, spouses (and their previous and subsequent marriages), and parents of spouses. Whenever any of this data is omitted, as is frequently the case, the missing facts were either unknown or unavailable. Frequently used sources were *Burke's Genealogical and Heraldic History of the Peerage, Baronetage, and Knightage* and *Debrett's Peerage, Baronetage, Knightage, and Companionage* (various editions of both); British and American *Who's Who* and *Who Was Who* volumes; the *Dictionary of American Biography* and *National Cyclopaedia of American Biography*; the *Times* (of London), the *New York Times*, the *New York Herald Tribune*, and other newspapers; Harvard, Yale, and other classbooks, especially 25th and 50th anniversary reports; *Social Register* volumes and city directories; *Daughters of the American Revolution Lineage Books*; federal censuses; and sundry unpublished wills, deeds, and birth, marriage, and death records from local courthouses, town halls, or state-wide repositories of vital statistics. Additional sources are listed at the end, and occasionally a note or two is added following each part.

This compilation of the Princess's near American relatives is by no means complete. Even as presented herein, however, it could not have been assembled without considerable assistance from both genealogical colleagues and the relatives themselves. Among the former I would like to acknowledge Timothy Field Beard and Neil D. Thompson of New York City (now of Roxbury, Connecticut, and Bronxville, New York respectively); John Insley Coddington of Bordentown, New Jersey; Meredith B. Colket, Jr., of Cleveland, Ohio; John R. Grabb of Chillicothe, Ohio; and especially Gary Boyd Roberts of Boston, Massachusetts. Among the relatives I wish to acknowledge William Barr, Joan Bishop, Sarah Cornell, John Gray, Elisabeth Hooker, Jane Maynard, Marie Morgan, Margaret Richardson, Schuyler Richardson, Cynthia Russell, Edward Uhler, and Virginia Wortley; and especially Abby Van Pelt Feldman, Ruth, Lady Fermoy, Peter Moore, Nancy Shaw, Cecily Slade, Alice Thompson, and Frances Wood.

Chart of the Immediate Ancestry of Frances Eleanor Work, Mrs. Burke Roche, American Great-Grandmother of The Princess of Wales

FRANCES ELEANOR WORK,
b. New York, N.Y.,
27 Oct. 1857,
d. New York, N.Y.,
26 Jan. 1947,
m. New York, N.Y.,
22 Sept. 1880,
div. Wilmington, Del.,
3 March 1891
James Boothby Burke Roche,
3rd Baron Fermoy,
b. Twyford Abbey, Middx.,
28 July 1851,
d. Westminster
30 Oct. 1920.

FRANK(LIN H.) WORK,
b. Chillicothe, O.,
10 Feb. 1819,
d. New York, N.Y.,
16 March 1911,
m. New York, N.Y.,
19 Feb. 1857,
ELLEN WOOD,
b. Chillicothe, O.,
18 July 1831,
d. New York, N.Y.,
22 Feb. 1877.

GREAT-GRANDPARENTS OF THE PRINCESS OF WALES

JOHN WARK,
b. Plymouth, Devon,
——— [1783],
d. Chillicothe, O.,
16 Apr. 1823,
m. ——— [1808],
SARAH DUNCAN BOUDE,
b. Elkridge Landing, Md.,
15 Dec. 1790,
d. Columbus, O.,
16 Dec. 1860.

JOHN WOOD,
b. [Sheperdstown, W.?] Va.,
29 July 1785,
d. Chillicothe, O.
29 Jan. 1848,
m. Chillicothe, O.,
13 March 1823,
ELEANOR STRONG,
b. Philadelphia, Pa.,
——— [1802/3],
d. New York, N.Y.,
9 July 1863.

——— WARK,
b. ———, d. ———,
m. ———,
———,
b. ———, d. ——— .

JOSEPH BOUDE,
b. ——— 13 Dec. 1740,
d. ———,
m. Baltimore, Md.,
——— [1781],
BARBARA BLACK,
b. ———, d. ——— .

GEORGE WOOD,
b. ———,
d. Ky., 23 Aug. 1802,
m. ———,
ELIZABETH CONNER,
b. ——— 1766,
d. Franklin Co., O.,
13 Aug. 1818.

JOSEPH STRONG,
b. S. Coventry, Ct.,
10 March 1770,
d. Philadelphia, Pa.,
24 Apr. 1812,
m. Philadelphia, Pa.,
8 Sept. 1796,
REBECCA YOUNG,
b. Philadelphia, Pa.,
5 May 1779,
d. Piqua, O.,
8 June 1862.

For the descendants of Frank Work and of Ellen Wood, see Part I.

FOURTH COUSINS OF THE PRINCESS OF WALES:

For other descendants of John Wark and of Sarah Duncan Boude, see Part II.
For other descendants of John Wood and of Eleanor Strong, see Part III.

FIFTH COUSINS OF THE PRINCESS OF WALES:

For other descendants of ——— Wark and of ———, see Part IV.
For other descendants of Joseph Boude and of Barbara Black, see Part V.
For other descendants of George Wood and of Elizabeth Conner, see Part VI.
For other descendants of Joseph Strong and of Rebecca Young, see Part VII.
For the siblings of Rebecca Young and the descendants of her second marriage, see Part VIII.

I

Descendants of Frank(lin H.) Work and of Ellen Wood

1. FRANK(LIN H.) WORK, dry goods merchant, stockbroker (see Part II, number 6, below), b. Chillicothe, Ohio, 10 Feb. 1819, d. New York, N.Y., 16 March 1911, son of John Wark and of Sarah Duncan Boude, m. New York, N.Y., 19 Feb. 1857, ELLEN WOOD (see Part III, number 3, below), b. Chillicothe, Ohio, 18 July 1831, d. New York, N.Y., 22 Feb. 1877, dau. of John Wood and of Eleanor Strong.

Issue (surname WORK):

2. a. FRANCES ELEANOR, b. New York, N.Y., 27 Oct. 1857, d. New York, N.Y., 26 Jan. 1947.

b. GEORGE PAUL, b. 8 Sept. 1858, d. Davos Platz, Kt. Grisons (Switz.), 25 Feb. 1900.

3. c. LUCY BOND, b. New York, N.Y., May 1860, d. New York, N.Y., 21 March 1934.

2. FRANCES ELEANOR WORK, b. New York, N.Y., 27 Oct. 1857, d. New York, N.Y., 26 Jan. 1947, m. (1) New York, N.Y., 22 Sept. 1880, div. Wilmington, Del., 3 March 1891, JAMES BOOTHBY BURKE ROCHE, from 10 Sept. 1856, Hon. James Boothby Burke Roche, from 1 Sept. 1920, 3rd BARON FERMOY, b. Twyford Abbey, Middx., 28 July 1851, d. Westminster 30 Oct. 1920, son of Edmund Burke Roche, 1st Baron Fermoy, and of Eliza Caroline Boothby; m. (2) New York, N.Y., 4 Aug. 1905, div. New York, N.Y., 5 Nov. 1909, as his second wife, AUREL BATONYI [he had m. (1) and div.], son of Leopold Batonyi.

Issue by first husband (surname BURKE ROCHE; styled from 1 Sept. 1920 "Hon."):

a. EILEEN, b. 1882, d. 1882.

4. b. CYNTHIA, b. London 10 Apr. 1884, d. Newport, R.I., 18 Dec. 1966.

5. c. EDMUND MAURICE, b. Chelsea 15 May 1885 (twin), d. King's Lynn 8 July 1955.

d. FRANCIS GEORGE, b. Chelsea 15 May 1885 (twin), d. Newport, R.I., 30 Oct. 1958.

3. LUCY BOND WORK, b. New York, N.Y., May 1860, d. New York, N.Y., 21 March 1934, m. New York, N.Y., 27 Apr. 1887, div. Dec.

1918, as his first wife, PETER COOPER HEWITT, engineer, b. New York, N.Y., 5 May 1861, d. Paris 25 Aug. 1921 [he later m. (2) Paterson, N.J., 21 Dec. 1918, Maryon Andrews, b. 1884, d. New York, N.Y., 30 Apr. 1939], son of Abram Stevens Hewitt and of Sarah Amelia Cooper.

No issue.

4. CYNTHIA BURKE ROCHE, from 1 Sept. 1920, Hon. Mrs. Burden, b. London 10 Apr. 1884, d. Newport, R.I., 18 Dec. 1966, m. (1) New York, N.Y., 11 June 1906, ARTHUR SCOTT BURDEN, b. Troy, N.Y., 11 Aug. 1879, d. White Plains, N.Y., 15 June 1921, son of James Abercrombie Burden and of Mary Proudfit Irvin; m. (2) Newport, R.I., 24 July 1922, GUY FAIRFAX CARY, b. New York, N.Y., 14 Nov. 1879, d. Newport, R.I., 27 Aug. 1950, son of Clarence Cary and of Elisabeth Miller Potter.

Issue: (a) by first husband (surname BURDEN):

6. a. EILEEN, b. New York, N.Y., 15 Oct. 1910, d. Darien, Conn., 24 March 1970.

(b) by second husband (surname CARY):

b. GUY FAIRFAX II, b. 11 July 1923.
7. c. CYNTHIA, b. New York, N.Y., 16 Oct. 1924.

5. EDMUND MAURICE BURKE ROCHE, from 1 Sept. 1920, Hon. Edmund Maurice Burke Roche, from 30 Oct. 1920, 4th BARON FERMOY, b. Chelsea 15 May 1885, d. King's Lynn 8 July 1955, m. Bieldside 17 Sept. 1931, RUTH SYLVIA GILL, b. Bieldside 2 Oct. 1908, dau. of Col. William Smith Gill and of Ruth Littlejohn.

Issue (surname BURKE ROCHE, styled "Hon."):

8. a. MARY CYNTHIA, b. Bieldside 19 Aug. 1934.
9. b. FRANCES RUTH, b. Sandringham 20 Jan. 1936.
10. c. EDMUND JAMES, b. London 20 March 1939.

6. EILEEN BURDEN, b. New York, N.Y., 15 Oct. 1910, d. Darien, Conn., 24 March 1970, m. (1) New York, N.Y., 9 Feb. 1932, div., as his first wife, WALTER MAYNARD, investment analyst, b. New York, N.Y., 19 Apr. 1906, d. New York, N.Y., 27 Nov. 1971 [he later m. (2) New York, N.Y., 26 Dec. 1957, Augusta M. Poe], son of Walter Effingham Maynard and of Eunice Ives; m. (2) New York, N.Y., 4 Apr. 1963, as his second wife, THOMAS ROBINS, Jr., b. New York, N.Y., Oct. 1896, d. Darien, Conn., 26 May 1977 [he had m. (1) Louisa Winslow Cogswell, d. Darien, Conn., 11 July 1962], son of Thomas Robins, Sr., and of Winifred Tucker.

Issue by first husband (surname MAYNARD):

11. a. WALTER, JR. (ROBIN), b. New York, N.Y., 14 Nov. 1932.
12. b. SHEILA, b. New York, N.Y., 1 Aug. 1936.
13. c. JOHN, b. New York, N.Y., 23 Feb. 1940.

7. CYNTHIA CARY, b. New York, N.Y., 16 Oct. 1924, m. (1) Newport, R.I., 23 Aug. 1947, div. 1972, as his first wife, CHARLES BINGHAM PENROSE VAN PELT, b. Philadelphia, Pa., 2 May 1922 [he later m. (2) Philadelphia, Pa., 24 Jan. 1976, Jane E. Eger], son of Andrew Van Pelt and of Sarah Hannah Boies Penrose; m. (2) 1976, as his third wife, EDWIN FAIRMAN RUSSELL, b. Elizabeth, N.J., 15 July 1914 [he had m. (1) Westminster 15 May 1943, div. Reno, Nev., 7 Oct. 1966, Lady Sarah Consuelo Spencer-Churchill, b. London 17 Dec. 1921, and had m. (2) Washington, D.C., 31 Oct. 1966, div. 1975, Iris Ada Smith, b. 1927], son of Lucius Thomas Russell and of Marian Cronin.

Issue by first husband (surname VAN PELT):

a. PETER TURNER, b. Philadelphia, Pa., 22 June 1948.
14. b. ABBY ANN, b. Newport, R.I., 23 Sept. 1950.
c. GUY FAIRFAX CARY, b. Morristown, N.J., 16 July 1956.

8. Hon. MARY CYNTHIA BURKE ROCHE, b. Bieldside 19 Aug. 1934, m. (1) Westminster 25 Nov. 1954, div. 1966, as his first wife, ANTHONY GEORGE BERRY, from 3 Feb. 1936, Hon. Anthony George Berry, b. 12 Feb. 1925 [he later m. (2) Chelsea 5 Apr. 1966, Sarah Anne Clifford-Turner], son of Sir James Gomer Berry, 1st Viscount Kemsley, and of Mary Lilian Holmes; m. (2) London [shortly before 13 July] 1973, DENNIS ROCHE GEOGHEGAN.

Issue by first husband (surname BERRY):

15. a. ALEXANDRA MARY, b. London 9 Sept. 1955.
b. ANTONIA RUTH, b. 2 Aug. 1957 (twin).
c. JOANNA CYNTHIA, b. 2 Aug. 1957 (twin).
d. EDWARD ANTHONY MORYS, b. 23 June 1960.

9. Hon. FRANCES RUTH BURKE ROCHE, b. Sandringham 20 Jan. 1936, m. (1) Westminster 1 June 1954, div. 1969, as his first wife, Hon. EDWARD JOHN SPENCER, from birth, Viscount Althorp, from 9 June 1975, 8th EARL SPENCER, b. London 24 Jan. 1924 [he later m. (2) London 14 July 1976, Raine McCorquodale, b. 9 Sept. 1929], son of Albert Edward John Spencer, 7th Earl Spencer, and of Lady Cynthia Elinor Beatrix Hamilton; m. (2) 2 May 1969, as his second wife, PETER SHAND KYDD [he had m. (1) and div., 1965, Janet ———].

Issue by first husband (surname SPENCER, styled "Hon."; from 9 June 1975 sons "Hon.", daughters "Lady"):

16. a. ELIZABETH SARAH LAVINIA (SARAH), b. [Althorp?], Northampton, 19 March 1955.
17. b. CYNTHIA JANE (JANE), b. King's Lynn 11 Feb. 1957.
c. JOHN, b. and d. 12 Jan. 1960.
18. d. DIANA FRANCES, b. Sandringham 1 July 1961.
e. CHARLES EDWARD MAURICE, from 9 June 1975, Viscount Althorp, b. London 20 May 1964.

10. Hon. EDMUND JAMES BURKE ROCHE, from 8 July 1955, 5th BARON FERMOY, b. London 20 March 1939, m. London 22 June 1964, LAVINIA FRANCES ELIZABETH PITMAN, b. 18 Apr. 1941, dau. of Capt. John Pitman and of Elizabeth Cattenach Donaldson.

Issue (surname BURKE ROCHE, styled "Hon."):

a. FRANCES CAROLINE, b. 31 March 1965.
b. ELIZABETH, b. 27 March 1966, d. 2 Apr. 1966.
c. PATRICK MAURICE, b. 11 Oct. 1967.
d. EDMUND HUGH (HUGH), b. 5 Feb. 1972.

11. WALTER MAYNARD, Jr. (Robin), b. New York, N.Y., 14 Nov. 1932, m. (1) Darlington, Md., 9 Oct. 1954, div. 1973, as her first husband, PAMELA STOKES SILVER, b. 1934 [she later m. (2) 19 June 1975, Sheridan Lord, b. 1926], dau. of John Archer Silver and of Pamela Nicholson Wright; m. (2) New York, N.Y., 22 Nov. 1974, as her second husband, JANE FRANCES HENDERSON, b. 29 March 1936 [she had m. (1) Manchester, Mass., 21 Sept. 1963, div., Peter Swords, b. 14 Apr. 1935], dau. of Warwick Henderson and of Elizabeth Davidson.

Issue by first wife (surname MAYNARD):

19. a. AUDREY, b. Camp Pendleton, Cal., 1 Sept. 1955.
b. WALTER ALEXANDER (ALEXANDER), b. Boston, Mass., 2 Apr. 1957.
c. THOMAS, b. 27 Feb. 1968, d. 17 Oct. 1976.

12. SHEILA MAYNARD, b. New York, N.Y., 1 Aug. 1936, m. Rhinebeck, N.Y., 28 June 1957, NICHOLAS PLATT, Sr., b. Mount Kisco, N.Y., 10 March 1936, son of Geoffrey Platt and of Helen Choate.

Issue (surname PLATT):

a. ADAM, b. Washington, D.C., 18 July 1958.
b. OLIVER, b. Windsor, Ont., 12 Jan. 1960.
c. NICHOLAS, Jr., b. Hong Kong 29 Apr. 1964.

13. JOHN MAYNARD, b. New York, N.Y., 23 Feb. 1940, m. Londiani, Kenya, 10 Feb. 1968, PENELOPE KIRTON, b. 16 Sept. 1941, dau. of James Kirton and of Frances Panter.

Issue (surname Maynard):

a. Geoffrey, b. 2 Oct. 1969.
b. Nicholas, b. 16 Sept. 1971.

14. Abby Ann Van Pelt, b. Newport, R.I., 23 Sept. 1950, m. Bryn Mawr, Pa., 3 July 1982, as his second wife, Jay Robert Feldman, b. Philadelphia, Pa., 28 May 1947 [he had m. (1) and div.], son of Martin Feldman and of Dorothy Abelson.

No issue yet.

15. Alexandra Mary Berry, b. London 9 Sept. 1955, m. 3 July 1982, Reinhold Bartz.

No issue yet.

16. Hon. Elizabeth Sarah Lavinia Spencer (Sarah), from 9 June 1975, Lady Sarah Spencer, b. [Althorp?], Northampton, 19 March 1955, m. Great Brington, Northampton, 17 May 1980, Neil McCorquodale, b. 10 Apr. 1951, son of Alastair McCorquodale and of Rosemary Turnor.

Issue (surname McCorquodale):

a. Emily Jane, bapt. 9 Oct. 1983.

17. Hon. Cynthia Jane Spencer (Jane), from 9 June 1975, Lady Jane Spencer, b. King's Lynn 11 Feb. 1957, m. London 20 Apr. 1978, Robert Fellowes, b. 11 Dec. 1941, son of Capt. Sir William Albemarle Fellowes and of Jane Charlotte Ferguson.

Issue (surname Fellowes):

a. Laura Jane, bapt. 20 Nov. 1980.
b. Alexander, b. 1983.

18. Hon. Diana Frances Spencer, from 9 June 1975, Lady Diana Spencer, b. Sandringham 1 July 1961, m. London 29 July 1981, H.R.H. Prince Charles Philip Arthur George, Prince of Great Britain and Northern Ireland, from birth, Earl of Merioneth, from 6 Feb. 1952, Duke of Cornwall, from 6 Feb. 1952, Duke of Rothesay, created, 26 July 1958, Prince of Wales and Earl of Chester, b. Buckingham Palace 14 Nov. 1948, son of H.R.H. Prince Philip, Prince of Great Britain and Northern Ireland, Duke of Edinburgh, and of H.M. Queen Elizabeth II, Queen of the United Kingdom of Great Britain and Northern Ireland.

Issue (Prince of Great Britain and Northern Ireland [H.R.H.]):

a. William Arthur Philip Louis, from birth, Baron Greenwich, b. Paddington 21 June 1982.

19. AUDREY MAYNARD, b. Camp Pendleton, Cal., 1 Sept. 1955, m. 18 Sept. 1982, KAIGHN SMITH, Jr., b. 12 Jan. 1956, son of Kaighn Smith, Sr., and of Ann Graham Robb.

No issue yet.

Notes

Number 3:
By his second wife, Mr. Hewitt had a daughter, Anne Cooper Hewitt, for whom see *Time* magazine, Jan. 20, 1936, pp. 42-47.

Number 5:
The engagement of Maurice Edmund Burke Roche to Ysabel d'Alcedo, dau. of the Marquis d'Alcedo, was announced in the *New York Times*, 19 Apr. 1913, p. 9, col. 2. She, Dona Isabel Quinones de Leon y Banuelos, III. Condesa de Banuelos (from 3 May 1911), b. Torquay, Devon, 5 Jan. 1892 (dau. of Don Fernando Quinones de Leon y Francesco Martin, III. Marques de San Carlos, I. Marques de Alcedo, and of Dona Antonia de Banuelos y Thorndike, II. Condesa de Banuelos), married at Biarritz 3 Jan. 1914, Don Pedro Christopherson y Alvear. See Marquis of Ruvigny (pseud.), *The Titled Nobility of Europe* (London, 1914), 295. In 1932 she was living in Buenos Aires. See *Guia Nobiliara de Espana* (Madrid, 1932), 138.

The *New York Times* later stated, 23 Aug. 1929, p. 12, col. 2, and 25 Aug. 1929, p. 27, col. 4, that Lord Fermoy was reported to be engaged to a Miss Mary Carter, whose father was a clerk in holy orders. At that time, Lord Fermoy was the only Member of Parliament who was a graduate of Harvard.

Number 12:
Mr. Platt is currently (1984) the United States Ambassador to Zambia.

II

Descendants of John Wark and of Sarah Duncan Boude

1. John Wark, civil engineer (see Part IV, number 2, below), b. Plymouth, Devon [1783?], d. Chillicothe, Ohio, 16 Apr. 1823, son of ——— Wark and of ———, m. [license to marry issued in Baltimore, Md., on 2 Feb. 1808], Sarah Duncan Boude (see Part V, number 3, below), b. Elkridge Landing, Md., 15 Dec. 1790, d. Columbus, Ohio, 17 Dec. 1860, dau. of Joseph Boude and of Barbara Black.

Issue (surname Work [order uncertain]):

- **2.** a. John Clinton (Clinton), b. Baltimore, Md., 17 March 1809, d. New York, N.Y., 29 Nov. 1887.
- **3.** b. Caroline Maria, b. Chillicothe, Ohio [1814?], d. [after 1877].
- **4.** c. George, d. [by 1902].
- **5.** d. Elizabeth, b. Columbus, Ohio, 1818, d. 1847.
- **6.** e. Frank(lin H.), b. Chillicothe, Ohio, 10 Feb. 1819, d. New York, N.Y., 16 March 1911.

2. John Clinton Work (Clinton), dry goods merchant, b. Baltimore, Md., 17 March 1809, d. New York, N.Y., 29 Nov. 1887, m. Hanover, Pa., 7 Apr. 1839, Jane Culbertson Sharon, b. [Derry?], Pa., 1825, d. New York, N.Y., 17 May 1898, dau. of Rev. James Sharon.

Issue (surname Work):

- a. Mary McCoy, d. ae. 4 years.
- **7.** b. John Clinton, Jr., b. Columbus, Ohio, 9 Feb. 1841, d. Charlestown, N.H., 30 Aug. 1888.
- **8.** c. Jane Sarah, b. Ohio, 1844, d. 1925.
- **9.** d. James Henry, b. New York, N.Y., 28 June 1846, d. Lawrence, N.Y., 22 Oct. 1916.
- **10.** e. Elisabeth, b. New York, N.Y., 1848, d. Farmington, Conn., 27 Sept. 1932.
- **11.** f. George Francis, later "Frank Work, Jr.", b. N.Y., Jan. 1851, d. Oyster Bay, N.Y., 13 Oct. 1908.

3. Caroline Maria Work, b. Chillicothe, Ohio [1814?], d. [after 1877], m. Chillicothe, Ohio, 4 Jan. 1832, John Cutler Merrick, b. Brookfield, Mass., 7 Dec. 1809, d. Columbus, Ohio, 15 May 1857, son of Pliny Merrick and of Ruth Cuthbert.

Issue (surname MERRICK):

a. MARIA C. (MAY), b. 1834, in 1911 living at 70 Jefferson Ave., Columbus, Ohio.
b. ELIZABETH K., b. 1840, in 1887 living in Columbus, Ohio.
12. c. FRANK W., b. Ohio, Apr. 1844, d. Columbus, Ohio, 29 Sept. 1904.
d. ELLEN W. (NELLIE), b. March 1850, in 1934 living at 70 Jefferson Ave., Columbus, Ohio.

4. GEORGE WORK, d. [by 1902], m. ———.

Issue (surname WORK):

a. WILLIAM, living 1902.
b. ——— (dau.), living 1902.

5. ELIZABETH WORK, b. Columbus, Ohio, 1818, d. 1847, m. Franklin Co., Ohio, Oct. 1841, as his first wife, JAMES KOOKEN, dry goods merchant, d. Columbus, Ohio, 17 Aug. 1872 [he later m. (2) (Logansport, Ind.?), 8 March 1871, Ruth A. Stewart], son of Capt. James Kooken and of Gertrude ———.

No issue.

6. FRANK(LIN H.) WORK, dry goods merchant, stockbroker, b. Chillicothe, Ohio, 10 Feb. 1819, d. New York, N.Y., 16 March 1911, m. New York, N.Y., 19 Feb. 1857, ELLEN WOOD (see Part III, number 3, below), b. Chillicothe, Ohio, 18 July 1831, d. New York, N.Y., 22 Feb. 1877, dau. of John Wood and of Eleanor Strong.

Issue: See Part I, above.

7. JOHN CLINTON WORK, Jr., b. Columbus, Ohio, 9 Feb. 1841, d. Charlestown, N.H., 30 Aug. 1888, m. 12 Aug. 1871, SUSIE D. DICKINSON, b. Charlestown, N.H., 20 Jan. 1854, in 1888 living in Charlestown, N.H., dau. of George M. Dickinson and Susan D. Clapp.

Issue (surname WORK):

13. a. GEORGINA DICKINSON, b. N.H., 26 Dec. 1873, living 1937.

8. JANE SARAH WORK, b. Ohio, 1844, d. 1925, m. 9 June 1869, HENRY OLCOTT, b. 21 Dec. 1840, d. [living 1893], son of George Olcott and of Emily Ann Silsbey.

Issue (surname OLCOTT):

14. a. ELIZABETH WORK, b. 10 Nov. 1870, d. Fort Worth, Tex., 13 Feb. 1931.

9. JAMES HENRY WORK, attorney, b. New York, N.Y., 28 June 1846, d. Lawrence, N.Y., 22 Oct. 1916, m. New York, N.Y., 28 May 1874, MARY PIERCE WARNER, b. New York, N.Y., 16 Sept. 1851, d. Lawrence, N.Y., 28 July 1927, dau. of Hiram Wolcott Warner and of Charlotte M. Strong.

Issue (surname WORK):

15. a. ALICE WARNER, b. N.Y., 20 May 1875, d. Lawrence, N.Y., 8 Feb. 1966.
b. MABEL WARNER, b. N.Y., 4 Oct. 1877, d. [between 1900 and 1910].
16. c. SALLIE DUNCAN, b. N.Y., 6 Feb. 1879, d. Wilton, Conn., 30 March 1972.
d. JEAN SHARON, b. N.Y., 29 Jan. 1882, d. 7 Feb. 1968.
e. MARY WARNER, b. N.Y., 10 Feb. 1884, d. Lawrence, N.Y., 13 July 1957.
17. f. JAMES HENRY, Jr., b. N.Y., 22 Dec. 1890, d. Lawrence, N.Y., 31 May 1954.
18. g. MARJORIE, b. N.Y., 2 Sept. 1892.

10. ELISABETH WORK, b. New York, N.Y., 1848, d. Farmington, Conn., 27 Sept. 1932, m. New York, N.Y., 24 Dec. 1879, WILLIAM AUGUSTUS HOOKER, b. Hartford, Conn., 4 Sept. 1845, d. [before 1932], son of William Throop Hooker and of Caroline Collins.

Issue (surname HOOKER):

19. a. WILLIAM BRIAN (BRIAN), b. New York, N.Y., 2 Nov. 1880, d. New London, Conn., 28 Dec. 1946.
b. JOAN CULBERTSON, b. New York, N.Y., 27 Feb. 1884, d. Truro, Mass., 4 May 1971.
20. c. DUNCAN COLLINS, b. New York, N.Y., 4 March 1885, d. Hartford, Conn., 26 July 1953.
21. d. RICHARD, b. 17 Feb. 1892, d. 27 Oct. 1969.

11. George Francis Work, later "FRANK WORK, Jr.", b. N.Y., Jan. 1851, d. Oyster Bay, N.Y., 13 Oct. 1908, m. 23 May 1879, EMMA MARBURY, b. N.Y., March 1851, d. Lakewood, N.J., 30 Dec. 1915, dau. of Francis F. Marbury and of Elizabeth McCann.

Issue (surname WORK):

22. a. JOHN CLINTON, b. New York, N.Y., Dec. 1881, d. St. Thomas, V.I., 30 Apr. 1959.

12. FRANK W. MERRICK, attorney, b. Ohio, Apr. 1844, d. Columbus, Ohio, 29 Sept. 1904, m. Franklin Co., Ohio, 4 Nov. 1885, as her second husband, MINNIE BELL, b. Ohio, Aug. 1859, in 1934 living at 1696 Merrick Rd., Columbus, Ohio [she had m. (1)].

No issue.

13. Georgina Dickinson Work, b. N.H., 26 Dec. 1873, living 1937, m. [by 1902], ——— Morton.

Issue, if any, unknown.

14. Elizabeth Work Olcott, b. 10 Nov. 1870, d. Fort Worth, Tex., 13 Feb. 1931, m. (1) New York, N.Y., 10 May 1893, John Prentiss Browning, son of S. G. Browning and of ——— Prentiss; m. (2) 19 July 1906, Frederic A. Potts, Jr., d. Lakewood, N.J., 24 March 1923, son of Frederic A. Potts, Sr.

Issue by second husband (surname Potts):

23. a. David C., later "Frederic A. Potts III".

15. Alice Warner Work, b. N.Y., 20 May 1875, d. Lawrence, N.Y., 8 Feb. 1966, m. 1895, John L. Lawrence, b. N.Y., 22 June 1857, d. Lawrence, N.Y., 17 Nov. 1930, son of Alfred Newbold Lawrence and of Elizabeth Woodhull Lawrence.

Issue (surname Lawrence):

a. Alice, b. N.Y., March 1898.
b. John L., Jr., b. N.Y., 1902, in 1945 living in W. Granby, Conn.
24. c. Alfred Newbold, b. N.Y., 1903.

16. Sallie Duncan Work, b. N.Y., 6 Feb. 1879, d. Wilton, Conn., 30 March 1972, m. [by 1903], Franklin Baker Lefferts, architect, b. N.Y., Jan. 1879, d. 1908, son of Marshall Clifford Lefferts and of Caroline Ella Baker.

Issue (surname Lefferts):

25. a. Dorothy C., b. N.Y., 13 May 1905, d. Stowe, Vt., 19 Sept. 1971.

17. James Henry Work, Jr., b. N.Y., 22 Dec. 1890, d. Lawrence, N.Y., 31 May 1954, m. Overbrook, Pa., 8 June 1916, Mary Layng Davis, b. 2 Dec. 1895, d. Greenwich, Conn., 8 June 1970, dau. of Nathan Hatfield Davis and of Nancy Harlan Doll.

Issue (surname Work):

26. a. Nancy Harlan, b. 18 May 1917.
27. b. Margaret Warner.

18. Marjorie Work, b. N.Y., 2 Sept. 1892, m. New York, N.Y., 1 March 1912, De Courcy Lawrence Hard, pharmaceutical manufacturer, b. Lawrence, N.Y., 1 Aug. 1887, d. Cedarhurst, N.Y., 12 July 1966, son of Anson Wales Hard and of Sarah Elizabeth Brown.

Issue (surname HARD [order unknown]):

a. STEPHEN B.
b. MARJORIE WOLCOTT (SUSAN).
28. c. BARBARA.
29. d. DE COURCY LAWRENCE, Jr.

19. WILLIAM BRIAN HOOKER (Brian), author, b. New York, N.Y., 2 Nov. 1880, d. New London, Conn., 28 Dec. 1946, m. Farmington, Conn., 18 Aug. 1911, DORIS REDFIELD COOPER, b. New York, N.Y., 29 Dec. 1890, d. Old Lyme, Conn., 2 July 1967, dau. of Frederick Taber Cooper and of Edith Redfield.

Issue (surname HOOKER):

a. Belinda, b. Farmington, Conn., 28 July 1912.
b. Elisabeth, b. New York, N.Y., 13 March 1914.
30. c. PAMELA, b. New York, N.Y., 23 Dec. 1917.

20. DUNCAN COLLINS HOOKER, firearms engineer, b. New York, N.Y., 4 March 1885, d. Hartford, Conn., 26 July 1953, m. IRENE SIMMONS, living 1953 in Granby, Conn.

No issue.

21. RICHARD HOOKER, b. 17 Feb. 1892, d. 27 Oct. 1969, m. 12 Aug. 1920, ISABEL PAINE, b. 18 Feb. 1901, dau. of Frederick Landon Paine and of Harriet Parks.

Issue (surname HOOKER):

31. a. ISABEL CRANE, b. 12 June 1921.
32. b. RICHARD, b. 20 July 1926.

22. JOHN CLINTON WORK, Commander, U.S.N., b. New York, N.Y., Dec. 1881, d. St. Thomas, V.I., 30 Apr. 1959, m. (1) New York, N.Y., 21 Jan. 1909, div., as her first husband, CECILY ISOLDE SHELDON, b. London 1885, d. Essex, Conn., 30 Apr. 1978 [she later m. (2) Salem, Mass., 16 Sept. 1933, Henry Suydam Satterlee, M.D., b. New York, N.Y., 4 June 1874, d. Newport, N.H., 9 Jan. 1967], dau. of James O. Sheldon and of Emily J. Adam; m. (2) Elizabeth Johnson.

Issue by first wife (surname WORK):

33. a. CECILY SHELDON, b. Morristown, N.J., 1 Nov. 1909.
34. b. JOHN CLINTON, Jr., b. 1914.

23. David C. Potts, later "FREDERIC A. POTTS III", m. (1) New York, N.Y., 8 Sept. 1933, MARTHA L. WOLFELT, dau. of Curtis H. Wolfelt; m. (2) 24 Dec. 1941, VIRGINIA COX.

Issue by second wife (surname POTTS):

a. SUSAN C., b. 1942.
b. ELIZABETH B., b. 1946.
c. JANE O., b. 1948.
d. FREDERIC A. IV, b. 1956.

24. ALFRED NEWBOLD LAWRENCE, b. N.Y., 1903, m. (1) New York, N.Y., 12 Nov. 1930, div., MARIANNA CASSERLY, dau. of John B. Casserly and of ——— Cudahy; m. (2) 16 Oct. 1950, ELSE KENNEDY.

Issue by first wife (surname LAWRENCE):

35. a. ALFRED NEWBOLD, Jr., b. 1931.

25. DOROTHY C. LEFFERTS, b. N.Y., 13 May 1905, d. Stowe, Vt., 19 Sept. 1971, m. Cedarhurst, N.Y., 14 Sept. 1928, as his first wife, LAWRENCE MOORE, b. 25 Nov. 1897 [he later m. (2) West Hartford, Conn., 29 Sept. 1973, Marjorie Lang], son of Frank Gardner Moore and of Anna B. White.

Issue (surname MOORE):

36. a. PETER L., b. New York, N.Y., 12 Sept. 1929.
37. b. SARA SANDYS, b. 13 Dec. 1934.

26. NANCY HARLAN WORK, b. 18 May 1917, m. (1) Lawrence, N.Y., 30 Apr. 1936, div. [1938?], MORGAN MACY, b. 1903, son of Sylvanus Jenkins Macy and of Susanne Morgan; m. (2) New York, N.Y., 20 Jan. 1939, div., ALFRED SEVERIN BOURNE, Jr., b. 20 March 1906, son of Alfred Severin Bourne, Sr., and of H. Louise Barnes; m. (3) Greenwich, Conn., 26 Nov. 1954, as his second wife, JOHN LATHROP GRAY, Jr., b. Elizabeth, N.J., 20 March 1905 [he had m. (1) 23 Aug. 1928, div. July 1954, Eleanor Reynolds Snow, b. Nov. 1904], son of John Lathrop Gray, Sr., and of Harriet Hamilton Cornell Tyng.

Issue by second husband (surname BOURNE):

38. a. FREDERICK HARLAN, b. Greenwich, Conn., 24 Dec. 1939.
39. b. NANCY ELLICOTT, b. 5 July 1943.
40. c. LYNNE SEVERIN, b. 16 Jan. 1947.

27. MARGARET WARNER WORK, m. Cedarhurst, N.Y., 20 June 1940, div., W. WARE LYNCH, son of Frank J. Lynch and of L. Ware.

Details of issue unknown (two children and three grandchildren).

28. BARBARA HARD, m. Cedarhurst, N.Y., 30 March 1946, JOHN MILTON URNER, son of Samuel Everett Urner.

Issue, if any, unknown.

29. De Courcy Lawrence Hard, Jr., m. Far Rockaway, N.Y., 10 July 1937, as her first husband, Anne Kathryn FitzSimmons [she later m. (2) Anglesey (Wales), 24 Aug. 1961, James Higginson Weekes, b. New York, N.Y., 11 Sept. 1911, d. 13 June 1977], dau. of Robert FitzSimmons.

Known issue (surname Hard):

a. Gaelynn Bridget.
b. De Courcy Lawrence III.

30. Pamela Hooker, b. New York, N.Y., 23 Dec. 1917, m. (1) 31 Aug. 1940, Philip Sands, b. Old Lyme, Conn., 2 July 1913, d. Old Lyme, Conn., 18 Aug. 1954, son of Joshua Sands and of Lucy Childs; m. (2) Hadlyme, Conn., 20 July 1971, Paul Warner Thomas, b. New London, Conn., 6 Aug. 1925.

Issue by first husband (surname Sands):

41. a. Sarah Anne, b. New London, Conn., 16 March 1943.
42. b. Philip Hooker, b. 17 Nov. 1949.

31. Isabel Crane Hooker, b. 12 June 1921, m. 16 May 1942, John Kent Cardwell.

Issue (surname Cardwell):

43. a. Cheryl Lynn, b. 8 Aug. 1944.
b. John Kent, b. 19 Apr. 1950.
c. Brian Hooker, b. 8 July 1957.

32. Richard Hooker, b. 20 July 1926, m. 17 Oct. 1953, Anna Wilson.

Issue (surname Hooker):

a. Sandra Ann, b. 28 Nov. 1961.
b. Richard Thomas, b. 13 Aug. 1964.

33. Cecily Sheldon Work, b. Morristown, N.J., 1 Nov. 1909, m. Cold Spring Harbor, N.Y., 12 May 1934, Howard Slade II, banker, b. Cambridge, Mass., 20 Aug. 1905, d. Essex, Conn., 11 Dec. 1965, son of Winthrop Slade and of Anne Abeel Hall.

Issue (surname Slade):

44. a. Cecily Sheldon, b. New York, N.Y., 20 June 1935.
b. Anne Abeel, b. New York, N.Y., 1 Feb. 1938.
45. c. Elizabeth Marbury, b. New York, N.Y., 3 Feb. 1941.

34. JOHN CLINTON WORK, Jr., b. 1914, m. (1) Westbury, N.Y., 2 March 1940, div., as her first husband, PRISCILLA GRANT [she later m. (2) 1959, John C. Timken], dau. of Robert Grant, Jr., and of Priscilla C. Stackpole; m. (2) Essex, Conn., 12 Dec. 1958, as her second husband, JULIA POWELL [she had m. (1) ——— Norton].

Issue by first wife (surname WORK):

46. a. PRISCILLA.
47. b. JOHN CLINTON III.
48. c. IAN GRANT.

35. ALFRED NEWBOLD LAWRENCE, Jr. (Mike), b. 1931, m. Hewlett, L.I., 28 Jan. 1961, MARY TERRY LIVINGSTON, dau. of John G. Livingston and of Mary Terry Harrison.

Issue (surname LAWRENCE):

a. PETER C., b. 1961.
b. CYNTHIA T., b. 1965.

36. PETER L. MOORE, b. New York, N.Y., 12 Sept. 1929, m. Ipswich, Mass., 31 Oct. 1964, ALICIA MARGUERITE HILLS, b. Salem, Mass., 26 Aug. 1930, dau. of Carroll B. Hills and of Consuelo Bates.

Issue, if any, unknown.

37. SARA SANDYS MOORE, b. 13 Dec. 1934, m. Wilton, Conn., 9 June 1956, LOUIS LONGACRE CORNELL, b. 5 Aug. 1934, son of Milton L. Cornell and of Mary Gaston.

Issue (surname CORNELL):

a. THOMAS L., b. 18 Dec. 1957.
b. STEPHEN L., b. 15 March 1959.
c. JOHN S., b. 22 Aug. 1962.

38. FREDERICK HARLAN BOURNE, b. Greenwich, Conn., 24 Dec. 1939, m. Riverside, Conn., 24 Nov. 1962, div. 18 Nov. 1981, JUDITH VERRIER, b. 5 June 1941, dau. of John Verrier and of Marjorie ———.

Issue (surname BOURNE):

a. PATRICIA ANNE, b. Greenwich, Conn., 15 Aug. 1963.
b. SUSAN ELIZABETH, b. Greenwich, Conn., 5 June 1965.
c. KATHRYN LEIGH, b. Greenwich, Conn., 31 Aug. 1968.

39. NANCY ELLICOTT BOURNE, b. 5 July 1943, m. 6 Apr. 1968, BOB DAVID SWAN, b. 21 Apr. 1939, son of David Earl Swan and of Edna Marie Mitchell.

Issue (surname SWAN):

a. TYRA LYNNE, b. 15 Jan. 1969.
b. TYLER WOODWARD, b. 12 June 1972.

40. LYNNE SEVERIN BOURNE, b. 16 Jan. 1947, m., div. 1981, ——— VAN ANTWERP.

Details of issue unknown (two children).

41. SARAH ANNE SANDS, b. New London, Conn., 16 March 1943, m. Salem, N.H., 14 Nov. 1963, RONALD EDWARD ROSE, b. Cambridge, Mass., 3 Nov. 1940, son of Edward Rose and of Mary R. Campbell.

Issue (surname ROSE):

a. REBECCA ELLEVA, b. Boston, Mass., 6 Apr. 1965.
b. ELISABETH EDNA, b. Boston, Mass., 24 Apr. 1975.

42. PHILIP HOOKER SANDS, b. 17 Nov. 1949, m. Norwich, Conn., 20 Dec. 1976, MARIE BERNADETTE COYLE, b. 22 Apr. 1951.

No issue yet.

43. CHERYL LYNN CARDWELL, b. 8 Aug. 1944, m. 12 July 1961, DAVID L. DELANEY.

Issue (surname DELANEY):

a. MICHAEL, b. 12 Jan. 1962.
b. CHRISTINE, b. 1 May 1969.

44. CECILY SHELDON SLADE, b. New York, N.Y., 20 June 1935, m. Cold Spring Harbor, N.Y., 7 Feb. 1959, ROBERT UPJOHN REDPATH III, b. Orange, N.J., 16 Dec. 1931, son of Robert Upjohn Redpath, Jr., and of Nancy Shaw Miller.

Issue (surname REDPATH):

a. IAN.

45. ELIZABETH MARBURY SLADE, b. New York, N.Y., 3 Feb. 1941, m. Cold Spring Harbor, N.Y., 6 June 1964, WILLIAM READ HARPER MARTIN, b. New York, N.Y., 20 Feb. 1938, son of John May Martin and of Helen Barker.

Issue (surname MARTIN):

a. READ.
b. ANNE.

46. Priscilla Work, m. C. F. O'Neill.
Details of issue unknown (three sons).

47. John Clinton Work III, m. ———.
Details of issue unknown (two daughters).

48. Ian Grant Work, m. ———.
Details of issue unknown (one son).

Notes

Number 1:
It has been suggested that John and Sarah Duncan (Boude) Wark had ten children, but this suggestion appears to be based on a confusion between the two different John Works in Ross County, Ohio. In the 1820 federal census of Ross County, the John Work enumerated on page 232 (City of Chillicothe) is the one who married Sarah Duncan Boude and had five children, while the John Work enumerated on page 238 (Union Township) is the one who had the ten children. The connection, if any, between these two John Works is unknown.

Number 3:
The first member of this family consistently to spell (and pronounce) the surname "Work" instead of "Wark" was John Clinton Work (number 2, above).

Number 4:
The family stories concerning George Work state that he went "out west", married an American Indian woman, and had two children, a boy and a girl. These two were sent back east to a boarding school, from which they escaped, and were never heard from again. The first codicil (dated 14 May 1902) to the will (Manhattan Surrogate's Court, Liber 909, pp. 270-340) of Frank Work (Part II, number 5) mentions the children of the wife of his brother, George Work, one named William Work, the other a girl whose name he (Frank) didn't know.

III

Descendants of John Wood and of Eleanor Strong

1 JOHN WOOD, porkpacker, councilman (see Part VI, number 2, below), b. [Sheperdstown, W.?] Va., 29 July 1785, d. Chillicothe, Ohio, 29 Jan. 1848, son of George Wood and of Elizabeth Conner, m. Chillicothe, Ohio, 13 March 1823, ELEANOR STRONG (see Part VII, number 3, below), b. Philadelphia, Pa. [1802/3], d. New York, N.Y., 9 July 1863, dau. of Joseph Strong and of Rebecca Young.

Issue (surname WOOD):

a. JOHN, b. 1825, d. 1826.
b. WILLIAM BOND, b. Chillicothe, Ohio, 17 Oct. 1826, d. Wabash Co., Ind., 20 Sept. 1876.
2. c. JOHN, bapt. Chillicothe, Ohio, 22 June 1828, d. Wabash, Ind., 17 Oct. 1865.
d. THOMAS JAMES, b. Chillicothe, Ohio, 1829, in 1850 living in Chillicothe, Ohio.
3. e. ELLEN, b. Chillicothe, Ohio, 18 July 1831, d. New York, N.Y., 22 Feb. 1877.
4. f. GEORGE, b. Chillicothe, Ohio, 17 Dec. 1832, d. New York, N.Y., 15 May 1897.
g. JOSEPH STRONG, bapt. Chillicothe, Ohio, 5 Sept. 1834, bur. Chillicothe, Ohio, 12 Sept. 1834.
h. CHARLES, b. Chillicothe, Ohio, 26 Feb. 1845, d. Ross Co., Ohio, 30 June 1853.

2. JOHN WOOD, bapt. Chillicothe, Ohio, 22 June 1828, d. Wabash, Ind., 17 Oct. 1865, m. Chillicothe, Ohio, 1852, as her first husband, JANE MARY DUN, b. Chillicothe, Ohio, 7 July 1830 [she later m. (2) Dec. 1866, Jay Lugsdin], dau. of Robert Dun and of Lucy Wortham Angus.

Issue (surname WOOD):

a. ELLEN, living 1871.
b. JOHN, living 1871.
c. LUCY, b. 1852, living 1871.

3. ELLEN WOOD, b. Chillicothe, Ohio, 18 July 1831, d. New York, N.Y., 22 Feb. 1877, m. New York, N.Y., 19 Feb. 1857, FRANK(LIN H.) WORK, dry goods merchant, stockbroker (see Part II, number

6, above), b. Chillicothe, Ohio, 10 Feb. 1819, d. New York, N.Y., 16 March 1911, son of John Wark and of Sarah Duncan Boude.

Issue: See Part I, above.

4. GEORGE WOOD, banker, b. Chillicothe, Ohio, 17 Dec. 1832, d. New York, N.Y., 15 May 1897, m. 27 June 1860, SARAH MCDONALD GERARD, b. New York, N.Y., 31 Aug. 1840, d. Bedford, N.Y., 2 Jan. 1929, dau. of William Gerard and of Sarah McDonald Bates.

Issue (surname WOOD):

5. a. GEORGE EDWARD, b. N.J., 24 Aug. 1861, d. 14 Nov. 1925.
6. b. ALICE GERARD, b. New York, N.Y., 24 Jan. 1863, d. Morristown, N.J., 8 May 1928.

5. GEORGE EDWARD WOOD, architect, b. N.J., 24 Aug. 1861, d. 14 Nov. 1925, m. St. Paul, Minn., 17 Nov. 1892, ISABELLA HADDEN BEND, b. N.Y., 1865, d. 1948, dau. of William Bradford Bend and of Isabella Tomes.

Issue (surname WOOD):

7. a. GERARD HADDEN, b. Minn., 12 Sept. 1893.
b. MEREDITH BEND, Rev., b. N.Y., 26 Jan. 1896, d. March 1965.
8. c. ISABELLA, b. N.Y., 28 Aug. 1902, d. 19 Sept. 1975.

6. ALICE GERARD WOOD, b. New York, N.Y., 24 Jan. 1863, d. Morristown, N.J., 8 May 1928, m. New York, N.Y., 26 Apr. 1886, WILLIAM WATSON SHIPPEN, Jr., banker, b. Hoboken, N.J., 13 June 1858, d. Philadelphia, Pa., 31 May 1922, son of William Watson Shippen, Sr., and of Georgina Elmina Morton.

Issue (surname SHIPPEN):

a. EDWARD, b. New York, N.Y., 29 Dec. 1887, d. Morristown, N.J., 10 Feb. 1923.

7. GERARD HADDEN WOOD, Sr., b. Minn., 12 Sept. 1893, m. Vancouver, B.C., 15 Aug. 1928, FRANCES DUYCINCK COOPER, b. 14 Sept. 1904, dau. of Charles Bryant Cooper and of Katharine Christie McGrew.

Issue (surname WOOD):

9. a. GERARD HADDEN, Jr. (Hadden), b. 28 Oct. 1931.
10. b. KATHERINE COOPER, b. 3 Oct. 1934.
11. c. ALICE ISABEL, b. Coronado, Cal., 13 June 1937.

8. ISABELLA WOOD, b. N.Y., 28 Aug. 1902, d. 19 Sept. 1975, m. New York, N.Y., 24 May 1924, RALPH MONTAGU-STUART-WORTLEY, b.

New York, N.Y., 12 March 1897, d. Uniontown, Pa., 8 Feb. 1961, son of Hon. Ralph Grenville Montagu-Stuart-Wortley and of Virginia Maria Schley.

Issue (surname MONTAGU-STUART-WORTLEY):

12. a. ELIZABETH ANNE (BETTY), b. 8 May 1925.
13. b. ALAN RALPH, b. 22 July 1927.
14. c. JOAN ISABELLA, b. 20 July 1928.

9. GERARD HADDEN WOOD, Jr. (Hadden), b. 28 Oct. 1931, m. 1956, as her second husband, DOROTHY BLOIS, b. 9 Apr. 1929 [she had m. (1) Minot Arthur Crofoot], dau. of William Blois and of Olga Gallas.

Issue (surname WOOD):

a. CURTIS CHRISTIE, b. 3 Jan. 1958.

10. KATHERINE COOPER WOOD, b. 3 Oct. 1934, m. Wailuku, Maui, Hawaii, 1959, JOHN COOPER MCCRILLIS, b. 30 May 1930.

Issue (surname MCCRILLIS):

a. LAURA COOPER, b. 26 Oct. 1960.
b. JOHN DAVID (DAVID), b. 1 March 1962.
c. WILLIAM GERARD, b. 21 Oct. 1964.

11. ALICE ISABEL WOOD, b. Coronado, Cal., 13 June 1937, m. Bedford, N.Y., 6 Sept. 1958, TRAVIS OGDEN THOMPSON, b. Mickleton, N.J., 2 May 1935, son of Raymond Thompson and of Helen Pettit.

Issue (surname THOMPSON):

a. TARN BRIAN, b. 16 Aug. 1959.
b. LYNNE SEDGWICK, b. 31 Dec. 1962.

12. ELIZABETH ANNE MONTAGU-STUART-WORTLEY (Betty), b. 8 May 1925, m. 27 Nov. 1948, div. 1963, CHESTER LYMAN KINGSBURY, Jr., son of Chester Lyman Kingsbury, Sr.

Issue (surname KINGSBURY):

a. CHESTER LYMAN III, b. 14 Feb. 1950.
b. MEREDITH ELLEN, b. 1 May 1952.
c. MICHELLE ELIZABETH, b. 8 Oct. 1957.

13. ALAN RALPH MONTAGU-STUART-WORTLEY, b. 22 July 1927, m. Brownsville, Pa., 23 Feb. 1952, VIRGINIA ANN CLAYBAUGH, b. 12 Aug. 1928, dau. of William Martin Claybaugh and of Mary Louise Steele.

Issue (surname MONTAGU-STUART-WORTLEY):

15. a. Richard Alan, b. 26 May 1953.
b. Anne Steele, b. 30 Jan. 1955.
c. William Ralph, b. 18 Apr. 1959.

14. Joan Isabella Montagu-Stuart-Wortley, b. 20 July 1928, m. Bedford Center, N.Y., 1 Dec. 1951, Harry Atwood Bishop, Jr., b. 9 July 1926, son of Harry Atwood Bishop, Sr., and of Georgia Elvetta Walters.

Issue (surname Bishop):

16. a. Wendy Ann Isabella, b. 16 June 1952.
17. b. Linda Walters, b. 9 Oct. 1953.
18. c. Harry Atwood III, b. 1 Feb. 1957.
d. Alan Stuart-Wortley, b. 3 June 1959.

15. Richard Alan Montagu-Stuart-Wortley, b. 26 May 1953, m. Peru, Vt., 22 Sept. 1979, Mary Elizabeth Reed, b. 23 Apr. 1951, dau. of William W. Reed and of Dorothy Gadsden.

Issue (surname Montagu-Stuart-Wortley):
a. Reed, b. 5 Feb. 1980.

16. Wendy Ann Isabella Bishop, b. 16 June 1952, m. 23 Aug. 1975, Dennis Charles Gillespie.

Issue (surname Gillespie):
a. Kelly Ann Isabella, b. 2 Nov. 1977.
b. Meghan Therese, b. 27 Apr. 1980.

17. Linda Walters Bishop, b. 9 Oct. 1953, m. 21 Feb. 1981, Nicolo Bimbo.

No issue yet.

18. Harry Atwood Bishop III, b. 1 Feb. 1957, m. 26 June 1982, Julie Sayre Mulligan, dau. of Leonard Charles Mulligan and of Carol Sayre Musk.

No issue yet.

Notes

Number 1:
John Wood's tombstone states, in part, "BORN / JULY 19, 1785. / DIED / JAN. 29, 1847.", but the year of death is wrong. His will was dated 21 Jan. 1848

and admitted to probate on 3 Feb. 1848 (*Ross Co.* [Ohio] *Will Book E&F*, p. 76); and the *Register* of St. Paul's Episcopal Church, Chillicothe, shows John Wood, age 61, buried on 31 Jan. 1848.

Number 1 d:
Thomas James Wood was enumerated in the 1850 federal census with his mother and siblings in Chillicothe, Ohio. Shortly thereafter he left for Texas and was never heard from again.

Number 13:
As of 1983, Mr. Wortley is the heir-presumptive to the titles of Earl of Wharncliffe, Viscount Carlton, and Baron Wharncliffe.

IV

Descendants of ——— Wark and of ———

1. ——— WARK, b. ———, d. ———, son of ——— Wark and of ———, m. ———, ———, b. ———, d. ———, dau. of ——— and of ———.

Known issue (surname WARK):

2. a. JOHN, b. Plymouth, Devon [1783?], d. Chillicothe, Ohio, 16 Apr. 1823.

2. JOHN WARK, civil engineer, b. Plymouth, Devon [1783?], d. Chillicothe, Ohio, 16 Apr. 1823, m. [license to marry issued in Baltimore, Md., on 2 Feb. 1808] SARAH DUNCAN BOUDE (see Part V, number 3, below), b. Elkridge Landing, Md., 15 Dec. 1790, d. Columbus, Ohio, 17 Dec. 1860, dau. of Joseph Boude and of Barbara Black.

Issue: See Part II, above.

Note

John Wark (number 2, above) was almost certainly the John Wark who was born on 28 Oct. 1781 and baptized at the Batter Street Presbyterian Church, Plymouth, 8 Nov. following, son of John and Sarah Wark. The entry for his burial, in the *Register* of St. Paul's Episcopal Church, Chillicothe, Ohio, on 17 Apr. 1823, incorrectly calls him "Joseph Wark."

V

Descendants of Joseph Boude and of Barbara Black

1. Joseph Boude (see chapter 3, above), b. ——— 13 Dec. 1740, d. ———, son of Thomas Boude and of Sarah Newbold, m. Baltimore, Md., ——— [license to marry issued on 11 Dec. 1781], Barbara Black, dau. of William Black and of [probably] Catharine ———.

Issue (surname Boude [order uncertain]):

2. a. Elizabeth, b. [ca. 1784-5], d. Howard Dist., Anne Arundel Co., Md., 13 Jan. 1852.
3. b. Sarah Duncan, b. Elkridge Landing, Md., 15 Dec. 1790, d. Columbus, Ohio, 17 Dec. 1860.
c. Charles, d. Baltimore, Md.
4. d. Rudolph Thomas Clarkson, b. Baltimore, Md. [1793-1794], d. Shenandoah Co., Va., 1862 [before 9 Dec.].

2. Elizabeth Boude, b. [ca. 1784-5], d. Howard Dist., Anne Arundel Co., Md., 13 Jan. 1852, m. [1810], Joshua Barlow, b. Md. [1767-9], d. Howard Dist., Anne Arundel Co., Md., 20 Jan. 1857.

Known issue (surname Barlow):

5. a. Joseph, b. Md. [ca. 1818], living 1880.
6. b. Joshua, b. Md. [ca. 1820], living 1850.
c. Sarah, b. Md. [ca. 1827], living 1850.

3. Sarah Duncan Boude, b. Elkridge Landing, Md., 15 Dec. 1790, d. Columbus, Ohio, 17 Dec. 1860, m. [license to marry issued in Baltimore, Md., on 2 Feb. 1808], John Wark, civil engineer (see Part IV, number 2, above), b. Plymouth, Devon [1783?], d. Chillicothe, Ohio, 16 Apr. 1823, son of ——— Wark and of ———.

Issue: See Part II, above.

4. Rudolph Thomas Clarkson Boude, shoemaker, b. Baltimore, Md. [1793–1794], d. Shenandoah Co., Va., 1862 [before 9 Dec.], m. (1) Frederick Co., Va. [ca. 1820], Elizabeth Ewing, d. 1843, dau. of Thomas Ewing and of Adah Crawford; m. (2) [by 1850], Margaret Warren, b. Va. [1814], dau. of ——— Warren and of [Polly?].

Issue: (a) by first wife (surname Boude [order unknown]):

7. a. SARAH MARANDA, d. Coshocton Co., Ohio.
8. b. CAROLINE LAURA, d. Holmes Co., Ohio.
9. c. ELIZABETH MINERVA.
10. d. JOSEPH THOMAS, d. Columbus, Ohio [by 1902].
11. e. SAMUEL KENNERLY, b. Va., 1831, d. Summers Co., W. Va., 15 Feb. 1896.
12. f. JOHN CLINTON WORK.
13. g. ADAM POE, b. Millwood, Va., 20 Feb. 1835, d. Stanley, Va., 29 Nov. 1919.
14. h. MARY JANE, b. Va., 1838, living 1900.

(b) by second wife (surname BOUDE):

15. i. MARTHA, b. Va. [ca. 1844], living 1907.
j. SUSAN, b. Va. [ca. 1847], d. [young, after 1850].

5. JOSEPH BARLOW, b. Md. [ca. 1818], in 1880 living in Third District, Howard Co., Md., m. 2 Jan. 1841, ARIANNA NORWOOD, b. Md. [ca. 1814/5], living in 1880.

Known issue (surname BARLOW):

16. a. CLINTON, b. Md. [ca. 1842], living 1900.
b. EMMA, b. Md. [ca. 1843/4], living 1860.
c. JAMES, b. Md. [ca. 1845], living 1850.
17. d. LEWIS, b. Md., Dec. 1845, living 1900.
e. JOSEPH BOUDE, b. Md., 26 May 1847, living 1860.
f. HENRY C., b. Md. [ca. 1849], living 1860.
18. g. Frank Work, b. Md., 27 Feb. 1852, living 1900.
h. ANNA, b. Md. [ca. 1853], living 1860.

6. JOSHUA BARLOW, b. Md. [ca. 1820], in 1850 living in Howard Dist., Anne Arundel Co., Md., m. HONOUR [NORWOOD?], b. Md. [ca. 1820], living in 1850.

Known issue (surname BARLOW):

19. a. WILLIAM F., b. Md. [1843], living 1880.
20. b. JOSEPH M., b. Md., March 1845, living 1900.
c. JEMIMA, b. Md. [1847], living 1850.
d. ACHSAH, b. Md. [1849], living 1850.

7. SARAH MARANDA BOUDE, d. Coshocton Co., Ohio, m. JOSEPH LUDWICK.

Issue, if any, unknown.

8. CAROLINE LAURA BOUDE, d. Holmes Co., Ohio, m. Rev. ELISHA PEER, d. Holmes Co., Ohio.

Issue (surname PEER):

a. RUDOLPH, Rev.

9. ELIZABETH MINERVA BOUDE, m. PHILIP BOWMAN, of Mount Clifton, Va.

Issue, if any, unknown.

10. JOSEPH THOMAS BOUDE, d. Columbus, Ohio [by 1902], m. SARAH J. ROHR, in 1905 living in Columbus, Ohio.

Issue (surname BOUDE [order unknown]):

a. JOHN S.
b. WILLIAM H., blacksmith.
c. ———.

11. SAMUEL KENNERLY BOUDE, b. Va., 1831, d. Summers Co., W. Va., 15 Feb. 1896, m. (1) SARAH J. NICKELL, b. W. Va.; m. (2) as her second husband, SARAH C. BOYD, b. W. Va., Oct. 1856, in 1907 living in Hinton, W. Va. [she had m. (1) James Scott], dau. of James Boyd and of Mary ———.

Issue: (a) by first wife (surname BOUDE [order unknown]):

21. a. WALTER H., b. W. Va., 23 Sept. 1860, living 1910.
22. b. (dau.), living 1896.
23. c. MARY E., b. W. Va., Nov. 1866, living 1900.
d. CLEO H., b. W. Va., May 1880, in 1900 living in Summers Co., W. Va.
e. (dau.), living 1896.
f. (dau.), living 1896.

(b) by second wife (surname BOUDE):

g. RETA, b. W. Va., Nov. 1889, living 1907.
h. MONA, b. W. Va., June 1891, living 1907.

12. JOHN CLINTON WORK BOUDE, clerk of the Circuit Court of Rockbridge Co., Va., m. MUSADORA A. PLUNKETT.

No issue.

13. ADAM POE BOUDE, minister of the Methodist Episcopal Church South, b. Millwood, Va., 20 Feb. 1835, d. Stanley, Va., 29 Nov. 1919, m. (1) LOUISA LEE PLUNKETT [sister of Musadora, above]; m. (2) IDA PENDERGAST, in 1927 living in Stanley, Va., dau. of J. T. Pendergast and of Eliza ———.

Issue by first wife (surname BOUDE):

a. RUDOLPH THOMAS CLINTON (CLINTON), b. Feb. 1867, d. 22 Aug. 1888.

14. MARY JANE BOUDE, b. Va., 1838, in 1900 living in Shenandoah

Co., Va., m. B. J. STANTON, b. Va., 1833, d. [between 1880 and 1900].

Issue (surname STANTON [order uncertain]):

a. EMMA J., b. Va., 1857, living 1880.
24. b. CHARLES S., b. Va., May 1864, living 1910.
25. c. JAMES C., b. Va., March 1866, living 1910.
d. WILLIS R., b. Va., 1868, living 1880.
26. e. EDGAR A. K., b. Va., Apr. 1871, living 1900.
f. ELIZABETH C., b. Va., Aug. 1875, living 1900.
g. CYRUS HARRY, b. Va., Nov. 1879, living 1900.
h. [child], d. young.
i. [child], d. young.
j. [child], d. young.

15. MARTHA BOUDE, b. Va. [ca. 1844], in 1907 living in Conicville, Va., m. GEORGE ESTEP, living in 1907.

Known issue (surname ESTEP):

a. ARTHUR, living 1927 in Conicville, Va.

16. CLINTON BARLOW, b. Md. [ca. 1842], in 1900 living in Howard Co., Md., m. (1) ELIZABETH ———, b. Md. [ca. 1855], d. [after 1880]; m. (2) 1883, MARTHA ———, b. Md., Jan. 1863, living in 1900.

Known issue: (a) by first wife (surname BARLOW):

a. HENRY C., b. Md. [1872], living 1880.
b. JANE F., b. Md. [1873], living 1880.
c. LEMUEL L., b. Md. [1875], living 1880.
d. EDWIN A., b. Md. [1878], living 1880.

(b) by second wife:

e. LEWIS B., b. Md., Apr. 1884, living 1900.
f. ESTELL B., b. Md., May 1888, living 1900.
g. CLINTON L., b. Md., Apr. 1898, living 1900.
h. WILLIAM M., b. Md., Jan. 1900, living 1900.

17. LEWIS BARLOW, b. Md., Dec. 1845, in 1900 living in Howard Co., Md., m. 1886, ELIZABETH ———, b. Md., July 1849, living in 1900.

Issue, if any, unknown.

18. FRANK WORK BARLOW, carpenter, b. Md., 27 Feb. 1852, in 1900 living in Baltimore Co., Md., m. [ca. 1883], CLARA ———, b. Md., May 1867, living in 1900.

Known issue (surname BARLOW):

a. ROSELA, seamstress, b. Md., June 1884, living 1900.
b. FRANK, b. Md., Feb. 1888, living 1900.

c. Annie, b. Md., Apr. 1889, living 1900.
d. Clara, b. Md., Feb. 1892, living 1900.
e. Louisa, b. Md., Apr. 1896, living 1900.
f. Gladys, b. Md., Feb. 1900, living 1900.

19. William F. Barlow, upholsterer, b. Md. [1843], in 1880 living at 172 Gay St., Baltimore, Md., m. Mellissa ———, b. Md. [1850], living in 1880.

Known issue (surname Barlow):

a. Edna, b. Md. [1875], living in 1880.
b. William F., b. Md. [1876], living in 1880.
c. Milton, b. Md. [1877], living in 1880.

20. Joseph M. Barlow, upholsterer, b. Md., March 1845, in 1900 living at 600 Brune St., Baltimore, Md., m. 1867, Catherine ——— (Kate), b. Md., May 1848, living in 1900.

Known issue (surname Barlow):

27. a. William F., b. Md., Aug. 1869, living in 1900.
28. b. Kate, b. Md. [1871], living in 1900.
29. c. Lillie M., b. Md. [1876], living in 1900.
d. Honor, straw hat maker, b. Md., Aug. 1880, living in 1900.
e. Ella G., stenographer, b. Md., Dec. 1882, living in 1900.

21. Walter H. Boude, clerk of the Circuit Court of Summers Co., W. Va., b. W. Va., 23 Sept. 1860, in 1910 living in Hinton, W. Va., m. 25 Oct. 1894, Cynthia Alice Ford, b. W. Va., Jan. 1869, living in 1910, dau. of William Harrison Ford and of Cynthia ———.

Issue (surname Boude):

a. Daisy Nickell, b. W. Va., March 1896, living in 1910.
b. Clinton Ford, b. 1901, living in 1910.
c. Mary Lee, b. 1904, living in 1910.

22. ——— Boude (dau.), living in 1896, m. A. T. Crawford, son of Thomas Crawford.

Issue, if any, unknown.

23. Mary E. Boude, b. W. Va., Nov. 1866, in 1900 living in Summers Co., W. Va., m. [1885], James W. Farrell, b. W. Va., May 1858, living in 1900, son of D. K. Farrell and of Celia A. Meader.

Issue (surname Farrell):

a. Eda C., b. W. Va., Feb. 1886, living in 1900.
b. David K., b. W. Va., Oct. 1887, living in 1900.

c. Ora L., b. W. Va., Apr. 1890, living in 1900.
d. Celia A., b. W. Va., Feb. 1892, living in 1900.
e. Roy M., b. W. Va., March 1895 (triplet), living in 1900.
f. Ruby M., b. W. Va., March 1895 (triplet), living in 1900.
g. Erastus P., b. W. Va., March 1895 (triplet), living in 1900.

24. Rev. Charles S. Stanton, b. Va., May 1864, in 1910 living in Jefferson Co., W. Va., m. 1884, Victoria E. ———, b. Va., Feb. 1865, living in 1910.

Issue (surname Stanton [order uncertain]):

a. Carleton C., b. Md., Sept. 1891, living in 1910.
b. Louise, b. Md., Sept. 1896, living in 1910.
c. Christine, b. Va., July 1898, living in 1910.
d. [child], d. before 1900.
e. [child], d. before 1900.

25. James C. Stanton, lime kiln foreman, b. Va., March 1886, in 1910 living in Shenandoah Co., Va., m. 1891, Ida E. ———, b. Va., March 1871, living in 1910.

Known issue (surname Stanton):

a. Charles W., cooper, b. Va., Dec. 1892, living in 1910.
b. Edna M., b. Va., Nov. 1897, living in 1910.
c. [child], d. before 1900.
d. [child], d. before 1900.
e. [child], d. before 1900.
f. Melvin, b. Va., 1902, living in 1910.
g. Madaline, b. Va., 1906, living in 1910.
h. Marguerite, b. Va., Feb. 1909, living in 1910.

26. Edgar A. K. Stanton, preacher, b. Va., Apr. 1871, in 1900 living in Greene Co., Va., m. 1897, Florence ———, b. Va., Apr. 1874, living in 1900.

Issue, if any, unknown.

27. William F. Barlow, upholsterer, b. Md., Aug. 1869, in 1900 living at 600 Brune St., Baltimore, Md., m. 1894, Mary A. ———, b. Md., June 1873, living in 1900.

Issue, if any, unknown.

28. Kate Barlow, b. Md. [1871], living in 1900, m. [before 1900], ———.

Issue, if any, unknown.

29. Lillie M. Barlow, b. Md. [1876], living in 1900, m. [before 1900], ———.

Issue, if any, unknown.

VI

Descendants of George Wood and of Elizabeth Conner

1. GEORGE WOOD, b. ———, d. ———, Ky., 23 Aug. 1802, son of ——— Wood and of ———, m. [ca. 1784], ELIZABETH CONNER, midwife in Sheperdstown, [W.] Va., b. ——— 1766, d. Franklin Co., Ohio, 13 Aug. 1818, dau. of ——— Conner and of ———.

Issue (surname WOOD):

2. a. JOHN, b. [Sheperdstown, W.?] Va., 29 July 1785, d. Chillicothe, Ohio, 29 Jan. 1848.
3. b. THOMAS, b. [Sheperdstown, W. Va.?], 1788, d. Franklin Co., Ohio, 1834.
4. c. CHARLES CONNER, b. [Sheperdstown, W. Va.?], 1790, d. Franklin Co., Ohio, 1838.
d. GEORGE, porkpacker, b. [Sheperdstown, W.?] Va., 7 March 1793, d. Chillicothe, Ohio, 14 Jan. 1861.
e. WILLIAM, b. [Sheperdstown, W. Va.?], 1796, d. ———.
5. f. SUSANNAH JAMES, b. Ky., 9 July 1798, d. 7 July 1872.
g. ANNA MARIA, b. Ky., 9 Dec. 1800, d. [young].

2. JOHN WOOD, porkpacker, councilman, b. [Sheperdstown, W.?] Va., 29 July 1785, d. Chillicothe, Ohio, 29 Jan. 1848, m. Chillicothe, Ohio, 13 March 1823, ELEANOR STRONG (see Part VII, number 3, below), b. Philadelphia, Pa. [1802/3], d. New York, N.Y., 9 July 1863, dau. of Joseph Strong and of Rebecca Young.

Issue: See Part III, above.

3. THOMAS WOOD, scout, spy, soldier, b. [Sheperdstown, W. Va.?], 1788, d. Franklin Co., Ohio, 1834, m. ELIZABETH RAMSEY, d. [before 1840].

Issue (surname WOOD):

6. a. SUSAN, d. [by 1892].
7. b. MARY, d. [by 1892].
8. c. GEORGE, Jr., b. Franklin Co., Ohio, 14 Dec. 1823, d. [1904?].
d. LEWIS C., in 1892 living in Colorado.
e. MARQUIS, d. [by 1892].

4. CHARLES CONNER WOOD, b. [Sheperdstown, W. Va.?], 1790, d. Franklin Co., Ohio, 1838, m. ———.

Issue, if any, unknown.

5. SUSANNAH JAMES WOOD, b. Ky., 9 July 1798, d. 7 July 1872, m. Ross Co., Ohio, 11 March 1819, THOMAS HOFFMAN, b. [Ky.?].

Issue (surname HOFFMAN):

9. a. ELIZABETH, b. Ohio, 27 July 1820, living 1877.
10. b. GEORGE WOOD, b. Chillicothe, Ohio, 7 Feb. 1823, d. Circleville, Ohio, 25 July 1864.

6. SUSAN WOOD, d. [by 1892], m. ——— WELTON.

Details of issue unknown (one son).

7. MARY WOOD, d. [by 1892], m. (1) ——— HALL; m. (2) ——— EDWARDS.

Details of issue unknown (six children).

8. GEORGE WOOD, Jr., b. Franklin Co., Ohio, 14 Dec. 1823, d. [1904?], m. Ross Co., Ohio, 8 Apr. 1852, HANNAH ELIZA INGHAM, b. Ohio, 1821, dau. of Hezekiah Ingham.

Issue (surname WOOD):

11. a. WILLIAM INGHAM, b. near Williamsport, Ohio, 7 Feb. 1853, d. [Pickaway Co., Ohio?], [fall] 1917.
b. CHARLES, b. Ohio, 15 June 1854, d. 12 Aug. 1861.
c. JOHN, b. Ohio, 18 Feb. 1857, d. 13 Aug. 1861.
12. d. NELLIE JUSTICE, b. Ohio, 18 June 1859, d. 29 March 1891.
13. e. MARY M., b. 12 Dec. 1861, d. 1935.
f. MARIA, b. 12 Apr. 1864, d. 26 March 1865.

9. ELIZABETH HOFFMAN, b. Ohio, 27 July 1820, in 1877 living in Chillicothe, Ohio, m. (1) 13 Nov. 1845, ABRAM JAMES, b. Ohio, 19 Apr. 1820, d. 27 Sept. 1861, son of Thomas James; m. (2) Ross Co., Ohio, 6 Nov. 1862, EDWIN N. CREEL, b. 9 May 1817, d. 26 June 1872, son of David Creel and of Elizabeth Neale.

Issue by first husband (surname JAMES):

14. a. SUSIE WOOD, b. Ohio, 31 Dec. 1848, d. 28 Oct. 1888.
15. b. LEMUEL BROWN, b. Ross Co., Ohio, 26 March 1851, d. Chicago, Ill., 9 Jan. 1918.

10. GEORGE WOOD HOFFMAN, b. Chillicothe, Ohio, 7 Feb. 1823, d. Circleville, Ohio, 25 July 1864, m. Ross Co., Ohio, 31 Aug. 1854, SARAH JANE CROUSE (Sallie), b. Ross Co., Ohio, Feb. 1830, in 1900 living in Pickaway Co., Ohio, dau. of David Crouse and of Elizabeth Boggs.

Issue (surname HOFFMAN):

a. WOOD, b. Ohio, 1856, in 1892 living in Chicago, Ill.
b. CROUSE, b. Ohio, July 1857, in 1900 living in Pickaway Co., Ohio.
16. c. GEORGIA, b. Ohio, May 1859, living in 1918.

11. WILLIAM INGHAM WOOD, b. near Williamsport, Ohio, 7 Feb. 1853, d. [Pickaway Co., Ohio?], [fall] 1917, m. 6 June 1906, as her second husband, MARTHA A., b. Ohio, 1867, d. [by 1943], [she had m. (1) ——— Hulse].

Issue of wife's first husband (surname HULSE):

a. ISIAH SMITH, b. Ohio, 1897, living in 1943.

12. NELLIE JUSTICE WOOD, b. Ohio, 18 June 1859, d. 29 March 1891, m. 1 May 1890, FRANK GARDINER THOMPSON.

Issue (surname THOMPSON):

a. GEORGE WOOD, b. 26 Feb. 1891, d. 29 March 1891.

13. MARY M. WOOD, b. 12 Dec. 1861, d. 1935, m. 26 Apr. 1906, as his second wife, JOSEPH A. SCHOEDINGER, b. 1870, d. 1932 [he had m. (1) ———, d. (before 1906)].

Issue of husband's first wife (surname SCHOEDINGER):

a. PAUL S., professor, U.N.H. at Durham, b. 1899, on 6 Sept. 1943 living at the University Club, Delaware, N.Y.

14. SUSIE WOOD JAMES, b. Ohio, 31 Dec. 1848, d. 28 Oct. 1888, m. Ross Co., Ohio, 12 Nov. 1868, Maj. CHARLES TAYLOE MASON, C.S.A., b. Fredericksburg, Va., 7 May 1832, d. Chillicothe, Ohio, 11 Dec. 1918, son of Charles Mason and Anna Tayloe Braxton.

No issue.

15. LEMUEL BROWN JAMES, b. Ross Co., Ohio, 26 March 1851, d. Chicago, Ill., 9 Jan. 1918, m. 1904, as her second husband, GEORGIA HOFFMAN [number 16, below], b. Ohio, May 1859, living in 1918 [she had m. (1) (by 1892), William C. Tompkins, d. (New York, N.Y.), (before 1900)], dau. of George Wood Hoffman and of Sarah Jane Crouse.

No issue.

16. GEORGIA HOFFMAN, b. Ohio, May 1859, living in 1918, m. (1) [by 1892], WILLIAM C. TOMPKINS, lithographer, d. [New York, N.Y.?] [before 1900]; m. (2) 1904, LEMUEL BROWN JAMES [number 15, above], b. Ross Co., Ohio, 26 March 1851, d. Chicago, Ill., 9 Jan. 1918, son of Abram James and of Elizabeth Hoffman.

No issue.

VII

Descendants of Joseph Strong and of Rebecca Young

1. JOSEPH STRONG, physician (see chapter 1, above), b. South Coventry, Conn., 10 March 1770, d. Philadelphia, Pa., 24 Apr. 1812, m. Philadelphia, Pa., 8 Sept. 1796, as her first husband, REBECCA YOUNG (see Part VIII, number 2, below), b. Philadelphia, Pa., 5 May 1779, d. Piqua, Ohio, 8 June 1862 [she m. (2) Peter Gardiner], dau. of Capt. Peter Young, mariner, and of Eleanor ———.

Issue (surname STRONG):

2. a. LUCY, b. Philadelphia, Pa., 17 Sept. 1797, d. Cincinnati, Ohio, 27 Aug. 1860.
b. JOSEPH, Jr., professor at Maryland Military Academy, b. Philadelphia, Pa., 26 June 1799, d. Baltimore, Md., 1857.
c. PETER YOUNG, U.S.N., b. Philadelphia, Pa., 28 Apr. 1801, living 30 Apr. 1817.
3. d. ELEANOR, b. Philadelphia, Pa. [1802/3], d. New York, N.Y., 9 July 1863.
e. WILLIAM, b. Philadelphia, Pa., 12 Dec. 1804, d. Philadelphia, Pa., 8 Sept. 1805.
4. f. WILLIAM YOUNG, b. Philadelphia, Pa., 26 June 1806, d. Terre Haute, Ind., 23 March 1866.
5. g. REBECCA, b. Philadelphia, Pa., 25 Sept. 1808, living 1870.
h. LAVINIA, b. Philadelphia, Pa., 19 Aug. 1810, d. [bur. Philadelphia, Pa., 12 March 1812].

2. LUCY STRONG, b. Philadelphia, Pa., 17 Sept. 1797, d. Cincinnati, Ohio, 27 Aug. 1860, m. Col. WILLIAM KEY BOND, judge, congressman, b. St. Mary's Co., Md., 2 Oct. 1792, d. Cincinnati, Ohio, 17 Feb. 1864.

Issue (surname BOND):

6. a. CECILIA, d. [1881–1905].
7. b. ELEANOR JONES, bapt. Chillicothe, Ohio, 27 July 1823, d. New York, N.Y., 13 Jan. 1856.
8. c. LUCY, bapt. Chillicothe, Ohio, 1828, d. New York, N.Y., 13 Dec. 1906.
9. d. JOSEPHINE, bapt. Chillicothe, Ohio, 22 July 1832, d. New York, N.Y., 5 Apr. 1911.
10. e. SUSAN KEY, bapt. Chillicothe, Ohio, 14 May 1837, d. New York, N.Y., 23 March 1910.

3. ELEANOR STRONG, b. Philadelphia, Pa. [1802/3], d. New York, N.Y., 9 July 1863, m. Chillicothe, Ohio, 13 March 1823, JOHN WOOD, porkpacker, councilman (see Part VI, number 2, above), b. [Sheperdstown, W.?] Va., 29 July 1785, d. Chillicothe, Ohio, 29 Jan. 1848, son of George Wood and of Elizabeth Conner.

Issue: See Part III, above.

4. WILLIAM YOUNG STRONG, b. Philadelphia, Pa., 26 June 1806, d. Terre Haute, Ind., 23 March 1866, m. Jefferson Co., Ky., 3 Feb. 1835, ANNIE MASSIE, b. Ohio, 10 Aug. 1809, d. Piqua, Ohio, 17 Aug. 1860, dau. of Gen. Nathaniel Massie and of Susan Everard Meade.

Issue (surname STRONG):

11. a. WILLIAM EVERARD, b. Chillicothe, Ohio, 11 Aug. 1836, d. New York, N.Y., 14 May 1905.
12. b. JOSEPH, b. Chillicothe, Ohio, 25 June 1839, d. 10 Jan. 1929.

5. REBECCA STRONG, b. Philadelphia, Pa., 25 Sept. 1808, in 1870 living in Memphis, Tenn., m. Chillicothe, Ohio, 30 Oct. 1834, OLIVER HAZARD PERRY ANDERSON, Sr., b. Frankfort, Ky., 1813, d. [ca. 1850], son of Reuben Anderson and of Sarah Runyon.

Issue (surname ANDERSON):

a. WILLIAM STRONG.
13. b. CHARLES LOCKWOOD, b. Ky., 1838, d. [1878/9].
c. OLIVER HAZARD PERRY, Jr., Lt., C.S.A.

6. CECILIA BOND, d. [1881–1905], m. as his second wife, HENRY STANBERY, Attorney General of the U.S., b. New York, N.Y., 20 Feb. 1803, d. New York, N.Y., 26 June 1881 [he had m. (1) Frances E. Beecher, d. 1840], son of Jonas Stanbery, M.D., and of Ann Lucy Seaman.

No issue.

7. ELEANOR JONES BOND, bapt. Chillicothe, Ohio, 27 July 1823, d. New York, N.Y., 13 Jan. 1856, m. 12 Oct. 1852, as his first wife, JOHN AUGUSTUS ROBINSON, merchant, b. Westboro, Mass., 12 Aug. 1802, d. New York, N.Y., 14 July 1872 [he later m. (2) Cincinnati, Ohio, 2 June 1858, Lucy Bond (number 8, below), bapt. Chillicothe, Ohio, 1828, d. New York, N.Y., 13 Dec. 1906], son of John Robinson and of Abigail Drury.

Issue (surname ROBINSON):

a. LUCY BOND, b. Paris 26 June 1853, d. New York, N.Y., 4 March 1854.
b. JOHN AUGUSTUS, Jr., b. New York, N.Y., 19 Sept. 1854, d. New York, N.Y., 24 Jan. 1856.
14. c. ELLEN BOND, b. New York, N.Y., 5 Jan. 1856, d. Pau, Basses-Pyrenees, 5 Dec. 1908.

8. LUCY BOND, bapt. Chillicothe, Ohio, 1828, d. New York, N.Y., 13 Dec. 1906, m. Cincinnati, Ohio, 2 June 1858, as his second wife, JOHN AUGUSTUS ROBINSON, merchant, b. Westboro, Mass., 12 Aug. 1802, d. New York, N.Y., 14 July 1872 [he had m. (1) 12 Oct. 1852, Eleanor Jones Bond (number 7, above), bapt. Chillicothe, Ohio, 27 July 1823, d. New York, N.Y., 13 Jan. 1856], son of John Robinson and of Abigail Drury.

No issue.

9. JOSEPHINE BOND, bapt. Chillicothe, Ohio, 22 July 1832, d. New York, N.Y., 5 Apr. 1911, m. 19 Jan. 1869, as his third wife, Rev. JARED BRADLEY FLAGG, painter, b. New Haven, Conn., 16 June 1820, d. New York, N.Y., 25 Sept. 1899 [he had m. (1) Hartford, Conn., 30 Dec. 1841, Sarah Robbins Montague, b. Mansfield, Conn., 21 July 1823, d. Hartford, Conn., 25 Jan. 1844, and had m. (2) Hartford, Conn., 1 Dec. 1846, Louisa Hart, b. New Britain, Conn., 5 Oct. 1828, d. New Haven, Conn., 18 Jan. 1867], son of Henry Collins Flagg and of Martha Whiting.

No issue.

10. SUSAN KEY BOND, bapt. Chillicothe, Ohio, 14 May 1837, d. New York, N.Y., 23 March 1910, m. Cincinnati, Ohio, 23 Dec. 1858, NATHANIEL WHITTIER EMERSON, cotton broker, b. Cincinnati, Ohio, Dec. 1828, d. New York, N.Y., 24 Jan. 1912, son of Henry Emerson and of Evelina Benbridge.

Issue (surname EMERSON):

15. a. WILLIAM KEY BOND, b. Ohio, Dec. 1860, d. Munich 13 Nov. 1932.
b. HENRY, d. [between 1871 and 1900].
c. JOSEPH ROBINSON, d. 1867.

11. WILLIAM EVERARD STRONG, stockbroker, b. Chillicothe, Ohio, 11 Aug. 1836, d. New York, N.Y., 14 May 1905, m. 1873, ALICE CORBIN SMITH, b. Alexandria, Va., 15 June 1848, d. New York, N.Y., 26 Nov. 1939, dau. of Francis Lee Smith and of Sarah Gosnell Vowell.

Issue (surname STRONG):

a. FRANCIS, b. N.J. [age 6 in 1880], d. [1880–1900].
16. b. ANNE MASSIE, b. N.Y., Nov. 1874, d. Lakewood, N.J., 12 Apr. 1915.
17. c. ALICE EVERARD, b. New York, N.Y., 15 Sept. 1876, d. Southampton, N.Y., 1 Aug. 1944.

12. JOSEPH STRONG, grocer, b. Chillicothe, Ohio, 25 June 1839, d. 10 Jan. 1929, m. 3 Dec. 1866, MARY BOURNE BLAKE, b. Terre Haute, Ind., June 1842, d. [after 1900], dau. of Richard Blake.

Issue (surname STRONG):

18. a. ANNIE MASSIE, b. Ind., 19 Oct. 1867.
19. b. RICHARD B., b. Ind., Nov. 1870, d. [by 1937].
20. c. HENRIETTA D., b. Ind., Feb. 1873, living 1956.
d. WILLIAM, b. Ind., 1876, d. [between 1880 and 1900].
21. e. FRANCESKA G., b. Terre Haute, Ind., Nov. 1877, living 1908.
22. f. SUSAN MEADE, b. Ind., Jan. 1879, living 1966.
23. g. ELIZABETH A. B., b. Ind., Jan. 1880, living 1961.

13. CHARLES LOCKWOOD ANDERSON, b. Ky., 1838, d. [1878/9], m. 1859, HARRIET WALLACE HOWORTH, b. Ky., March 1838, d. 1908, dau. of George Milburn Howorth and of Harriet W. Graham.

Issue (surname ANDERSON):

24. a. MARY, b. Memphis, Tenn., Nov. 1859, living in 1939.
b. GERTRUDE, b. Ky., March 1863, living in 1940.
25. c. ELISA, b. Germantown, Tenn., Apr. 1875, living in 1900.

14. ELLEN BOND ROBINSON, b. New York, N.Y., 5 Jan. 1856, d. Pau, Basses-Pyrenees, 5 Dec. 1908, m. New York, N.Y., 25 Apr. 1876, WILLIAM FORBES MORGAN, attorney, b. Selma, Ala., 1841, d. Mayfair, London, 14 Dec. 1916.

Issue (surname MORGAN):

26. a. ETHEL, b. New York, N.Y., 30 Apr. 1877, d. Biarritz, 29 May 1953.
27. b. LUCY BOND, b. New York, N.Y., 5 Aug. 1878.
28. c. WILLIAM FORBES, Jr., b. New York, N.Y., 22 Sept. 1879, d. Columbus, Ohio, 20 Apr. 1937.
29. d. HAROLD, b. 1 Oct. 1884, d. [Honolulu, Hawaii?].

15. WILLIAM KEY BOND EMERSON, b. Ohio, Dec. 1860, d. Munich, 13 Nov. 1932, m. 1893, MARIA HOLMES FURMAN, b. Westchester, N.Y., June 1869, d. New York, N.Y., 17 May 1943, dau. of John M. Furman and of Virginia D. Holmes.

Issue (surname EMERSON):

a. WILLIAM KEY BOND, Jr., b. New York, N.Y., 9 Apr. 1894, slain near Toul, Meurthe-et-Moselle, 14 May 1918.
30. b. RUPERT, b. Rye, N.Y., 20 Aug. 1899, d. Cambridge, Mass., 9 Feb. 1979.

16. ANNE MASSIE STRONG, b. N.Y., Nov. 1874, d. Lakewood, N.J., 12 Apr. 1915, m. New York, N.Y., 8 Oct. 1902, as his first wife, MORETON FOLEY GAGE, b. 12 Jan. 1873, d. 6 July 1953 [he later m. (2) Paris 30 Sept. 1916, Frances Lippitt, d. 14 June 1955], son of Hon. Edward Thomas Gage and of Ella Henrietta Maxse.

Issue (surname GAGE):

31. a. BERKELEY EVERARD FOLEY, b. 27 Feb. 1904.
32. b. EDWARD FITZHARDINGE PEYTON, b. London 3 July 1906.

17. ALICE EVERARD STRONG, b. New York, N.Y., 15 Sept. 1876, d. Southampton, N.Y., 1 Aug. 1944, m. Saranac Lake, N.Y., 10 Oct. 1911, CHARLES TIFFANY RICHARDSON (Tiffany), stockbroker, b. New York, N.Y., 12 May 1880, d. New York, N.Y., 31 July 1967, son of William A. Richardson and of Sarah Matilda Anderson.

Issue (surname RICHARDSON):

33. a. WILLIAM EVERARD, b. New York, N.Y., 14 Nov. 1912.
34. b. ANNE SCHUYLER, b. 20 Nov. 1914.
35. c. CHARLES TIFFANY, Jr., b. 15 March 1917.

18. ANNIE MASSIE STRONG, b. Ind., 19 Oct. 1867, m. 20 Oct. 1891, BENJAMIN MCKEEN, railway official, b. Terre Haute, Ind., 23 June 1864, d. Dec. 1947, son of William Riley McKeen and of Ann Crawford.

Issue (surname MCKEEN):

a. MARY JOSEPHINE, b. Ind., Jan. 1900.

19. RICHARD B. STRONG, b. Ind., Nov. 1870, d. [by 1937], m. 1895, CATHERINE CARLTON, b. Ind., July 1872, in 1958 living in Terre Haute, Ind., dau. of Ambrose Carlton and of Mary R. ———.

Issue, if any, unknown.

20. HENRIETTA D. STRONG, b. Ind., Feb. 1873, in 1956 living in Terre Haute, Ind., m. [1896/7], SAMUEL CRAWFORD MCKEEN, banker, b. Ind., Dec. 1862, d. [by 1937].

Known issue (surname MCKEEN):

36. a. WILLIAM R., b. Ind., July 1897.
b. JOSEPH S., b. Ind., May 1899, in 1931 living in Annendale, Ind.

21. FRANCESKA G. STRONG, b. Terre Haute, Ind., Nov. 1877, in 1908 living in Haverhill, Mass., m. [after 1900], GRANT H. FAIRBANKS, b. Joplin, Mo., living in 1908.

Known issue (surname FAIRBANKS):

a. WILLIAM CRAWFORD, b. Haverhill, Mass., 5 Aug. 1903.
b. PAULINE, b. Haverhill, Mass., 29 Nov. 1908.

22. SUSAN MEADE STRONG, b. Ind., Jan. 1879, in 1966 living in Terre Haute, Ind., m. Terre Haute, Ind., 12 June 1907, JAMES ATHENIAN COOPER, Jr., attorney, b. New Harmony, Ind., 27 Dec. 1874, d. Terre Haute, Ind., 12 Nov. 1931, son of James Athenian Cooper and of Emma Williams Stewart.

Issue (surname COOPER):

a. STEWART BLAKE.
b. DAVID MEADE.

23. ELIZABETH A. B. STRONG, b. Ind., Jan. 1880, in 1961 living in Terre Haute, Ind., m. [after 1900], JOHN L. CRAWFORD, d. [by 1922].

Issue, if any, unknown.

24. MARY ANDERSON, b. Memphis, Tenn., Nov. 1859, living in 1939, m. 1881, EDWARD TIPTON BARR, b. Ind., Nov. 1855, living in 1939, son of Thomas Barr and of Martha McC. Tipton.

Issue (surname BARR):

37. a. LOCKWOOD ANDERSON, b. Bowling Green, Ky., 2 Apr. 1883, d. [1968?].
38. b. E. WALLACE, b. Ky., March 1887, d. 1962.
39. c. CORINNE MCCREARY, b. Bowling Green, Ky., 5 May 1890, d. Baton Rouge, La., Nov. 1964.

25. ELISA ANDERSON, b. Germantown, Tenn., Apr. 1875, in 1900 living in Louisville, Ky., m. 1896, CLEMENS GREY HEWETT, b. Ky., Dec. 1870, living in 1900.

Issue (surname HEWITT):

a. PERRY A., b. Ky., May 1897.

26. ETHEL MORGAN, b. New York, N.Y., 30 Apr. 1877, d. Biarritz 27 May 1953, m. (1) London 12 Oct. 1899, div. Feb. 1913, WILFRED CONSTANTINE CHAPMAN, b. [26 Dec. 1874?], d. Paris 17 Apr. 1931, son of Frederick Barclay Chapman and of Augusta Marion Miller-Mundy; m. (2) 1915, FERNANDO DE SORIANO, d. 1979, son of ——— de Soriano, Marques de Ivanrey.

Issue by first husband (surname CHAPMAN):

40. a. BRIDGET MURIEL, b. Pau, Basses-Pyrenees, 20 May 1902.

27. LUCY BOND MORGAN, b. New York, N.Y., 5 Aug. 1878, d. ———, m. (1) Pau, Basses-Pyrenees, 6 Sept. 1900, div., as his first wife, HENRY MARION WARD, attorney, b. 1870, d. Washington, D.C., 7 Feb. 1949 [he later m. (2) Gloucester, Mass., 30 Aug. 1913, Rhoda Olive Nicholls], son of Charles Henry Ward and of Mary Montague Parmly; m. (2) ——— MILLER.

Issue: (a) by first husband (surname WARD):

41. a. HENRY MORGAN, b. 1902, d. Duarte, Cal., 26 June 1963.
42. b. SAMUEL, b. 28 March 1905, d. 7 July 1982.

(b) by second husband (surname MILLER):

43. c. ROBERT RUSH, b. Colorado Springs, Col., 23 Apr. 1916.
d. MALCOLM.

28. WILLIAM FORBES MORGAN, Jr., Secretary of the Democratic National Committee, b. New York, N.Y., 22 Sept. 1879, d. Columbus, Ohio, 20 Apr. 1937, m. (1) 19 Feb. 1904, EDITH LIVINGSTON HALL, b. 26 Sept. 1873, d. New York, N.Y., 4 Feb. 1920, dau. of Valentine Gill Hall and of Mary Livingston Ludlow; m. (2) Washington, D.C., 5 Sept. 1933, as her second husband, SARAH BRANCH JACKSON, b. 1910 [she had m. (1) Boston, Mass., 30 May 1930, div. 1932, John Clark Coonley, b. Riverside, Ill., 24 Sept. 1904, d. (1960s), and later m. (3) Baltimore, Md., 14 Dec. 1942, M. Dorland Doyle, b. Chicago, Ill., 1899, d. New York, N.Y., 6 Feb. 1977], dau. of Robert Jackson and of Dorothy Branch.

Issue by first wife (surname MORGAN):

a. BARBARA, b. 1905, d. New York, N.Y., 4 Feb. 1920.
44. b. WILLIAM FORBES III, b. 3 July 1907, d. at sea [Pacific Ocean] 8 Oct. 1945.
c. ELLEN, b. 25 Aug. 1909, d. New York, N.Y., 4 Feb. 1920.

29. HAROLD MORGAN, b. 1 Oct. 1884, d. [Honolulu, Hawaii?], m. ———.

No issue.

30. RUPERT EMERSON, professor, b. Rye, N.Y., 20 Aug. 1899, d. Cambridge, Mass., 9 Feb. 1979, m. London 14 Sept. 1925, ALLA JULIEVNA GROSJEAN, dau. of Jules Grosjean.

Issue (surname EMERSON):

45. a. WILLIAM KEY BOND III, b. Port Chester, N.Y., 20 May 1927.

46. b. NINA ULE.
47. c. NATASHA MARIA.
48. d. RUPERT ALLAN.

31. BERKELEY EVERARD FOLEY GAGE, from 1955, Sir Berkeley Gage, K.C.M.G., b. 27 Feb. 1904, m. (1) London 15 Jan. 1931, div. 1954, as her first husband, HEDWIG GERTRUD EVA MARIA VON CHAPPUIS, recognized as Kniazhna Romanovskaya, b. Habelschwerdt, Germany, 6 Dec. 1905 [she later m. (2) London 19 Nov. 1954, E. V. Kniazh Rostislav Aleksandrovich, Kniazh Rossiiski, b. Aitodor, Crimea, 11/24 Nov. 1902, d. Cannes 30 July 1978], dau. of Karl von Chappuis and of Gertrud, Freiin von Richthofen; m. (2) 4 Oct. 1954, as her second husband, LILLIAN VUKMIROVICH [she had m. (1), div., ——— Riggs-Miller], dau. of Vladimir Vukmirovich.

Issue by first wife (surname GAGE):

49. a. ANTHONY ST. CLERE BERKELEY, b. 9 Nov. 1931.
50. b. ULICK CHARLES CHRISTOPHER, b. 7 Jan. 1938.

32. EDWARD FITZHARDINGE PEYTON GAGE, b. London 3 July 1906, m. London 21 Jan. 1931, THALIA WESTCOTT MILLETT, b. Irvington, N.Y., 9 Feb. 1906, dau. of Stephen Caldwell Millett and of Thalia Westcott.

Issue (surname GAGE):

51. a. ANNE CAROLINE THALIA, b. London 25 Nov. 1931.
52. b. ROBERT WESTCOTT MORETON, b. London 19 Apr. 1934.
53. c. ELIZABETH ESTLING, b. London 31 Dec. 1937.

33. WILLIAM EVERARD RICHARDSON, b. New York, N.Y., 14 Nov. 1912, m. (1) Brookline, Mass., 27 June 1936, div., as her first husband, HELEN S. WATERS, d. 1973 [she later m. (2) New York, N.Y., 27 May 1939, John Elting, and later m. (3) 1951, Duncan Steuart Ellsworth, b. Watkins, N.Y., 23 Nov. 1898, d. Salisbury, Conn., 3 Dec. 1967], dau. of Bertram G. Waters and of Helen K. Shaw; m. (2) Alexandria, Va. [by 1939], div., CLARA AUGEROT (Bonnie), b. the Bronx, N.Y., 29 May 1912, d. Harrison, N.Y., 15 March 1960, dau. of Peter William Augerot and of Clara Falkman; m. (3) Stamford, Conn., 30 Apr. 1949, div., as her first husband, MARY LYONS (Gibbie), b. Washington, D.C., 12 Aug. 1925 [she later m. (2) Stamford, Conn., 21 July 1973, John Francis Moynahan, b. Boston, Mass., 11 Apr. 1912], dau. of Gibbs Lyons and of Anna Mary Powers; m. (4) San Juan, P.R., 25 Oct. 1958, MARGARET ELINOR THOMAS, b. Warren, Ohio, 24 Sept. 1925, dau. of Carl Farnsworth Thomas and of Elinor Hull.

Issue: (a) by second wife (surname RICHARDSON):

54. a. WILLIAM TIFFANY, b. New York, N.Y., 15 Dec. 1939.
b. PAMELA CLARE, b. New York, N.Y., 13 Nov. 1941.

(b) by third wife (surname RICHARDSON):

c. KENT LYONS, b. Stamford, Conn., 7 Jan. 1955.

(c) by fourth wife (surname RICHARDSON):

d. ALICE ELINOR, b. Greenwich, Conn., 10 Apr. 1961.
e. ELIZABETH ANNE, b. Greenwich, Conn., 27 Sept. 1962.
f. CHARLES THOMAS, b. Greenwich, Conn., 18 Oct. 1963.

34. ANNE SCHUYLER RICHARDSON, b. 20 Nov. 1914, m. New York, N.Y., 12 Feb. 1945, MORIS T. HOVERSTEN, son of Albert Hoversten.

Issue (surname HOVERSTEN):

55. a. PHILIP.
b. BARBARA.
c. PETER.
d. NANCY.

35. CHARLES TIFFANY RICHARDSON, Jr. (Tiffany), b. 15 March 1917, m. Washington, D.C., 10 June 1950, div. 1962, ELLEN B. COSTELLO, d. 1964, dau. of Henry Nicholas Costello and of Rosemary Mason.

Issue (surname RICHARDSON):

a. SCHUYLER MASON, b. 1950.

Ward (surname SANTOS):

b. AMADO, b. Panama, 15 Sept. 1957.

36. WILLIAM R. MCKEEN, banker, b. Ind., July 1897, d. ———, m. [by 1931], HENRIETTA G. ———.

No issue.

37. LOCKWOOD ANDERSON BARR, publicist, b. Bowling Green, Ky., 2 Apr. 1883, d. [1968?], m. Kansas City, Kansas, 9 Oct. 1912, BERNICE OWENS, b. St. Louis Mo., 12 Feb. 1885, d. ———, dau. of William Thomas Owens and of Florence Chappell.

Issue (surname BARR):

56. a. LOCKWOOD CHAPPELL, b. Brooklyn, N.Y., 3 March 1914, d. Rowayton, Conn., 25 June 1951.
57. b. WILLIAM EDWARD, b. Brooklyn, N.Y., 10 July 1915.

38. E. WALLACE BARR (Wallace), b. Ky., March 1887, d. 1962, m. ———.

Issue (surname BARR):

a. E. WALLACE, JR.
b. ROBERT MOSELEY.

39. CORINNE MCCREARY BARR, b. Bowling Green, Ky., 5 May 1890, d. Baton Rouge, La., Nov. 1964, m. Bowling Green, Ky., 12 Jan. 1918, JOHN EARLE UHLER, professor, b. Media, Pa., 20 June 1891, d. Baton Rouge, La., Nov. 1962, son of William Jackson Uhler and of Anne Wittig.

Issue (surname UHLER):

58. a. JOHN EARLE, Jr., b. Baltimore, Md., 12 Nov. 1918, d. Plaquemine, La., July 1969.
59. b. MILBURN EDWARD BARR, b. Baltimore, Md., 3 Nov. 1922.

40. BRIDGET MURIEL CHAPMAN, b. Pau, Basses-Pyrenees, 20 May 1902, m. London 14 Nov. 1935, COLERIDGE EUSTACE HILLS, b. 3 Aug. 1912, d. 17 Dec. 1941, son of Eustace Gilbert Hills and of Hon. Nina Louisa Shuttleworth.

No issue.

41. HENRY MORGAN WARD (Morgan), professor, b. 1902, d. Duarte, Cal., 26 June 1963, m. as her first husband, SIGRID ——— [she later m. (2) Harry C. Hart].

Issue (surname WARD [order unknown]):

60. a. (dau.).
61. b. ERIC B.
c. RICHARD.
62. d. SAMUEL, b. Los Angeles, Cal., 29 Sept. 1944.

42. SAMUEL WARD, bookdealer, b. 28 March 1905, d. 7 July 1982, m. (1) ———; m. (2) 1974, LUCY ———.

No issue.

43. ROBERT RUSH MILLER, b. Colorado Springs, Col., 23 Apr. 1916, m. 1940, FRANCES H. ———.

Details of issue unknown (five children).

44. WILLIAM FORBES MORGAN III, b. 3 July 1907, d. at sea [Pacific Ocean] 8 Oct. 1945, m. 7 Aug. 1937, MARIE NEWSOME, b. Shawnee, Okla., dau. of William E. Newsome and of Caroline O. Fox.

Issue (surname MORGAN):

63. a. BARBARA, b. 2 Oct. 1941.
b. WILLIAM FORBES IV, b. 23 Aug. 1945.

45. WILLIAM KEY BOND EMERSON III, b. Port Chester, N.Y., 20 May 1927, m. (1) Lobito, Angola, 15 Oct. 1954, MARIA REGINA VIANA SERRAO; m. (2) 3 Jan. 1976, LYNN ERNESTINE CATOE.

Issue by first wife (surname EMERSON):

a. WILLIAM KEY BOND IV, b. 8 March 1956.
b. ISABEL SERRAO, b. 14 July 1965 (twin).
c. PAOLA SERRAO, b. 14 July 1965 (twin).

46. NINA ULE EMERSON, m. WILLIAM ANDREW OPEL.

Known issue (surname OPEL):

a. DEBORAH E.

47. NATASHA MARIA EMERSON, m. Rochester, N.Y., 21 March 1964, ERIC ARMIN PFEIFFER, b. Rauenthal, Germany, 15 Sept. 1935, son of Fritz Pfeiffer and of Emma Saborowska.

Issue (surname PFEIFFER [order unknown]):

a. ERIC ALEXANDER.
b. MICHAEL DAVID.
c. MARK ARMIN.

48. RUPERT ALLAN EMERSON, m. Cleveland, Ohio, 2 Sept. 1968, NICOLENE CARONITE.

Known issue (surname EMERSON):

a. JOY ROSE, b. 1975.

49. ANTHONY ST. CLERE BERKELEY GAGE, b. 9 Nov. 1931, m. Buckfast, Devon, 1 May 1965, VIRGINIA MARY FERENS, dau. of Denis Henry Ferens.

Issue (surname GAGE):

a. BENJAMIN FRANCIS, b. 3 May 1969.
b. GREGORY BERNARD, b. 1971.
c. OLIVER, b. 1973.

50. ULICK CHARLES CHRISTOPHER GAGE, b. 7 Jan. 1938, m. London 12 Dec. 1964, HELEN MARY JANET HOWELL, dau. of Evelyn Michael Thomas Howell and of Helen Joan Hayes.

Issue (surname GAGE):

a. ULICIA MARY, b. 23 May 1965.
b. MARIUS BERKELEY, b. 21 Sept. 1966.

51. ANNE CAROLINE THALIA GAGE, b. London 25 Nov. 1931, m. London 25 Feb. 1960, ROBIN ALEXANDER BARING, from 27 March 1938, Hon. Robin A. Baring, b. 15 Jan. 1931, son of Alexander Francis St. Vincent Baring, 6th Baron Ashburton, and of Hon. Doris Mary Therese Harcourt.

Issue (surname BARING):

a. FRANCESCA RHIANNON, b. London 6 Dec. 1963.

52. ROBERT WESTCOTT MORETON GAGE, b. London 19 Apr. 1934, m. Santander, Spain, 4 Apr. 1964, MARIA TERESA FRANCISCA DIAZ-CANEJA, dau. of Don Emilio Diaz-Caneja and of Dona Maria Bettencourt.

Issue (surname GAGE):

a. DOLORES ISABELLA, b. London 2 March 1965.
b. HENRY ST. CLERE ROKEWOOD, b. London 12 June 1966.

53. ELIZABETH ESTLING GAGE, b. London 31 Dec. 1937, m. (1) London 5 Dec. 1957, div. 1965, as his first wife, DAVID VERNON RUSSELL, b. 11 July 1929 [he later m. (2) 1 Oct. 1965, Lady Mary Katherine Baillie-Hamilton, b. 13 Jan. 1934], son of Hugh Edward Russell, D.S.O., Brig.; m. (2) London 21 March 1970, div., as his ——— wife, DAVID BRUCE DOUGLAS LOWE, b. 3 Apr. 1933 [he later m. 1978, Dagmar Bosse], son of Douglas Gordon Arthur Lowe, Q.C., and of Karen Thamsen; m. (3) London 4 March 1974, RICHARD FRANKLIN PERKINS, son of Donald Marsh Perkins and of Katherine Hewitt Neal.

No issue yet.

54. WILLIAM TIFFANY RICHARDSON, b. New York, N.Y., 15 Dec. 1939, m. Louisville, Ky., 22 Aug. 1981, DEBORAH JEAN WOODS, b. Louisville, Ky., 31 Aug. 1951, dau. of Hubert William Woods and of Norma Jean Sieveking.

No issue yet.

55. PHILIP HOVERSTEN, m. ———.

Issue (surname HOVERSTEN):

a. TIFFANY.
b. SCHUYLER.

56. LOCKWOOD CHAPPELL BARR, b. Brooklyn, N.Y., 3 March 1914, d. Rowayton, Conn., 25 June 1951, m. Pelham Manor, N.Y., 23 June 1937, JANE SHAW CHURCHILL, dau. of Lawrence Whitfield Churchill.

Issue (surname BARR [order unknown]):

a. LOCKWOOD CHURCHILL.
b. BETSY KENDALL.

57. WILLIAM EDWARD BARR, b. Brooklyn, N.Y., 10 July 1915, m. 12 Dec. 1942, CLAIRE BRYANT.

Issue (surname BARR):

64. a. BERENICE FLORENCE, b. 26 Apr. 1947.
65. b. WILLIAM EDWARD, Jr., b. 13 Dec. 1948.
c. ALLEN MORFORD, b. 11 Oct. 1953.

58. JOHN EARLE UHLER, Jr., b. Baltimore, Md., 12 Nov. 1918, d. Plaquemine, La., July 1969, m. (1) Greenville, Miss., 1939, NELL ROBERTSHAW; m. (2), as her second husband, ETHEL GRUBY [she had m. (1) ——— Langford]; m. (3) Franklinton, La., 1959, as her first husband, GLENNA KNIGHT [she later m. (2) E. Bruce Lusk].

Issue: (a) by first wife (surname UHLER):

66. a. ELLEN, b. Greenville, Miss., 24 Aug. 1942.
67. b. JAN, b. 16 Nov. 1947.

(b) by third wife (surname UHLER):

c. ANN, b. Plaquemine, La., 28 Oct. 1960.
68. d. CAMILLE ALLANA, b. Plaquemine, La., 8 Apr. 1965.

59. MILBURN EDWARD BARR UHLER (Edward), b. Baltimore, Md., 3 Nov. 1922, m. (1) New York, N.Y., 14 Apr. 1956, CONSTANCE MAY LINCOLN; m. (2) HELEN GERTRUDE OUTLER.

Issue by first wife (surname UHLER):

69. a. VALERIE FRANCES, b. Hackensack, N.J., 31 Dec. 1957.

60. ——— WARD, m. RICHARD GRAY.

Issue, if any, unknown.

61. ERIC B. WARD, m. ANN L. ———.

Issue, if any, unknown.

62. SAMUEL WARD, b. Los Angeles, Cal., 29 Sept. 1944, m. 1966, ———.

Details of issue unknown (one child).

63. BARBARA MORGAN, b. 2 Oct. 1941, m. (1) ——— COLE; m. (2) ——— ALDERSON.

Issue by first husband (surname COLE):

a. CAROLINE.

64. BERENICE FLORENCE BARR, b. 26 Apr. 1947, m. DONALD EDMUND CODY, b. 1 Sept. 1947.

No issue yet.

65. WILLIAM EDWARD BARR, Jr., b. 13 Dec. 1948, m. BARBARA PARK, b. 15 Sept. 1949.

Issue (surname BARR):

a. WILLIAM EDWARD III.
b. MATTHEW SCOTT.

66. ELLEN UHLER, b. Greenville, Miss., 24 Aug. 1942, m. 1 June 1963, ROBERT L. ERWIN.

Issue, if any, unknown.

67. JAN UHLER, b. 16 Nov. 1947, m. 29 May 1971, JAY TURNER.

Issue (surname TURNER):

a. JOHN OLIN, b. Friona, Tex., 3 Aug. 1974.
b. JAIME CORINNE, b. Friona, Tex., 15 June 1977.

68. CAMILLE ALLANA UHLER, b. Plaquemine, La., 8 Apr. 1965, m. Plaquemine, La., 2 July 1982, KEVIN JOSEPH NAVARRE.

No issue yet.

69. VALERIE FRANCES UHLER, b. Hackensack, N.J., 31 Dec. 1957, m. Sacramento, Cal., Aug. 1981, CHRISTOPHER RUPERT.

No issue yet.

Note

Number 31:
Sir Berkeley Gage was the British Ambassador to Thailand from 1954 to 1957 and the British Ambassador to Peru from 1957 to 1963.

VIII

Descendants of Peter Young and of Eleanor ———

1. Capt. PETER YOUNG, mariner, b. ——— [Scotland?], ——— [ca. 1739], d. ——— [between 11 Dec. 1781 and 12 Nov. 1784], son of ——— Young and of ———, m. ———, ELEANOR ———, b. ———, d. ——— [after 21 Oct. 1796], dau. of ——— and of ———.

Issue (surname YOUNG):

- a. DAVID, b. 25 July 1762.
- b. ELEANOR, b. 13 Nov. 1767.
- c. SARAH, b. 9 July 1768.
- d. PETER Jr., b. Philadelphia, Pa., 22 June 1771 (twin).
- e. MARGARET, b. Philadelphia, Pa., 22 June 1771 (twin).
- f. JAMES, b. Philadelphia, Pa., 8 Jan. 1773.
- g. PETER, b. Philadelphia, Pa., 8 Nov. 1774, bur. Philadelphia, Pa., 1 Sept. 1776.
- **2.** h. REBECCA, b. Philadelphia, Pa., 5 May 1779, d. Piqua, Ohio, 8 June 1862.
- i. WILLIAM, b. Philadelphia, Pa., 21 Jan. 1782, d. Philadelphia, Pa., 19 Nov. 1851.

2. REBECCA YOUNG, b. Philadelphia, Pa., 5 May 1779, d. Piqua, Ohio, 8 June 1862, m. (1) Philadelphia, Pa., 8 Sept. 1796, JOSEPH STRONG, physician (see Part VII, number 1, above), b. South Coventry, Conn., 10 March 1770, d. Philadelphia, Pa., 24 Apr. 1812, son of Benajah Strong and of Lucy Bishop; m. (2) PETER GARDINER.

Issue: (a) by first husband (surname STRONG):
See Part VII, above.

(b) by second husband (surname GARDINER):

- **3.** i. RICHARD J., b. Philadelphia, Pa., 15 Feb. 1818, d. Chillicothe, Ohio, 22 June 1892.

3. RICHARD J. GARDINER, b. Philadelphia, Pa., 15 Feb. 1818, d. Chillicothe, Ohio, 22 June 1892, m. MARGARET ———, b. 20 Sept. 1824, d. 10 March 1872.

Known issue (surname GARDINER):

- **4.** a. RICHARD J., Jr.

b. MAGGIE H., b. 9 Sept. 1854, d. 23 Sept. 1855.
5. c. MARY H., b. Ohio, Jan. 1856, d. 1943.
d. HUNTER, b. 27 July 1857, d. 4 Aug. 1857.
6. e. CLARA R., b. 4 Oct. 1858, d. 2 May 1879.
7. f. REBECCA, b. 6 March 1860, d. 12 May 1883.
g. WILLIAM R., b. 20 Oct. 1866, d. 22 Oct. 1866.

4. RICHARD J. GARDINER, Jr., m. Ross Co., Ohio, 13 July 1882, SUSIE E. ROBERTS.

Issue, if any, unknown.

5. MARY H. GARDINER, b. Ohio, Jan. 1856, d. 1943, m. Ross Co., Ohio, 24 Jan. 1878, VALENTINE L. BLANKENSHIP, engineer, b. Ohio, May 1850, d. 1930.

Issue (surname BLANKENSHIP):

a. ADA G., b. Ohio, Aug. 1878, living 1900.
b. MAE CLARA, b. Ohio, March 1880, d. North Hollywood, Cal., 20 Aug. 1967.
c. OLIVE J., b. Ohio, 1883, d. 1935.
8. d. WALTER D., b. Ohio, Jan. 1886, living 1969.
e. MARIE, b. Ohio, Nov. 1888, living 1907.

6. CLARA R. GARDINER, b. 4 Oct. 1858, d. 2 May 1879, m. Ross Co., Ohio, 21 March 1878, JOHN T. O'CONNOR.

Issue, if any, unknown.

7. REBECCA GARDINER, b. 6 March 1860, d. 12 May 1883, m. Ross Co., Ohio, 23 Feb. 1882, GEORGE BERTHOLD.

Issue, if any, unknown.

8. WALTER D. BLANKENSHIP, M.D., b. Ohio, Jan. 1886, in 1969 living at 31 Sunset Pl., Lancaster, Pa., m. WINIFRED B. ———, living 1969.

Issue, if any, unknown.

Note

Letters of Marque were issued by the Continental Congress to Capt. Peter Young as Master of the *Neptune* on 5 Aug. 1779, as Master of the *Havannah* on 3 July 1780, and as Master of the *Nancy* on 11 Dec. 1781. See *Naval Records of the American Revolution, 1775–1788* (Washington, 1906), 402, 328, 400; and *Letters of Marque* (*Pennsylvania Archives*, 5th Series, Vol. 1, Harrisburg, 1906), 616, 619, 646, 647. All of the descendants of Capt. Peter Young are thus eligible for membership in the National Society of the Daughters of the American Revolution and the National Society of the Sons of the American Revolution.

Additional Sources: A Selected List

I. **Published Genealogies**

1. Craine, J. Robert T., and Harry W. Hazard. *The Ancestry and Posterity of Matthew Clarkson (1664–1702)*. N.p., 1971. Pp. 384, 385 (Part II).
2. Dwight, Benjamin Woodbridge. *The History of the Descendants of Elder John Dwight of Northampton, Mass.* 2 vols. Albany, N.Y., 1871. Reprint. Baltimore, 1975. Pp. 414-416 (Parts III and VII).
3. Robinson Family Association. *Robinson Genealogy*, Vol. 12: *William Robinson of Dorchester, Massachusetts*. N.p., n.d. Pp. 11, 26, 44 (Part VII).

II. **County Histories**

1. *Portrait and Biographical Record of Fayette, Pickaway, and Madison Counties, Ohio, Containing Biographical Sketches of Prominent and Representative Citizens*. Chicago, 1892. Pp. 237, 238, 830, 831 (Part VI).
2. *History of Franklin and Pickaway Counties, Ohio, with Illustrations and Biographical Sketches of Some of the Prominent Men and Pioneers*. Cleveland, 1880. P. 293, between 531 and 532 (Parts II and VI).
3. Miller, James H. *History of Summers County, West Virginia from the Earliest Settlement to the Present Time*. Hinton, Va., 1908. Pp. 698-704 (Part V).
4. Van Cleaf, Aaron R. *History of Pickaway County, Ohio and Representative Citizens*. Chicago, 1906. P. 875 (Part VI).
5. Wayland, John W. *A History of Shenandoah County, Virginia*. Strasburg, Va., 1927. Pp. 158, 510 (Part V).

III. **Ohio Newspapers**

1. *Chillicothe Gazette*, various items (Part VIII).
2. *Columbus Evening Dispatch*, 29 Sept. 1904, p. 1 (Part II).
3. *Scioto Gazette* (Chillicothe, Ohio), 29 Jan. 1861, p. 3, col. 2 (Part VI).

IV. **Family Papers, Primary Materials, Etc.**

1. Various writings of Lockwood Anderson Barr (see Part VII,

number 37), several cited elsewhere (Parts VII and VIII).

2. Manuscript notes of Miss Martha Bennett at the Ross County Historical Society, Chillicothe, Ohio (Part VI).
3. Information from Mr. William S. Dun (Part III).
4. Genealogical material collected by Capt. Gerard Hadden Wood (see Part III, number 7) (Parts III and VI).
5. Ross County, Ohio Will Book E and F, pp. 544-560 (Part VI).
6. Register of St. Paul's Episcopal Church, Chillicothe, Ohio (Parts III and VII).
7. Death certificates of Frank(lin H.) Work, Ellen Wood Work, and Eleanor (Ellen) Strong Wood, cited elsewhere (Parts I, III, and VII).
8. Inscriptions from Grandview Cemetery, Chillicothe, Ohio, confirmed by personal visit (Parts III and VIII).

Appendix

The Royal Descents of H.R.H. The Princess of Wales Through the Immigrant Mrs. Alice Freeman Thompson Parke of Roxbury, Massachusetts

Generation

1. Ethelred II, King of England, d. 1016 = 1) Alfflaid
2. Elgiva of England = 3) Uchtred, Earl of Northumberland
3. Edith of Northumberland = Maldred, Lord of Carlisle & Allerdale, brother of Duncan, King of Scots, d. 1040
4. Gospatrick I, Earl of Northumberland & Dunbar = ———, sister of Edmund
5. Gospatrick II, 2nd Earl of Dunbar = Sybil Morel
6. Juliana of Dunbar = Ralph de Merlay
7. Roger de Merlay = Alice de Stuteville
8. Agnes de Merlay = Richard Gobion
9. Hugh Gobion = Matilda ———
10. Joan Gobion = John de Morteyn
11. Sir John de Morteyn = Joan de Rothwell
12. Lucy de Morteyn = Sir John Giffard
13. Sir Thomas Giffard = Elizabeth de Missenden
14. Roger Giffard = 3) Isabel Stretle
15. Thomas Giffard = Eleanor Vaux
16. John Giffard = Agnes Winslow, daughter of Thomas Winslow & Agnes Throckmorton, daughter of Sir John Throckmorton & Eleanor Spinney
17. Thomas Giffard = Joan Langston, a Capetian descendant, as follows:

1. Hugh Capet, King of France, d. 996 = Adelaide of Poitou
2. Edith of France = Rainier IV, Count of Hainault
3. Beatrix of Hainault = 1) Ebles I, Count of Roucy
4. Alice of Roucy = Hildouin IV, Count of Montdidier
5. Margaret of Montdidier = Hugh I, Count of Clermont
6. Adeliza of Clermont = Gilbert de Clare
7. Baldwin Fitz Gilbert de Clare = Adelina de Rullos
8. Emma de Clare = Hugh Wake
9. Geoffrey Wake = ———
10. ——— Wake (daughter) = William de Duston
11. William de Duston = Mary ———
12. Isabel de Duston = Sir Walter de Grey of Rotherfield
13. Sir Robert de Grey of Rotherfield = Joan de Valoines
14. Thomas de Grey = ———
15. Joan de Grey = Guy le Breton

16. Katherine le Breton = Thomas Quatremain
17. Thomas Quatremain = Joan Russell
18. Maud Quatremain = John Bruley
19. Joan Bruley = John Danvers
20. Amy Danvers = John Langston
21. Joan Langston = Thomas Giffard, see above & below

17. Thomas Giffard = 21. Joan Langston
18, 22. Amy Giffard = Richard Samwell
19, 23. Susanna Samwell = Peter Edwards
20, 24. Edward Edwards = Ursula Coles
21, 25. Margaret Edwards = Henry Freeman
22, 26. Alice Freeman of Roxbury, Massachusetts = 1) John Thompson 2) Robert Parke
23, 27. (by 1) Dorothy Thompson = Thomas Parke, her step-brother
24, 28. Dorothy Parke = Joseph Morgan
25, 29. Margaret Morgan = Ebenezer Hibbard
26, 30. Keziah Hibbard = Caleb Bishop
27, 31. Lucy Bishop = Benajah Strong
28, 32. Dr. Joseph Strong = Rebecca Young
29, 33. Eleanor Strong = John Wood
30, 34. Ellen Wood = Frank(lin H.) Work
31, 35. Frances Eleanor (Ellen) Work = 1) James Boothby Burke Roche, 3rd Baron Fermoy
32, 36. Edmund Maurice Burke Roche, 4th Baron Fermoy = Ruth Sylvia Gill
33, 37. Hon. Frances Ruth Burke Roche = 1) Edward John Spencer, 8th Earl Spencer
34, 38. Lady Diana Frances Spencer, now H.R.H. The Princess of Wales, b. 1961 = 1981 H.R.H. Prince Charles Philip Arthur George, Prince of Wales, b. 1948
35, 39. H.R.H. Prince William Arthur Philip Louis of Wales, b. 1982

For sources see page 32.

Index